OFF THE BEATEN PATH® S

Idaho

FOURTH EDITION

Off the Beaten Path®

by Julie Fanselow

The Globe Pequot Press

Guilford, Connecticut

For Natalie, who was born to travel.

Maps created by Equator Graphics © The Globe Pequot Press
Illustrations by Carole Drong
Text design by Laura Augustine

ISSN 1535-4431
ISBN 0–7627–2266–5

Manufactured in the United States of America
Fourth Edtion/Third Printing

Acknowledgments

Many Idahoans too numerous to name recommended special spots throughout the Gem State for this book. My thanks to all. I'd also like to acknowledge the help of Georgia Smith, Karen Ballard, and Ron Gardner of the Idaho Department of Commerce and everyone at the local chambers of commerce and visitors bureaus who keep me up to date on what's happening around Idaho. Thanks, too, to the people at The Globe Pequot Press and the staff of *Sunset* Magazine, for whom I regularly cover Idaho.

As always, my deepest gratitude goes to my family. My husband, Bruce Whiting; our daughter, Natalie Fanselow Whiting; and most recently my father, Byron Fanselow (an Idahoan since 1998) have accompanied me to many of the places described in this book. Our trips are usually whirlwinds of activity, covering hundreds of miles each day with a stay each night in a different motel. Natalie, born in 1994, has already visited all of Idaho's forty-four counties, many of them several times. When you figure many people spend their lives in one place, without even seeing the next state, I believe that's quite an achievement. But at the same time, I sometimes feel our knowledge of Idaho runs a mile wide and an inch deep. So it's my hope that we'll someday be able to spend an entire week together rafting the Salmon River, a long weekend in a cabin at Warren, or just an entire afternoon on the beach at Pend Oreille.

About the Author

An Idaho resident since 1989, Julie Fanselow is among the state's most widely published writers. Her other guidebooks include *Traveling the Lewis and Clark Trail* and *Traveling the Oregon Trail* (Falcon Press/Globe Pequot), *British Columbia* and *Texas* (Lonely Planet), and *The Unofficial Guide to the Northwest With Kids* (Hungry Minds). A regular contributor to *Sunset* magazine, Julie also is a cofounder of guidebookwriters.com, the Internet's top source of proven travel-writing talent. Julie is a member of the American Society of Journalists and Authors and the Society of American Travel Writers.

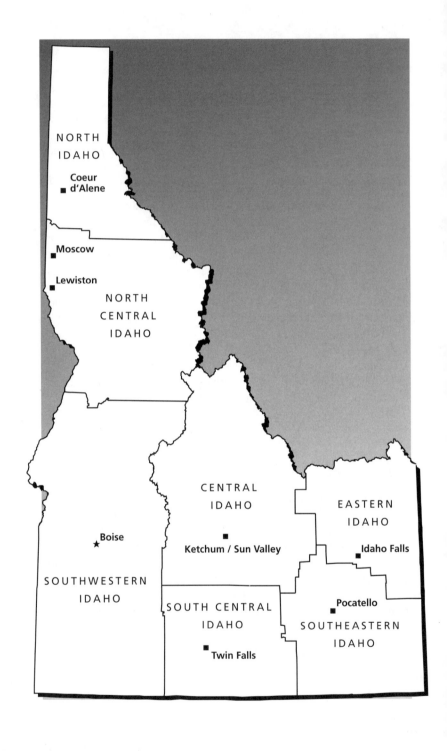

Contents

Introduction

When I first moved to Idaho, I had about two weeks before I was scheduled to start my job at the newspaper in Twin Falls. What better way to spend the time, I figured, than on a quick orientation trip around my new home state? Two weeks would be plenty of time to take a drive through Idaho's mountainous midsection, followed by a beeline for the Canadian border, a detour through Montana to Salmon, and a swing through Eastern Idaho.

Or so I thought. A week or so later, I'd meandered across maybe a quarter of my intended route. As someone who had grown up on the fringes of Pennsylvania suburbia and come of age in rural Ohio, I knew more than a little bit about back roads and small towns. But I knew next to nothing about a landscape that would force me, by virtue of geography and scenery, to really slow down and savor the journey, not to mention a piece of huckleberry pie here and a buffalo burger there. More than a dozen years later, I still haven't seen all Idaho has to offer. I expect it will take a lifetime, and that's fine.

In a sense, all of Idaho could be considered off the beaten path. It's true that here—like elsewhere—interstates now cross the state from east to west. But Highway 12, the only route across North Central Idaho, didn't link Lewiston to Missoula, Montana, until 1961. The White Bird Grade on the state's only major north-south road, Highway 95, wasn't completed until 1975. When it's closed by bad weather or rock slides, travelers must make a five-hour detour through Oregon and Washington. And until the early 1990s, it was nonstop cross-country from Boston to Seattle on I–90, except for one stoplight in the town of Wallace, Idaho.

Idaho was the last of the continental United States to be settled by whites pushing westward (although Native Americans were here 10,000 to 15,000 years ago). When pioneers pressed west on the Oregon and California trails, most kept right on going through what would become Idaho. When British fur traders staked their claims in the Northwest, they did so hundreds of miles west near the mouth of the great Columbia River. Idaho's first permanent town, Franklin, wasn't settled until 1860, and many of today's communities didn't exist at all until early in the twentieth century.

The state's tourism slogans of recent years tell the story, too: "Idaho: The Undiscovered America" and "Idaho Is What America Was." The state's population is swelling, most notably in the southwestern corner, where

Boise—frequently touted as one of America's most desirable places to live—is giving way to a creeping urban sprawl that is home to about a third of the state's population. But no matter where you are in Idaho, you don't have to travel far to escape: Owyhee County, south of Boise, and the Central Idaho Rockies, northeast of the capital city, remain so sparsely settled they could qualify as frontier. All across Idaho residents and visitors have plenty of opportunities to get happily lost for a day, a weekend, or longer, on a seldom-traveled forest road, in an abandoned mountaintop fire tower, in a country antiques store, or in a tucked-away cafe.

A few notes on how to use this book: There are seven chapters, each covering one of the tourism regions designated by the Idaho Travel Council. Each chapter leads off with a general overview of the region. With roads few and far between in many areas of Idaho, it is impossible to avoid retracing a route once in a while, but I've tried to keep backtracking to a minimum. Although each chapter leads off with a general map of the region and its attractions, you will want to use a more detailed map in planning your travels. You can get a free highway map by calling (800) 434–3246. Maps are also available via the state's travel Web site at www. visitid.org, or by writing the Idaho Travel Council at 700 West State Street, Boise 83720. *The Idaho Atlas & Gazetteer*, published by DeLorme Mapping, P.O. Box 298, Freeport, ME 04032, is another excellent reference, as are the maps published by the various units of the U.S. Forest Service in Idaho.

It's still possible to travel 50 miles or more in Idaho without passing a gas station. And just because a town is listed on a map or road sign, that's no guarantee you'll find a filling station or other services there. So before you set out off the beaten path, make sure your vehicle is in good shape and the fuel tank is full. Carry a good full-size spare tire and jack, a gasoline can, and a basic emergency kit, including flashers. A shovel and ax also can come in handy on unpaved back roads, the former in case you encounter a snow drift, the latter in the event a tree has fallen in your path. (Both these things happen not infrequently on Forest Service roads in Idaho's high country, even in the dead of summer.) Most of the places mentioned in this book are accessible using any two-wheel drive vehicle in good condition, but a few are unsuitable for large RVs or vehicles towing trailers. When in doubt, inquire locally before setting off on an unfamiliar back road.

I've tried to list prices for most attractions, but bear in mind these are subject to change. Use the prices as a guideline, and call ahead for updates or more information. Also remember that Idaho, unique among states, is divided north-south into two time zones. The northern part of the state is on Pacific time, while the south runs on Mountain time. (The Salmon River between North Fork in the east and Riggins in the west is the rough dividing point.)

Finally, it should be noted that Idaho has more federally designated wilderness lands—nearly four million acres—than any other state in the lower forty-eight, with an additional nine million acres of roadless public land. Much of Idaho is, therefore, accessible only by boat, on horseback, on foot, or by chartered plane flown into a backcountry airstrip. For more information about exploring Idaho's wilderness areas, contact the Idaho Outfitters and Guides Association, P.O. Box 95, Boise 83701. The phone number is (208) 342–1919; the Web site is at www.ioga.org/. If, after reading this book, you'd like more help planning an Idaho vacation, I am available for personalized advice and itinerary planning services. You can contact me via www.guidebookwriters.com (follow the links to Idaho), or by writing Julie Fanselow, P.O. Box 1593, Twin Falls, ID 83303-1593.

It is my hope that *Idaho: Off the Beaten Path* will inspire you to hit the open road and discover this great state. Whether you seek an unusual family vacation destination, a romantic weekend rendezvous, or a fun one-day getaway; whether you desire mountain peaks, high desert stillness, or crystalline lakes, Idaho awaits your exploration. If, in your own travels, you come across changes in the information listed here or a great place that might be mentioned in a future edition of this book, drop me a line in care of The Globe Pequot Press, P.O. Box 480, Guilford, Connecticut 06437. Thanks—and happy travels!

Idaho Facts

Population (2000 census): 1,293,953

Statewide tourism information: (800) 434–3246 or www.visitid.org/

Major newspapers:

The Idaho Statesman (Boise)
Boise Weekly (alternative news and views)
The Times-News (Twin Falls)
The Idaho State Journal (Pocatello)
The Post Register (Idaho Falls)
The Coeur d'Alene Press
Lewiston Morning Tribune
The Idaho Spokesman-Review (North Idaho)

Helpful statewide phone numbers and Web sites:

State of Idaho Home Page—www.accessidaho.org
Idaho weather—www.wrh.noaa.gov/boise/
Road conditions report—(208) 336–6600 or
    www2.state.id.us/itd/ida-road/index.asp
Idaho Department of Parks and Recreation—(208) 334–4199 or
    www.idahoparks.org
Idaho Department of Fish and Game—(800) 635–7820 or
    www.state.id.us/fishgame/fishgame.html
United States Forest Service—(208) 373–4100 or
    www.fs.fed.us
Idaho RV Campgrounds Association—(800) RV–IDAHO or
    www.gocampingamerica.com/idaho/

Transportation:

Air: Idaho's major airport is in Boise, which is served by Alaska, America West, Delta, United, Northwest, and Southwest Airlines. Other airports with scheduled service—sometimes via commuter carriers—include Hailey (Sun Valley), Idaho Falls, Lewiston, Twin Falls, and Pocatello. Many people traveling to North Idaho choose to fly into Spokane, Washington (just 33 miles from Coeur d'Alene). And the airport in Salt Lake City (161 miles from Pocatello) is reasonably convenient to destinations in the Southeastern, Eastern, and South Central regions of Idaho.

Bus: Greyhound serves many Idaho cities along Interstates 15, 84, and 90, including Boise, Burley, Coeur d'Alene, Kellogg, Idaho Falls, Mountain Home, Nampa, Pocatello, Twin Falls, and Wallace. For more information call (800) 229–9424.

Train: Amtrak's Empire Builder route passes through Sandpoint in North Idaho.

Climate:

Because Idaho is so big, its climate cannot be easily summed up in a paragraph. But generally Idaho is drier than the Pacific Northwest and milder than the rest of the Rocky Mountain region. In Boise, daytime highs range from about 90° F in July to the mid-30s in January, with nighttime lows in the 50s in summertime and the 20s December through February. In the panhandle region, summer daytime temperatures are typically in the 80s, dipping to about 50° F at night. In the winter expect North Idaho daytime highs at just about the freezing mark and lows about 20° F. Humidity is low around most of the state.

Precipitation varies widely, from only 9 inches of rain and 17 inches of snow falling annually at Twin Falls in South Central Idaho to 30 inches of rain and 75 inches of snow at Sandpoint. The best time to visit depends on your interests, but generally spring and fall are especially pleasant in the southern regions while mid-July through mid-September are the best times to visit North Idaho and the Central Idaho mountains. The high country often has snow until after the Fourth of July.

Famous Idahoans:

Famous Idahoans include former Mormon church president Ezra Taft Benson, Edgar Rice Burroughs (author of *Tarzan*), Philo Farnsworth (inventor of television), baseball great Harmon Killebrew, writer Ezra Pound, businessman J. R. Simplot, skier Picabo Street, and actress Lana Turner. Other celebrities who have made homes in the state include Jamie Lee Curtis, Patty Duke, Ernest Hemingway, Patrick McManus, Steve Miller, Demi Moore, and Bruce Willis.

Recommended Reading:

Guidebooks and travel

Hiking Idaho by Jackie and Ralph Maughan (2nd edition; Falcon Press, 2001). The latest edition of a classic statewide guide.

Idaho for the Curious by Cort Conley (Backeddy Books, 1982). The first modern Idaho guidebook, it concentrates on history along the state's highways.

Moon Handbook: Idaho by Don Root (4th edition; Avanlon Travel Publishing, 2001). If you buy only one other travel guidebook, this should be your choice. Exhaustive and witty.

Traveling the Lewis and Clark Trail and *Traveling the Oregon Trail* by Julie Fanselow (2nd edition; Falcon Press, 2000 and 2001, respectively). Comprehensive modern travel guides to the famous trails, both of which run through Idaho.

History

Building Idaho: An Architectural History by Jennifer Eastman Attebery (University of Idaho Press, 1991).

Camera Eye on Idaho by Arthur A. Hart (Caxton Press, 1990). A fascinating survey of pioneer photography in the state from 1863 through 1913.

History of Idaho by Leonard J. Arrington (1994, University of Idaho Press/Idaho State Historical Society). This two-volume set was completed as part of the state's Centennial celebration in 1990.

Roadside History of Idaho by Betty Derig (Mountain Press Publishing, 1996).

Natural history

Idaho Wildlife Viewing Guide by Aimee Pope (2nd edition; Falcon Press, 2001). Describes ninety-four viewing sites statewide.

Roadside Geology of Idaho by David Alt and Donald W. Hyndman (Mountain Press, 1989).

Rocks, Rails and Trails by Paul Karl Link and E. Chilton Phoenix (Idaho Museum of Natural History, 1996). A photo-packed look at the geology, geography, and history of Eastern and Southern Idaho.

Literature and miscellaneous

Idaho Loners: Hermits, Solitaries, and Individualists by Cort Conley (Backeddy Books, 1994). Idaho is a state of individualists, and veteran writer Conley interviewed some of the most singular for these profiles.

Is Idaho in Iowa? by Tim Woodward (Backeddy Books,1994). The popular *Idaho Statesman* columnist takes a humorous look at this frequent geographical blunder.

Idaho's Poetry: A Centennial Anthology edited by Ronald E. McFarland and William Studebaker (University of Idaho Press, 1989)

So Incredibly Idaho! by Carlos A. Schwantes (University of Idaho Press, 1996). A photographic and literary tour of Idaho's varied landscapes.

Where the Morning Light's Still Blue: Personal Essays About Idaho edited by William Studebaker and Richard Ardinger (University of Idaho Press, 1994).

Written on Water: Essays on Idaho Rivers edited by Mary Clearman Blew (University of Idaho Press, 2001).

For children

Idaho (Hello USA series) by Kathy Pelta (Lerner, 1995) and *Idaho* (Portrait of America) by Kathleen Thompson (Steck-Vaughn, 1996) are two children's books about the state. *The Story of Idaho* by Virgil M. Young (University of Idaho Press, 1990) is a textbook frequently used in the state's schools.

Other Fast Facts:

- Idaho is among the nation's fastest-growing states. The population rose 28 percent between 1990 and 2000.

- Idaho has more white water than any other state, with 3,250 miles of river rapids.

- Idaho is the only state with an official seal designed by a woman.

- Hells Canyon on the Idaho/Oregon border is the deepest gorge in North America.

- Idaho elected the nation's first Jewish governor.

- Yes, Idaho is the nation's leading potato producer. But you knew that.

> The prices and rates listed in this guidebook were confirmed at press time. We recommend, however, that you call establishments before traveling to obtain current information.

North Idaho

For decades, the lakes of North Idaho were a private playground for the people of the Northwest. If you grew up in eastern Washington, Idaho, or Montana, chances are your family vacationed on the shores of Lake Coeur d'Alene at least once. If you didn't, your neighbors probably did. But outside this corner of the country, few people had North Idaho on their radar screens.

Today, however, North Idaho has been discovered. Coeur d'Alene and, to a slightly lesser degree, Sandpoint are hot spots. Even scruffy old Wallace and Kellogg, long the victims of declining mining fortunes, are enjoying a tourism-centered renaissance. Consequently, you may need to work a bit harder to get off the beaten path in this region. But it can be done.

I–90 runs through Coeur d'Alene and the Silver Valley surrounding Wallace, and it's the only high-speed road in the region. Elsewhere, even on U.S. Highways 2 and 95, two-lane stretches, stunning scenery, and occasionally heavy traffic are apt to slow you down. If you'd really like to leave the crowds behind, try the road up the east side of Priest Lake, the Coeur d'Alene Scenic Byway (State Routes 97 and especially 3), or the State Highway 200 east of Sandpoint (the Pend Oreille Scenic Byway).

For more North Idaho travel information, call (888) 333–3737 or write the North Idaho Tourism Alliance, P.O. Box 850, Coeur d'Alene 83816.

Lakes and Forests

The northernmost reach of Idaho's panhandle is almost 500 miles from the state capital, Boise. The Idaho-Canada border is more than 100 miles from even the regional center of Coeur d'Alene. Is there anything way up here worth driving those kind of distances?

Good grief, yes. Actually, Good Grief is the name of a tavern on Highway 95 just a few miles south of the U.S.–Canadian border. People up this way pride themselves on their individualism, and the folks you'll meet at the ***Good Grief Tavern*** are about as singular as can be. Take "Thelma

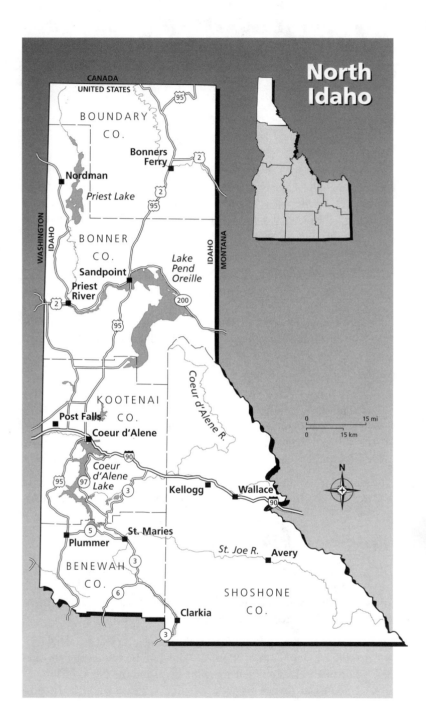

and Louise," protagonists of the Good Grief Massacre a few years back. Seems a few young fellas from Bonners Ferry came up looking for trouble one night and Thelma and Louise—those are their nicknames, anyway—wound up having to defend themselves with clubs. By the time the men got back to Bonners Ferry to tell the tale, their two mild-mannered, middle-aged assailants had turned into ten tough Canadian loggers.

It's possible to kill a lot of time at the Good Grief Tavern, not necessarily by drinking but by cracking wise with the regulars. The tavern caters to a motley crew of loggers, snowmobilers, hunters, and anglers. It was even mentioned on the country comedy TV show *Hee Haw* back in the 1970s. The bar serves a menu of pizza, hamburgers, and sandwiches. Other diversions include a great collection of license plates (including one from Montana that reads REPENT), a pool table, and darts. Ring up the Good Grief Tavern at (208) 267–2804 to check on hours.

A short drive north on Highway 95, maybe a mile south of the Eastport border, a turnoff for the Copper Creek Forest Service campground leads to the short and scenic *Copper Falls* trail. Only 8/10 of a mile in length, this loop winds through stands of Western red cedar, Douglas fir, birch, and Western larch to a delicate 80-foot waterfall. An overlook makes a pleasant place for a picnic. Look for an interpretive brochure at the trailhead, or get one by writing the Bonners Ferry Ranger District, Route 4, Box 4860, Bonners Ferry 83805.

Everywhere you look in North Idaho, you see either dense forests, expansive lakes, or both. This part of the state is most noted for its three large lakes—Coeur d'Alene, Pend Oreille, and Priest Lake (which actually is two lakes) —and the recreation-oriented resort towns on their shores. But rivers also run through this country, their Indian names music to the ears, their wild rapids and placid pools pure tonic for the soul. Two of these rivers—the Kootenai and the Moyie—meet at Bonners Ferry, the seat of Boundary County. East of town under a bridge spanning U.S. Highway 2, the Moyie flows through one of Idaho's most impressive canyons. The 1,223-foot-long steel truss *Moyie River Bridge,* built in 1964, is the second highest in the state, just 12 feet shy of the Perrine Bridge over the Snake River Canyon at Twin Falls. Stop at the rest area just east of the bridge for a good view of the span, or take the road to Upper and Lower Moyie Falls, two cascades that drop 100 feet and 40 feet, respectively.

The *Deer Ridge Lookout Tower,* one of several current or former Idaho fire lookouts available for rent from the U.S. Forest Service, sits 26 miles northeast of Bonners Ferry. Deer Ridge and other Idaho fire lookouts and cabins are great alternatives to traditional camping, offering solitude, a roof over one's head, and unparalleled views. Deer Ridge, a 40-foot-high lookout in the Purcell Mountains, is generally available from June 15 through the end of September. Visitors are treated to a panorama featuring the Selkirk Mountains to the west and the Moyie River Valley below.

Deer Ridge is reached via the Deer Creek or Meadow Creek roads east of Bonners Ferry, but the last mile is rough and narrow and caution is advised. Four people can stay in the tower, which rents for $25 a night, but visitors are discouraged from bringing small children because of the tower's height. For more information call (208) 267–5561 or write the Bonners Ferry Ranger District, Route 4, Box 4860, Bonners Ferry 83805. For a directory of lookouts and cabins available for rent throughout Northern Idaho and surrounding states, write the U.S. Forest Service's Northern Region Headquarters, P.O. Box 7669, Missoula, MT 59807.

If you happen to be within driving distance of Bonners Ferry at the end of September, check out the traditional Norwegian smorgasbord at Trinity Lutheran Church on U.S. Highway 95. This longtime event, held either the last Thursday night of each September or the first Thursday evening in October, features such delectable Scandinavian dishes as Swedish meatballs, lefse, pork roast, and pickled herring. The event typically draws a crowd of about 500 people (in a town of 2,200), and you can really fill up for about $6.00 a person. Call the church at (208) 267–2894 for this year's date.

The largest motel in Bonners Ferry, the Best Western Kootenai River Inn, is owned by the Kootenai Indians. Like Idaho's other tribes, the Kootenai help fund their economy with gambling, so the Kootenai Inn boasts its own hotel casino. Try your luck on about 400 slot machines, or sit down for some bingo action. The Kootenai River Inn also has a restaurant and lounge, indoor pool, game room, and exercise area. Call (800) 346–5668 for more information or reservations.

Ten miles south of Bonners Ferry, the small town of Naples sits just west of Highway 95. Naples in turn lies near a spot known as Ruby Ridge, which will forever be known as the setting of the 1992 confrontation between federal agents and Randy Weaver (see sidebar, page 6).

But Naples is also the setting of North Idaho's only Hostelling International–American Youth Hostel accommodation. Built as a dance hall a half-century ago, *Hostelling International–Naples* includes the town general store and laundromat. Bunks here cost just $10 per night, which includes access to kitchen facilities. The hostel also has four private rooms, available on a first-come, first-served basis for $10 per person per night. This makes a great, cheap base camp for exploring the panhandle. Reservations aren't necessary, but you can ensure a spot by calling (208) 267–2947 between 8:00 and 10:00 A.M. or 3:00 and 8:00 P.M. Pacific Time.

Although much smaller than Coeur d'Alene, Sandpoint rivals its neighbor as the most interesting town in Northern Idaho. Sandpoint's abundant natural attractions include Lake Pend Oreille, Idaho's largest, and *Schweitzer Mountain Resort.* Schweitzer is one of the West's biggest ski areas, with 2,350 skiable acres; that and its fairly remote location help make it one of the least crowded. From the top, skiers are treated to unbeatable views of Lake Pend Oreille. At the bottom, guests can relax at the slopeside Selkirk Lodge or party in Sandpoint. Schweitzer has recently expanded its offerings to the warmer months, too. Summertime visitors can picnic atop the mountain, take a half-day or overnight guided llama trek, go mountain biking, or play golf. For more information on Schweitzer call (800) 831–8810.

Sandpoint is a shopping paradise, with a bevy of unique stores. Even people who don't like to shop will find this town hard to resist. The epicenter of creative commerce is *Coldwater Creek,* run by the booming Sandpoint-based mail-order company of the same name on the Cedar Street Bridge downtown. The bridge was built over Sand Creek in 1906 and used for vehicles until 1971, when a new bridge opened. The city subsequently condemned the Cedar Street Bridge, but it was saved by a local businessman who turned it into an enclosed shopping plaza—the first of its kind in the United States. Coldwater Creek took over in 1995.

The bridge now showcases Coldwater Creek items, of course, with separate stores for all the company's varied wares. Northcountry sells moderately priced apparel and accessories for women, while Spirit of the West (upstairs) features upscale clothing. There's also a deli, an outlet store, an espresso cafe and a wine bar, along with lovely, wood-filled decor and a near open-air feel. Following a tip from my fellow guidebook author Don Root (of Moon's *Idaho Handbook*), I just had to check out the second-floor rest rooms. Sure enough the last stalls for each gender look out onto Sand Creek—"the best view of any commode in Idaho," indeed. Coldwater Creek is open seven days a week year-round. Call (208) 263–2265 for hours or more info.

Elsewhere downtown, ***From Sea to Si Imports*** is another top shopping stop. Everything in the store—sweaters, hats, home accessories, kids' clothing, pillows, purses, jewelry, and more—is from Ecuador. What's more, the prices are extremely reasonable, much less than you'd expect from a shop in a resort town. From Sea to Si is owned by Yamil and Tina Arliss. Yamil is a native of Otavalo, Ecuador, where many of that nation's great markets are located; Tina, who grew up in Lewiston, Idaho, met him while studying for a master's degree in Quito. They settled on Sandpoint as the place to open their shop, and it's a great addition to the town's eclectic, internationally flavored mix.

Echoes of Ruby Ridge

*R*andy Weaver and his family moved to remote North Idaho in 1983 to live off the land, practice a radical brand of Christian fundamentalism, and turn up at the occasional gathering of the state's fringe neo-Nazi movement. Because most Idahoans have a live-and-let-live philosophy, the Weavers didn't attract much attention—until 1990, when Randy was caught selling illegal arms to an undercover Bureau of Alcohol, Tobacco, and Firearms agent. Released after a court appearance, he decided to hole up on his property and make the law come to him. After a year and a half of surveillance, federal marshals moved in. It's never been proven who shot first, but by the time the gunfire ended, three people were dead: decorated U.S. Marshal William Degan; Weaver's fourteen-year-old son,

Samuel; and Weaver's wife, Vicki, who was holding her baby when she fell. Following an eleven-day standoff, Weaver surrendered. He subsequently went to trial on murder and conspiracy charges, beating all but a failure-to-appear rap with the aid of flamboyant defense attorney Gerry Spence, and he left Idaho.

The story of Ruby Ridge still echoes loudly in North Idaho. Local businesspeople and residents are still asked about the incident and the location of the Weavers' cabin. (The property was long a site for curiosity-seekers, but now under new ownership, it's off limits.) Most Idahoans are eager to put the episode behind them, but it may take many more years before Ruby Ridge is erased from Idaho's collective consciousness.

(Nearby, shoppers also will find wares from such foreign lands as Scandinavia and Texas.) From Sea to Si is located at 105 Main Street. The phone number is (208) 265–1609.

Sandpoint's pride and joy is the **Panida Theater,** originally opened in 1927 and dedicated to "the people of the Panhandle of Idaho," thus the name. For years the Panida was considered one of the premier movie palaces of the Northwest, but like many theaters, it fell on hard times in the late 1970s and early 1980s. The community rallied to buy and restore the Panida, and it now is home to a full calendar of films and performing arts. For example, one month the Panida's entertainment menu included the Ballet Folklorico de Mexico, blues artist Charlie Musselwhite, and screenings of *A Hard Day's Night* and the latest Warren Miller ski film. The theater is located along First Street, and patrons are welcome to bring in espresso purchased at the coffee shop next door. The Panida's box office phone number is (208) 263–9191. **The Festival at Sandpoint** is another staple of the local arts scene. Held midsummer on Lake Pend Oreille, the concert series features an inspired menu of music ranging from Branford Marsalis to Lee Ann Womack to Blue Rodeo. For tickets, call (888) 265–4554.

Lake Pend Oreille is the center of sea kayaking activity in Idaho, and **Full Spectrum Tours** was the state's first licensed outfitter for the sport. The company offers rentals, lessons, and a wide menu of trips. If you have only a day, consider a Full Moon Paddle or Goat 'n' Boat trip, on which paddlers scope out mountain goats on the lake's south shore at Farragut State Park. Travelers with more time may want to arrange a combination paddling-camping trip or "lake to lodge" package featuring overnight accommodations at a guest ranch. For more information, call (208) 263–5975, visit Full Spectrum's Web site at www.kayaking.net, or stop in the store at 405 North Fourth Street in Sandpoint.

State Highway 200 runs east from Sandpoint through the communities of Hope and East Hope, both recreational gateways to the northeastern reaches of Lake Pend Oreille. Near here, in 1809, Canadian explorer David Thompson established Kullyspell House, the earliest fur trade post in the American Pacific Northwest. Nothing remains of the post, but a monument to Thompson's efforts sits along the highway at Hope.

Clark Fork, 8 miles from the Montana border on Highway 200, is home to the University of Idaho's **Clark Fork Field Campus.** Located at the base of Antelope Mountain, the campus holds one-day workshops on topics ranging from fishing to home landscaping to environmental issues, as well as longer programs such as Elderhostel for senior citizens.

Overnight accommodations for up to fifty people make Clark Fork Campus a good spot for retreats, too. More information is available by writing to P.O. Box 87, Clark Fork 83811 or by calling (208) 266–1452.

In Cocolalla, 11 miles south of Sandpoint, a roadside business called **Wolf People** offers travelers an easy chance to stop and meet these misunderstood creatures. Up to ten wolves usually live on the premises at any one time and may be viewed free of charge. Bill and Nancy Taylor have been raising wolves since 1987, and they now offer a gift shop, educational programs, and wolf sponsorships. All in all, Wolf People is a whole lot more commercial than the nonprofit Wolf Education and Research Visitor Center down in Winchester (see the North Central Idaho chapter for information), but the Taylors seem to have their hearts in the right place. Visit the Web site at www.wolfpeople.com, or call (800) 404–9653 for more information and current hours of operation.

Southwest of Sandpoint, Lake Pend Oreille flows into Priest River, toward a town of the same name. Head north from the town of Priest River to **Priest Lake,** Northern Idaho's least-used big lake. Named for the Jesuit priests who came to Northern Idaho to spread their gospel among the Native Americans, Priest Lake is bordered to the east by the Selkirk Mountain Range, whose more than 7,000-foot peaks stand majestic against the lake's altitude of some 2,400 feet above sea level. Priest Lake is actually two lakes—the main body of water and Upper Priest Lake, which is connected to the much larger lower lake by a 2-mile-long water thoroughfare. Area marinas rent boats and other watercraft that can be used to ply the lakes and thoroughfare as well as explore island campsites dotting the water. The eastern shore is almost entirely undeveloped save for **Priest Lake State Park** and a few marinas. Nevertheless, this was where Nell Shipman—an early silent film star—had a studio during the 1920s, way up at Lionhead on the lake's northeastern tip.

At the south end of Priest Lake, **The Old Northern Inn** welcomes vacationers to a gracious, antique-filled bed-and-breakfast. Amenities include a small private marina, a swimming and sunning beach, and a deck overlooking the lake. The inn is open Memorial Day through mid-October, with four rooms and two suites, all with private baths. Rates range from $90 to $140 double occupancy, including a home-cooked breakfast for two and afternoon refreshments. For more information or reservations, call (208) 443–2426 or write The Old Northern Inn, P.O. Box 177, Coolin 83821.

The west side of Priest Lake has more commercial development than the east side, but still nothing compared to the shores of Coeur d'Alene and Pend Oreille. **Hill's Resort** has been welcoming guests to Luby Bay since 1946 and has won wide acclaim for catering to families. Aside from water-based activities, Hill's is accessible to good hiking, mountain biking, volleyball, golf, tennis, hunting, cross-country skiing, and about 400 miles of groomed snowmobile trails. And then there's the food. Baby back ribs, Margarita shrimp, and huckleberry pie are among the specialties, and the view of Priest Lake is a welcome side dish. Hill's has lakefront housekeeping units in four buildings, along with cabins that sleep between six and ten people. Call (208) 443–2551 for reservations or more information.

Huckleberries are plentiful in Northern Idaho, and some of the best berry patches are located along Priest Lake. Because huckleberries need sunlight to ripen, the best picking is often along abandoned logging roads and areas opened to sunshine by forest fires. Look for shrubs about 1 to 5 feet tall, with tiny pink or white urn-shaped flowers that

Idaho on Film

*L*ights ... camera ... disaster! With its wide range of unspoiled scenery, Idaho has landed some major roles in Hollywood, although it sometimes seems the state's involvement in movies has calamitous connections of one sort or another.

For example, the town of Wallace served as the setting for Dante's Peak, *the 1997, exploding volcano film starring Pierce Brosnan and Linda Hamilton. Despite lukewarm reviews, Wallace is proud of* Peak, *and you can still buy souvenirs of the film at many businesses around town. The same can't be said for* Heaven's Gate, *which was partially made in Wallace in 1979. The film is often cited among Hollywood's all-time biggest flops. But disaster movies, whether intentional or not, are nothing new in North Idaho: A silent film,* Tornado, *was filmed in the 1920s on the St. Joe River.*

On the other end of the dramatic scale, Idaho was the setting for one small film that escaped most moviegoers' notice when it was released in 1992. Dark Horse *is an engaging family film about the redemption of a troubled teen-age girl. Set in the Carey-Picabo area south of Sun Valley, the picture stars Ed Begley Jr. and Mimi Rogers, and it's well worth a video rental. Other films made entirely or partially in Idaho include Clint Eastwood's* Bronco Billy *and* Pale Rider; Northwest Passage *with Spencer Tracy;* Continental Divide *(with John Belushi in a tender-hearted role); Nell Shipman's* Told in the Hills; River of No Return *with Marilyn Monroe;* Breakheart Pass; Sun Valley Serenade; *and* Town & Country. *For information on film-making in Idaho, visit the Idaho Film Bureau's Web site at www.filmidaho. org or call (208) 334–2470.*

blossom in June or July. The berries themselves are purplish black to wine red in color, and they generally ripen in July or August, although some berries on slopes facing north may linger as late as October.

Humans like huckleberries a lot, but so do black bears and grizzly bears. The Selkirk Mountains are one of a handful of places where the legendary grizzlies still range in the United States, so caution must always be used. (Wear bells, keep a clean camp, and retreat from the area should a bear turn up.) For a pamphlet showing prime berry picking areas and a few recipes, contact the Kaniksu National Forest's Priest Lake Ranger District, 32203 Highway 57, Priest River 83856.

The Coeur d'Alenes

Idaho has its share of gourmet restaurants in unlikely locations, and *Chef in the Forest* certainly fits that description. Set on Hauser Lake north of the town of Post Falls, this chalet-style destination restaurant draws many patrons from eastern Washington and Montana's Flathead Valley as well as from all over Northern Idaho.

Chef in the Forest changes its menu regularly, but diners are likely to find such entrées as house specialty roast duckling with fresh brandied raspberry sauce; rack of lamb; and German sauerbraten, a Bavarian marinated pot roast complete with gingersnap sauce, potato pancakes, and braised red cabbage. Senior chef Richard Hubik (who owns Chef in the Forest with his wife, Deborah) considers himself a classical chef, steeped in traditional French and German dishes, while chef Jim Jensen specializes in pastas. Check out Cioppino, an award-winning dish featuring lobster, crab, scallops, and shrimp baked in an earthenware crock and served with rice pilaf and garlic bread.

Entrées at Chef in the Forest range in price from $16 to $36. A tempting variety of appetizers and desserts complements each main course, and the wine list has about fifty-five selections. To get to Chef in the Forest, watch for the sign on State Highway 53 west of Rathdrum; the restaurant is located at 12008 Woodland Beach Drive. Chef in the Forest is open for dinner only from 5:00 P.M. Wednesday through Sunday. For reservations, which are suggested, call (208) 773–3654.

Post Falls, one of Idaho's fastest-growing towns, is best known for its factory outlet stores and Templin's Resort. But the town boasts another, much less heralded and more obscure attraction, unless you're a musician—then chances are you've heard of *Vintage Guitars.*

Chef in the Forest

James Bowers started collecting guitars in 1960 and found it "a great hobby but a lousy business." Nevertheless, he's still buying, selling, and trading all manner of stringed instruments from his unassuming shop at 316 East Fifth Avenue in Post Falls. Among his 300 instruments are a guitar once played by Elvis Presley, an acoustic guitar dating back to 1850, a Gibson "harp" guitar from 1917, and many other unusual models.

Although it's tucked away on one of Post Falls's older streets, Vintage Guitars is visible from I–90, so if Bowers's reputation doesn't pull 'em in, the small neon sign in the window often will. Noted pickers who have stopped by include Leo Kottke, David Grissom, John Hartford, "and most of the guys from Asleep at the Wheel at one time or another," Bowers says. The Kentucky Headhunters once parked their tour bus right across the street and all came in together, Bowers says. Vintage Guitars is open from 9:00 A.M. to 6:00 P.M. Monday through Saturday "except when I'm closed." Call (208) 773–2387.

On a hot day, many Post Falls residents can be found at **Q'Emilin Park,** with its grassy lawn and beach. (*Q'Emilin,* pronounced "ka-MEE-lin," is an Indian term meaning "throat of the river.") Few, however, know that a magnificent canyon nearby awaits exploration. The gorge is also home to an outcropping of rocks popular with local rock climbers. To find the canyon, just stroll back beyond the boat dock and parking area.

One of Idaho's most storied state parks can be found near the town of Athol at the south end of big Lake Pend Oreille. In 1941 the U.S. Navy built the second-largest naval training center in the world on this site at the foot of the Coeur d'Alene Mountains. Over fifteen months during World War II, 293,381 sailors received basic training at Farragut Naval Training Station. Following the war the site served for a time as a college before being transformed into *Farragut State Park* in 1965. Since then the park—one of Idaho's largest—also has hosted several national Boy Scout and Girl Scout gatherings.

The park visitor center displays exhibits detailing the Navy presence at Farragut, which hasn't disappeared entirely: The military still uses 1,200-foot-deep Lake Pend Oreille as a submarine testing site. But recreation reigns at Farragut these days, with good opportunities for camping, hiking, cross-country skiing, boating, and wildlife viewing. Mountain goats patrol the steep peaks along Pend Oreille's south shore, and deer, moose, elk, and bear are also in residence. Farragut State Park is open year-round, with a $3.00-per-vehicle state park admission charge. For information call (208) 683–2425; write Farragut State Park, East 13400 Ranger Road, Athol 83801; or visit www.idahoparks.org/parks/farragut.html.

The Coeur d'Alene area takes the title as Idaho's bed-and-breakfast capital, with more than a dozen establishments providing homey hospitality and new ones opening all the time. One reason for this may be Idaho's relaxed marriage laws. No waiting period is required either before or after the license is obtained, so couples from Washington, Canada, Montana, and other spots often steal away to the Gem State to seal their vows, and Coeur d'Alene is a favorite destination. There's even a local bed-and-breakfast association available to offer information on all the local establishments, whether you are newlyweds, nearly-weds, or traveling on business. The association's accommodations hotline is at (800) 773–0323.

Although many of the area's inns do cater to couples, one welcomes families and even horses. Indoors, *Bridle Path Manor* has a decidedly upscale feel, but outside it's one big playground. Guests of all ages can take horseback lessons and then set off on a trail ride; try out the trampoline; hide in the tree house; or just play with the dogs and pygmy goats. Bridle Path Manor has thirty acres of its own and permission to use 685 adjacent acres, so there are miles of trails for riding, running, walking, cross-country skiing, and snowshoeing.

Bridle Path Manor has five guest rooms ranging in price from $90 to $160. Of these, the most expensive room—actually a suite—is best for families since it can accommodate up to five people. Room rates include a full breakfast. Horses may be boarded in the twelve-stall stable at the rate of $15 per night, which includes feed. The manor grounds also are available for all kinds of gatherings of up to 160 people. For more information call (208) 762–3126; write to 1305 East Lancaster Road, Hayden Lake 83835; or see the inn's Web site at www.bridle.com.

Farther east along Hayden Lake, the **Clark House** is among the most elegant inns in the Northwest. In the late 1980s the F. Lewis Clark Mansion on the shores of Hayden Lake was scheduled to be burned down after years of neglect and rampant vandalism. The mansion was completed in 1910 as a summer home for Spokane flour mill magnate F. Lewis Clark and his wife, Winifred. Clark was an unusually astute businessman who, fresh out of Harvard, built the C & C Mill in Spokane, later selling it for $200,000 more than he had invested. Clark knew Spokane would grow to the east, so he turned his attention to buying land in the Idaho panhandle. Here, too, his investments proved shrewd, turning Clark into a millionaire.

The 15,000-square-foot Hayden Lake villa was considered the most grand and expensive in Idaho when it was completed in 1912. Everything about the home was opulent, from the French hand-painted wallpaper to the Czechoslovakian crystal chandeliers. Unfortunately tragedy struck the Clarks not long after the mansion's completion. In 1914, while wintering in California, Clark disappeared while walking on the beach in Santa Barbara. His hat was found on the beach, but a body was never recovered, and authorities never determined whether the death was an accident or a suicide. Just a few years later, Winifred Clark was forced to leave the mansion in foreclosure proceedings.

The mansion played many roles over the next decades, serving as a children's home, church retreat center, military convalescence center, and a restaurant. But the grand building had stood vacant for many years when Monty Danner purchased it in 1989. Eighteen months later, after he replaced more than 1,000 window panes, installed new heating and electrical systems, and attended to countless other details, Danner rechristened the mansion the Clark House.

The inn has ten guest rooms—some the size of midsize apartments— ranging in price from $100 to $225 per night, double occupancy, including breakfast. All have private baths, some with Roman tubs for two; four have their own fireplaces; and the larger rooms are stocked liberally with books. The F. Lewis Clark Suite, the inn's showplace, features such sumptuous furnishings as a king-size canopied bed and billowing gold draperies hung on walnut rods. But even the more modest rooms are memorable and welcoming.

The guest quarters are hard to leave, but the rest of the house is worth a long look, too. Especially noteworthy are the murals by acclaimed artist Jack McCullagh, a frequent Academy Awards nominee for film set design (and winner of the scenic design prize at the Cannes film festival in France). Guests also are free to wander the twelve acres of grounds, play croquet, take in the lake views from the verandah, or soak in an enclosed hot tub.

In recent years, Clark House has become as well known for its food as for its lodging. Multicourse gourmet dinners are served seven nights a week by reservation, and the inn frequently hosts weddings, corporate retreats and business meetings, private dinner parties, and other events for up to fifty people. The Clark House is geared to adults and is considered "inappropriate for children under twelve." A two-day minimum stay is required weekends from Memorial Day through Labor Day. For reservations call (800) 765–4593, write the Clark House, 5250 East Hayden Lake Road, Hayden Lake 83835, or see www.clarkhouse.com.

South of Coeur d'Alene, **Berry Patch Inn** was once mentioned in *National Geographic Traveler* as one of the top twenty bed-and-breakfasts in the Rocky Mountain region. Surrounded by pines, this mountaintop chalet-style home is near Lake Coeur d'Alene's Cougar Bay and the headwaters of the Spokane River. As its name implies, Berry Patch Inn has its own fruit orchard. Guests can pick their own or watch deer browse among the berries, and a nightcap of berry liqueur is offered each evening. Badminton, kites, and a golf net provide warm-weather diversions, while sledding is a favorite winter pastime.

Berry Patch Inn has three guest rooms, each with a private bath. One room, the "Waterberry," has a separate entrance situated at the base of a waterfall. The inn is geared to adults, and smoking is prohibited. Call (208) 765–4994 for more information or write the Berry Patch Inn, 862 South Four Winds Road, Coeur d'Alene 83814.

Coeur d'Alene has plenty of good restaurants. One of the best (and least pretentious) is **Moon Time,** a neighborhood-style pub about a mile from the lakefront at 1602 Sherman Avenue. Menu favorites include spicy gumbo, salmon cakes, and a great array of sandwiches. Try the handmade Anasazi Bean Burger with a side of jalapeño fries and a Moon Unit brownie for dessert. Moon Time has live music and $1.00 pints of beer most Thursday nights. For more information, call (208) 667–2331.

In 1990 readers of *Condé Nast Traveler* magazine voted the **Coeur d'Alene Resort** the best resort in the continental United States. The

Coeur d'Alene isn't exactly off the beaten path—its copper-topped presence dominates the city's lakefront—but it does have one amenity no other resort in the world can claim: the *Floating Green* on the resort golf course. The brainchild of resort co-owner Duane Hagadone, the green is a par three on the fourteenth hole. It's also a moving target, floating between 100 and 175 yards from the blue (longest) tees. The movement is controlled by a computer, with the hole's length displayed each day at the tee. More than 30,000 golfers play the course each year, and during one memorable season, 22,000 golf balls, fifty golf clubs, and two golfers landed in the lake. The golf balls are removed from the lake weekly by salvage divers, but there's no word on what happens to errant golf clubs or golfers!

The Coeur d'Alene Resort Golf Course is notable for other elements of its design, too. The links were constructed on the site of a former sawmill, and planners strove to incorporate as much of the natural

Norman, Is That You?

*S*un Valley aside, Coeur d'Alene is about as fancy as Idaho gets. But never let it be forgotten that this town, famous for its pricey bed-and-breakfasts and posh resort, is also home to—scary movie music, please—the **Bates Motel.**

OK, so this mom-and-pop-style motor court at 2018 Sherman Avenue wasn't the setting for Alfred Hitchcock's immortal 1960 film Psycho. That hasn't stopped the Bates Motel from putting a shower curtain on its business cards, nor from doing a brisk business in souvenir towels, keychains, and T-shirts. As manager Mike Paradis explains, when former owner Randy Bates bought the old Highway 10 Motel years ago, he thought he'd have fun with the place and rename it.

The Bates Motel is one of Coeur d'Alene's best lodging bargains. The

rooms, originally used as cabins up at Farragut Naval Station, rent for just $30 to $45, and each has a refrigerator, microwave, and TV. "We cater to older couples who want a clean, quiet place to stay," Paradis says. In fact Paradis is choosy about his tenants, and he won't rent to anyone sight unseen. Too many people just want to come and party here, he adds. So if you're interested in staying a night, just show up to see if you pass muster.

Still, it helps to have a sense of humor at the Bates Motel. One summer evening two guests were picnicking on the front lawn when they needed something to slice their watermelon. They asked Paradis whether he could help, and he returned with the biggest, nastiest-looking knife he could find. Anthony Perkins would be proud.

environment into the course as possible. An osprey nest perches on a piling beside the thirteenth tee, and Fernan Creek and its trout spawning beds parallel the eleventh fairway. For these efforts the course was given a special award for environmental sensitivity from the Urban Land Institute. Alas, the Coeur d'Alene golf experience doesn't come cheap. Greens fees are $160 for resort guests and $210 for everyone else. The fee includes eighteen holes, caddy service, a custom-designed golf cart for each twosome, range balls, tees, and a personalized bag tag. For more information or reservations, call (208) 667–4653.

Exit 22 off of I–90 just east of Coeur d'Alene is the access point for the east and south shores of Lake Coeur d'Alene, including State Highway 97 (the Lake Coeur d'Alene Scenic Byway), the Wolf Lodge district, and the town of Harrison. At the end of a back road out of Harrison, **Hidden Creek Ranch** features six-night stays aimed at helping guests forget all about the outside world. Activities include lots of horseback riding, fly-fishing, hiking, stargazing, mountain biking—even such special programs as a sweat lodge ceremony and earth medicine workshops, plus plenty of programs just for kids. But everything is done on guests' own terms, and if all you want to do is laze about in a hammock, that's perfectly all right. Make sure you show up for meals, though: Most evenings, dinner is a "mere" four courses, but on one night, Hidden Creek really does it up with a seven-course candlelight feast featuring regional Northwest cuisine.

Hidden Creek Ranch is open May through October, with the six-night stay priced at $1,969 per person double occupancy June through August and $1,629 May, September, and October. (Rates for children ages three through eleven are $1,615 in high season; kids under three stay free, no children are allowed during the shoulder season.) Winter programs are available November through April. The ranch is run by John Muir, a direct descendant of the famous naturalist, and Iris Behr. For more information call (208) 689–3209 or (800) 446–3833; write Hidden Creek Ranch, 7600 East Blue Lake Road, Harrison 83833; or see the ranch's Web site at www.hiddencreek.com.

The oldest standing building in Idaho is preserved handsomely at **Old Mission State Park,** accessible via exit 39 off I–90. The Sacred Heart Mission was built between 1848 and 1853, the work of Coeur d'Alene Indians laboring under the supervision of Father Antonio Ravalli, a Jesuit missionary. The tribe called the mission "The House of the Great Spirit." Begin your tour by asking to see a slide presentation of the same name at the park visitor center.

The Coeur d'Alene Indians welcomed the Jesuits, for they believed the "Big Prayer" brought by the priests would give them an advantage over their enemies. There proved to be many parallels between the Native Americans and the Catholics: Each had a sense of the miraculous, the crucifix and rosaries were akin to the Indians' sacred charms, the chants of the Jesuit priests weren't unlike the natives' tribal songs, and the Catholics' incense, like the Indians' sage, were both said to help carry prayers skyward.

Ravalli designed the mission in classical Roman Doric style. In addition to serving as architect, he helped adorn the inside with devotional paintings and European-style chandeliers fashioned from tin cans. Wooden ceiling panels were stained blue with huckleberry juice to resemble the sky. Incredibly, when the Coeur d'Alenes were sent to a reservation, the boundaries drawn did not include their beloved mission. A new mission was built at DeSmet, 60 miles away. But the Sacred Heart Mission (also called the Cataldo Mission) remains an important site for history buffs, as well as for Catholics and the Coeur d'Alenes who make a pilgrimage to the site each year for the Feast of the Assumption. This event, held every August 15, includes a Mass, barbecue, and Indian dancing. Other annual happenings include a Historic Skills Fair with living history demonstrations the second Sunday each July and a Mountain Man Rendezvous the third weekend of August. Old Mission State Park is open year-round 8:00 A.M. to 6:00 P.M. June through August and 9:00 A.M. to 5:00 P.M. the rest of the year. Admission is $3.00 per vehicle. Phone (208) 682–3814 or look at the park Web site at www.idahoparks.org/parks/oldmission.html for more information.

Silver and Garnets

For more than a century, Idaho's Silver Valley—also known as the Coeur d'Alene Mining District—was the undisputed world leader in silver, lead, and zinc production. By 1985, a hundred years after mining began, the region had produced one billion ounces of silver, and the total value of wealth coaxed from the mines had topped $5 billion. Mining has fallen on hard times in recent years, with foreign competition forcing prices down below the North Idaho mines' cost of production. These days, like many Western areas formerly dependent on natural resources, the Silver Valley is looking to recreation and tourism to rebuild its economy. The region's location along I–90 has proven a blessing, with many attractions visible from the freeway, but a few places require a detour from the four-lane.

The **Enaville Resort** is one such spot. Dining in this restaurant is kind of like eating at a flea market. The walls are covered with collectors' plates, NASA memorabilia, and black velvet paintings, and patrons sit at extrarustic furniture amid bulbous tree burls. The decor leaves a bit to be desired, frankly, but the food keeps people coming back. The special here is Rocky Mountain Oysters. ("Make sure we have them. Sometimes the bulls don't cooperate," the menu cautions.) A full portion served with bread, soup or salad bar, and choice of potatoes costs $10.95, and a side order goes for $5.95. Other options include steaks priced from $8.95 to $29.95 for the Sweetheart Steak, which is big enough for two; a good selection of seafood; chicken-fried steak; and buffalo burgers. A smorgasbord of salmon, cod, oysters, shrimp, barbecued chicken and ribs, and sautéed mushrooms is available Fridays from 5:00 to 9:00 P.M.

For much of its 115-year history, Enaville Resort also has been known as "The Snake Pit." Ask five people why, and you'll likely get five different answers. One popular tale recalls when water snakes used to inhabit the area around the outdoor privies used before indoor plumbing came along. Patrons occasionally caught the snakes, put them in a container, and brought them inside. The business also served as a way station for railroaders, miners, and loggers. In addition to food they sometimes sought female companionship, and the women available at the roadhouse were supposedly called "snakes." The Enaville Resort is open daily for breakfast, lunch, and dinner. It's located 1½ miles from exit 43 off of I–90, up the Coeur d'Alene River Road. For more information call (208) 682–3453.

Nearby, the **Kingston 5 Ranch** may sound like a place to join the cattle drive, but it's actually a classy country-style bed-and-breakfast. Travelers have a choice of two rooms: the romantic Rose Room with vaulted ceilings, mountain views, and a jetted bathtub or the Reflections Suite, which opens onto a deck with a private hot tub and sitting area. Rates start at $125. Breakfast at Kingston 5 might include Belgian waffles with berries from the backyard patch, fresh homemade breads, and country-style meats, eggs, and potatoes. The ranch name isn't a total misnomer: Guests can do some horseback riding (stables are available and rental mounts may be found nearby), and hosts Walt and Pat Gentry raise their own beef. For more information call (800) 254–1852; write Kingston 5 Ranch, 42297 Silver Valley Road, Kingston 83839; or check out the Web site at www.k5ranch.com.

Sitting atop the old, mostly dormant Bunker Hill Mine in Kellogg, **Silver Mountain** resort has made a name for itself with the world's longest single-stage people-carrying gondola. Each car transports eight people on a nineteen-minute, 3-mile ride covering 3,400 vertical feet. The gondola runs in the summer as well as in the winter. After reaching the top, many warm-weather riders like to either hike or bike down the mountain on trails ranging from 2 to 22 miles long. Skiers have their choice of fifty-two runs covering 1,500 acres. For more information on Silver Mountain, call (208) 783–1111 or see www.silvermt.com.

Kellogg is doing its best to augment Silver Mountain with other attractions. Its small downtown features some interesting locally owned shops such as *Bitterroot Mercantile,* which stocks everything from Idaho-made goods to birdhouses and many beautiful antiques. It's at 117 McKinley Avenue.

Leave the interstate at exit 54 east of Kellogg to see the *Sunshine Mine Memorial,* which recalls the worst U.S. hard-rock mining disaster since 1917. On May 2, 1972, a fire broke out in the mine and, although eighty-five made it out safely and two were later found alive, ninety-one people died in the blaze. The monument features a miner hoisting a jack leg and a poem penned by then-state Senator Phil Batt (later Idaho's governor). Small memorials placed by the miners' families are scattered beneath the trees on each side.

Wallace, Kellogg's neighbor to the east, seems to be having more success than Kellogg in mining its glory days. The entire town is listed on the National Register of Historic Places, and it's well worth a day or two of exploration. The *Sierra Silver Mine Tour* is billed as the only one of its kind in the Northwest. Visitors ride a trolley-style bus to the mine portal, where hard hats are issued for the trip underground. Once in the mine the tour guides—themselves experienced miners—talk about and demonstrate the equipment and techniques used to mine silver ore. Interestingly this mine was once used as a working classroom for Wallace High School students who wanted to pursue a career underground.

Along with the mine visit, tour patrons are treated to a drive-around orientation of Wallace. Although billed as a family tour, children under four years old aren't permitted. (Guess no one makes hard hats that small.) But for everyone else, the one-hour tours leave every thirty minutes from 420 Fifth Street in Wallace. Tours are given from 9:00 A.M. to 4:00 P.M. mid-May through September, except during July and August, when trips leave until 6:00 P.M. Cost is $9.00 for adults, $8.00 for senior citizens age sixty-two and up, $7.00 for children ages four to sixteen, or $32.00 for a family of two adults with two or more children. Bring a jacket because mine temperatures average about 38° to 40° F. For more information call (208) 752–5151, or write Sierra Silver Mine Tour Inc., P.O. Box 712, Wallace 83873.

Just down the street from the mine tour office, the **Wallace District Mining Museum** at 509 Bank Street is a good spot to learn more about the mining industry and other area history. A short film, "North Idaho's Silver Legacy," is packed with interesting tales from Wallace's past. Exhibits include several mine models, a beautiful local history quilt, and the world's largest silver dollar (3 feet in diameter, with a weight of 150 pounds). It's also the usual final resting place of "Old Blinky," which until September 1991 was the last stoplight on I-90 between Seattle and Boston. The old stoplight is currently on loan to the Northwest Museum of Arts and Culture in Spokane, but should be back in Wallace by the end of 2003.

The mining museum is open daily from 8:00 A.M. to 8:00 P.M. in July and August and daily from 8:00 A.M. to 6:00 P.M. in May, June, and September. The rest of the year, it is open from 9:00 A.M. to 4:00 P.M. weekdays and 10:00 A.M. to 3:00 P.M. on Saturday, though hours may change, so call ahead. The cost is $2.00 for ages sixteen to fifty-five, $1.50 for senior citizens, 50 cents for kids ages six to fifteen, or $5.00 for a family. For more information, call (208) 556–1592.

On the same block at 524 Bank Street, **Silver Capital Arts** displays and sells collectible minerals and fossils, antiques, Idaho-made silver and gold jewelry, mining souvenirs, and more. **Indelible Tidbits** at 604 Bank Street doubles as a one-hour photo processing lab and a fly-tying shop. Owner Shauna Hillman offers a Fly of the Month Club, featuring a different angling aid sent to your favorite fly-fisher. For more information call her at (208) 753–0591.

Train fans will enjoy a stop at the **Northern Pacific Depot Railroad Museum** at 219 Sixth Street in Wallace. The last train ran out of the Wallace depot in 1980; since then, the facility has been moved to accommodate the freeway and renovated to tell all about the Northern Pacific, which at one time boasted "2,000 miles of startling beauty." There is an extensive collection of Northern Pacific memorabilia, even a quilt bearing the railway's famous red-and-black, yin-yang symbol.

The chateau-style Wallace depot has a fascinating history all its own. Built in 1901 with 15,000 bricks salvaged from what was to be a grand hotel in Tacoma, Washington, the station was visited two years later by then-President Theodore Roosevelt. It also has survived a string of

Northern Pacific Depot Railroad Museum

near disasters: a 1906 flood, a 1910 fire that burned half of Wallace, and a 1914 runaway train that crashed only a few feet from the depot. The Northern Pacific Depot Railroad Museum is open daily from 9:00 A.M. to 7:00 P.M. June through August. In May and September, hours are 9:00 A.M. to 5:00 P.M. In April and early October, the museum is open daily except Sunday from 10:00 A.M. to 3:00 P.M. Admission is $2.00 for adults, $1.50 for seniors age sixty and up, and $1.00 for children ages six through sixteen. Children age five and under get in free. The museum is closed mid-October through March. Call (208) 752–0111 for more information.

Last but certainly not least, the ***Oasis Rooms Bordello Museum*** at 605 Cedar Street documents another formerly important Wallace industry, one that thrived until just a decade ago. The Oasis Rooms were hardly unique; at one time five brothels stood along Wallace's main street, and prostitution was an acceptable misdemeanor in the eyes of local law enforcement. After all, Wallace had three times as many men as it did women, "so women had an opportunity and the townspeople didn't seem to object if the women stayed to themselves," explains Michelle Mayfield, who runs the museum with her husband, Jack.

But in 1973, according to *The New York Times,* Democratic Governor Cecil Andrus ordered that Wallace's brothels be shut down, possibly in response to an *Idaho Statesman* article in which Republican attorney Stanley Crow charged that Andrus had agreed to go easy on gambling and prostitution in North Idaho in return for a $25,000 campaign contribution. (Andrus denied the charge.) After the fuss subsided, the brothels quietly went back into business. But by the late 1980s, beset by the AIDS crisis and the faltering mining economy, only one house was left. The Oasis Rooms' employees would often make themselves scarce for a few days if FBI agents were rumored to be in town—and in January 1988, they left and never came back.

For that reason, the Oasis Rooms tour is a fascinating look at how these women worked and lived. The rooms are pretty much as the "girls" left them, with clothing, jewelry, and makeup strewn about. Mayfield opens a drawer in the office to reveal a pile of timers, each with a different woman's name affixed. A box of Mr. Bubble sits on the bathtub ledge, "Heather" written on it.

Mayfield explains that in the brothel's heyday, an employee might make $1,000 to $2,500 a week, and some women put themselves through college with their earnings. (The Oasis Rooms would not hire anyone from Wallace or the surrounding area.) But it's clear they worked hard for their money. A menu left on the wall when the Oasis Rooms closed revealed different services priced from $15 (for eight minutes of "straight, no frills") to $80 (for a bubble bath and an hour-long encounter). The madam kept 40 percent of all fees.

The Oasis Rooms Bordello Museum is open daily May through October

Home Strange Home

*I*t's not advertised in the Wallace tourism brochures, but **Jerry McKinnon's house** is easily the most offbeat spot in town. To get there just walk under the I–90 overpass by the Northern Pacific Depot Railroad Museum and past the Down by the Depot RV Park. Then look up to your right on the hillside, and you can't miss it. See the spaceship on the roof? When the wind blows just so, it rotates. And those huge, primitive paintings of favorite cartoon characters? Who's to say they won't someday wind up in a museum, touted as a leading example of late-twentieth-century folk art?

McKinnon keeps to himself most of the time and could not be interviewed for this book. "He likes his privacy," says Jeanne Grebil, who runs the adjacent RV park with her husband, Don. But Grebil does say that McKinnon's life has changed over the past few years. He once generated electricity with a paddlewheel on Nine Mile Creek below his home and recycled aluminum cans for grocery money—but now, since his Social Security checks started arriving, he's hooked up to the power company and cable television, just like everyone else. Still it seems doubtful that Jerry McKinnon will be replacing his Goofy and Popeye murals with beige siding any time soon.

from 10:00 A.M. to 5:00 P.M. It is open Thursday through Sunday in March, April, November, and December, and by appointment only in January and February. The tour costs $5.00 per person. For more information, call (208) 753–0801. To schedule a group tour or make an off-season appointment, phone (208) 752–3721.

Photos from the past are displayed at *The Beale House Bed and Breakfast,* located 4 blocks from downtown in one of Wallace's most prominent old buildings. Hosts Jim and Linda See have collected pictures from their home's past owners, as well as from the University of Idaho's Barnard-Stockbridge Photographic Collection. Beale House has five guest rooms, one with a fireplace, another with a balcony, another with two full walls of windows. Room rates start at $105, including breakfast. Children and pets should stay with grandma. For more information call (208) 752–7151, or write The Beale House, 107 Cedar Street, Wallace 83873.

East of Wallace, the *Route of the Hiawatha* mountain bike trail has stirred big excitement among cyclists. The 15-mile trail was built atop what was once the Milwaukee Road rail bed. Riders cross trestles (all with good guardrails) and pass through tunnels, including the 1.7-mile-long Taft Tunnel, which is why cyclists need to have a headlamp on their helmets. The mountain vistas are spectacular, and there's a fair chance you'll see wildlife. But the ride's biggest plus is that, with the help of a shuttle service, it's all downhill—actually a gentle grade of about 2 percent—making the Route of the Hiawatha a good choice for families. The trail is overseen by *Lookout Pass Ski and Recreation Area* located at I–90 exit 0 on the Idaho-Montana border. To get to the East Portal trailhead, where most people start, take I–90 over the Montana state line to exit 5 (Taft) and follow the signs. Trail day passes cost $7.00 per person, $3.00 for kids ages three to thirteen. The shuttle costs $9.00 for adults, $6.00 for children. The trail is open for riding or hiking late May through early October, and you can rent bikes, helmets, and lights here. For more information, see www.skilookout.com/home_bike.html or call (208) 744–1301.

From Wallace backtrack along I–90 to State Highway 3, the *White Pine Scenic Byway.* This route leads through country crisscrossed by the St. Joe and St. Maries Rivers. The St. Joe in particular is interesting; at about 2,200 feet above sea level, it is reportedly the highest navigable river in the world. These days it's also gaining renown for its fly-fishing and challenging rapids.

Hearty Scandinavian hospitality is the specialty at *Knoll Hus,* a guest house west of St. Maries overlooking Round Lake. Visitors stay in a cottage about 400 feet from the home of hosts Gene and Vicki Hedlund, who provide everything from a canoe and sandy beach to two mountain bikes. Knoll Hus can sleep up to four people; the rate for lodging is $110 per night for two, with additional people $10 apiece extra. Vicki requests a three-night minimum stay, and she can provide dinners with advance notice. Guests are on their own for breakfast, however, since Vicki also runs a shop in town. For more information or reservations, write Knoll Hus, P.O. Box 572, St. Maries 83861 or call (208) 245–4137.

Southeast of St. Maries on State Highway 3, look for two great places to have fun and maybe pick up some unique Idaho souvenirs (if you don't mind getting your hands dirty). The star garnet is found in only two places in the world, Idaho and India. And in Idaho the best place to dig for these dark beauties is the *Emerald Creek Garnet Area* 6 miles west of Clarkia on Forest Road 447. Star garnets are so named because they have rays that seem to dance across the gem's purple- or plum-colored surface. There are usually four rays, but some gems—the most valuable kind—have six. In ancient times, people believed garnets conferred a sense of calm and protection from wounds.

Garnets are typically found in alluvial deposits of gravel or sand just above bedrock, anywhere from 1 to 10 feet underground. The deposits along the East Fork of Emerald Creek are particularly rich, and visitors are invited to dig for fun and profit. First, however, a permit must be obtained at the A-frame building on the site, which is a half-mile hike from the parking lot. Permits are good for one day, and the cost is $10.00 for adults and $5.00 for children twelve and under.

The digging areas are open from 9:00 A.M. to 5:00 P.M. Friday through Tuesday, Memorial Day weekend through Labor Day, and a Forest Service campground is situated nearby. People planning to dig should bring the following: rubber boots, waders, or old tennis shoes; a change of clothes; a standard shovel; a bucket for bailing water; a container for holding garnets; and a screen box with quarter-inch wire mesh for washing gravel. Motorized equipment is not allowed at the site. For more information call the Forest Service in St. Maries at (208) 245–2531.

Also near Clarkia is the locally famous *Fossil Bowl,* just south of town. The Fossil Bowl was first and foremost a motorcycle racing track, but when owner Francis Kienbaum was bulldozing a new turn on the track in 1971, he unearthed a prime fossil area with a world-class stash of fifteen-million-year-old leaves, as well as a few fossilized insects, fish, and flowers. For $5.00 per person (no charge for young children), anyone can dig at the site. The fossils are found by chopping blocks from the soft clay hillside, then prying apart the layers with a knife. Some undisturbed layers that have yet to be exposed to the elements can yield magnificent leaves in their original dark green or red—until the air turns them black, usually within a minute.

The Fossil Bowl still hosts motorcycle races on Sundays mid-April through October, and anyone visiting on those days will get double for their entertainment dollar. The original fossil site is right by the racetrack, making for some dusty digging on race days, but another site farther from the commotion is now available as well. Digging is permitted year-round, but the Kienbaums suggest you call first to check on hours.

Visitors also may be interested in the Fossil Bowl's antiques collection, which includes century-old woodworking machinery. Although it's situated on Highway 3, the Fossil Bowl's legal address is Eighty-fifth and Plum—"85 miles out in the sticks and Plum the hell away from everything," Francis's son, Kenneth, explains. For more information call (208) 245–3608.

PLACES TO STAY IN NORTH IDAHO

BONNERS FERRY
Best Western Kootenai River Inn, Highway 95, (800) 346–5668, fax: (208) 267–3744

Bonners Ferry Log Inn, Highway 95 North, (208) 267–3986

SANDPOINT
Edgewater Resort, 56 Bridge Street, (800) 635–2534, fax: (208) 263–3194

Hawthorn Inn and Suites, 415 Cedar Street, (800) 282–0660, fax: (208) 263–3395

K2 Inn, 501 North Fourth, (208) 263–3441, fax: (208) 263–5718

Sandpoint Super 8, 3245 Highway 95, (800) 800–8000, fax: (208) 263–2210

Selkirk Lodge, at Schweitzer Mountain, (800) 831–8810, fax: (208) 263–7961

PRIEST LAKE (NORDMAN)
Elkins, HCO–1, Box 40, (208) 443–2432

Hill's Resort, 4777 West Lakeshore Road, (208) 443–2551

The Old Northern Inn, (208) 443–2426 (see text)

POST FALLS
WestCoast Templin's Hotel, 414 East First Avenue, (800) 325–4000, fax: (208) 773–4192

Riverbend Inn, 4105 West Riverbend Avenue, (800) 243–ROOM, fax: (208) 773–1306

Sleep Inn, 100 Pleasant View Road, (800) 851–3178, fax: (208) 777–8994

HAYDEN LAKE
Bridle Path Manor Bed & Breakfast, 1305 East Lancaster Road, (208) 762–3126 (see text)

Clark House, 5250 East Hayden Lake Road, (800) 765–4593 (see text)

COEUR D'ALENE
Bates Motel,
2018 Sherman Avenue,
(208) 667–1411 (see text)

Berry Patch Inn,
862 South Four Winds
Road, (208) 765–4994,
fax: (208) 664–0374
(see text)

Coeur d'Alene Inn &
Conference Center, 414
West Appleway Avenue,
(800) 251–7829,
fax: (208) 664–1962

Coeur d'Alene Resort,
115 South Second Avenue,
(800) 688–5253,
fax: (208) 664–7278

Garden Motel,
1808 Northwest Boulevard,
(208) 664–2743

Holiday Inn Express,
2209 East Sherman Avenue,
(800) HOLIDAY,
fax: (208) 769–7332

Shilo Inn,
702 West Appleway Avenue,
(800) 222–2244,
fax: (208) 667–2863

HARRISON
Hidden Creek Ranch,
7600 East Blue Lake Road,
(800) 446–DUDE,
fax: (208) 689–9115
(see text)

Squaw Bay Resort,
(208) 664–6782

KINGSTON
Kingston 5 Ranch,
42297 Silver Valley Road,
(208) 682–4862 (see text)

KELLOGG
Silverhorn Motor Inn,
699 West Cameron Avenue,
(208) 783–1151,
fax: (208) 784–5081

Super 8,
at the base of
Silver Mountain Gondola,
(800) 785–5443

WALLACE
Beale House Bed and
Breakfast, 107 Cedar Street,
(208) 752–7151

Best Western Wallace Inn,
100 Front Street,
(800) N–IDA–FUN,
fax: (208) 753–0981

The Brooks Hotel,
500 Cedar Street,
(800) 752–0469

ST. MARIES
The Pines Motel,
1117 Main, (208) 245–2545

Helpful Web sites

North Idaho Visitor Information—
www.visitnorthidaho.com

Sandpoint Chamber of Commerce—
www.sandpointchamber.com

Coeur d'Alene Visitor and
Convention Services—
www.coeurdalene.org

Idaho Spokesman–Review—
www.spokesmanreview.com

Worth Seeing

Factory outlets—*Post Falls*

Silverwood Amusement Park—
north of Coeur d'Alene

Wild Waters—*Coeur d'Alene*

Brooks Sea Planes—*Coeur d'Alene*

Coeur d'Alene Tribal Bingo/Casino—*Worley*

**PLACES TO EAT
IN NORTH IDAHO**

BONNERS FERRY
The Creamery (deli/coffee-house), 6428 Kootenai Street, (208) 267-2690

Springs Restaurant (American), in the Kootenai River Inn, (208) 267-8511

SANDPOINT
Eichardt's Pub Grill (American), 212 Cedar Street, (208) 263-4005

Fifth Avenue Restaurant (family), 807 North Fifth Avenue, (208) 263-0596

Hydra Restaurant (steak/seafood), 115 Lake, (208) 263-7123

Powerhouse Bar & Grill (American), 120 East Lake Street, (208) 265-2449

Swan's Landing (Northwest), Highway 95 (south end of the Long Bridge), (208) 265-2000

Several fast-food restaurants, located mainly along Highway 95 North

PRIEST LAKE
Elkins (American), HCO-1, Box 40, (208) 443-2432

Hill's Resort (American), 4777 West Lakeshore Road, (208) 443-2551

HAUSER LAKE
Chef in the Forest (fine dining), 12008 Woodland Beach Drive, (208) 773-3654 (see text)

POST FALLS
Bobby's Cafe (family), 103 West Seltice, (208) 773-9912

Casey's Pub & Grill (brewpub), 315 Ross Point, (208) 777-7047

Mallard's Restaurant (American), at Templin's Resort, (208) 773-1611

HAYDEN LAKE
Clark House(fine dining), 5250 East Hayden Lake Road, (800) 765-4593 (see text, reservations necessary)

COEUR D'ALENE
Beverly's (fine dining), in the Coeur d'Alene Resort, (208) 765-4000

Cedars Floating Restaurant (seafood), off Highway 95 south of town, (208) 664-2922

Java on Sherman (coffee house), 324 Sherman Avenue, (208) 667-0010

Jimmy D's (Northwest), 320 Sherman Avenue, (208) 664-9774

Moon Time (casual pub), 1602 Sherman Avenue, (208) 667-2331 (see text)

Mulligan's (American), in the Coeur d'Alene Inn & Convention Center, 414 West Appleway Avenue, (208) 765-3200

T.W. Fisher's (brewpub), 204 North Second Avenue, (208) 664-BREW

Takara (Japanese), 309 Lakeside, (208) 765-8014

Village Inn (family), Highway 95 North, (208) 664-3349

The Wine Cellar (Mediterranean), 313 Sherman, (208) 664-WINE

Most major fast-food chain restaurants, located mainly along Appleway Avenue

HARRISON
Gateway Resort & Marina (American), (208) 689-3387

KINGSTON
Enaville Resort (family), I-90 exit 43, (208) 682-3453 (see text)

KELLOGG
McDonald's (fast food), 820 West Cameron, (208) 784-4431

Mojo Espresso (coffee house), 124 McKinley, (208) 784-6025

Patrick's Steakhouse and Inn (American), 305 South Division Street, (208) 786-2311

Zany's at Silver Mountain
(pizza), 610 Bunker
Avenue, (208) 784–1144

WALLACE
Albi's Steakhouse
(American),
Sixth and Pine Streets,
(208) 753–3071

The Garden Restaurant
(American),
at The Brooks Hotel,
500 Cedar Street,
(800) 752–0469

The Jameson Restaurant &
Saloon (American),
304 Sixth Street,
(208) 556–6000
(closed winters)

ST. MARIES
Bud's Drive–In
(American), 101 College,
(208) 245–3312

North Central Idaho

I n Idaho, geography has decreed that there are simply some places where roads cannot go—or where travelers can pass only with much effort. In North Central Idaho, nature has made the rules and humans play along as well as we're able. Consequently there is only one east-west road, U.S. Highway 12, across this region—and it was not completed until 1962. The major north-south route, U.S. Highway 95, also evolved according to geography.

It's 196 miles from Moscow to McCall, but you're not going to make this trip in four hours. Between long hill climbs and river-hugging curves, it's slow, scenic going wherever you travel in North Central Idaho. The main routes are alluring enough, but plan to explore some of the secondary roads, too. The Lolo Highway, the Elk City Wagon Road, and the climb to the Hells Canyon Rim at Heaven's Gate are just a few of this region's many great byways.

For more North Central Idaho travel information, call (800) 473–3543; write the North Central Idaho Travel Association, P.O. Box 2018, Lewiston 83501; or see www.idahonwp.org.

Palouse and Clearwater Country

N orth Central Idaho is a land of contrast, and nowhere is this fact more visible than in Latah and Clearwater Counties, where rolling farmlands seamlessly give way to dense forests. This is the Palouse (pronounced pah-LOOSE), a rich agricultural region that spills across the Idaho-Washington border. And there are few better places to start a tour of the area than *Mary Minerva McCroskey State Park.* To get there from Moscow, drive 25 miles north on U.S. Highway 95, and watch for the Skyline Drive sign atop a hill not far north of the state rest area. Turn left, or west, and follow the road through thick pine forests into the preserve, such as it is.

Although it's among Idaho's largest and oldest state parks, McCroskey is also the state's most forgotten, until recently going unmentioned on

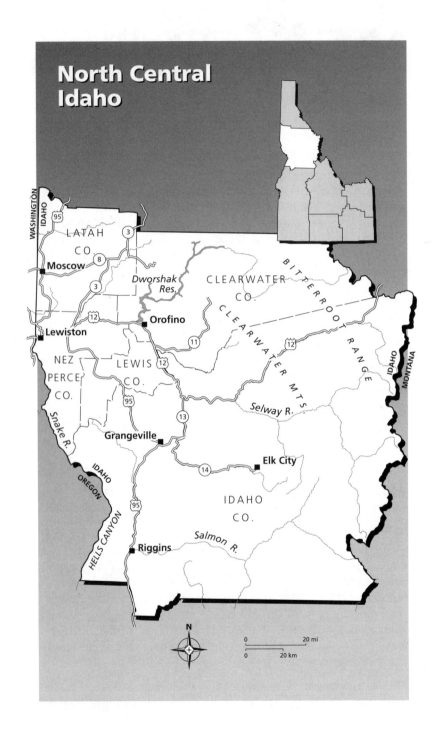

North Central Idaho

JULIE'S FAVORITES

Lolo Motorway—
North of Highway 12

Nez Perce National
Historic Park—regionwide

Wolf Education and
Research Visitor Center—
Winchester

Heaven's Gate—west
of Riggins

Backcountry B&B—Warren

most maps and parks literature. Virgil T. McCroskey grew up looking at this ridge from his boyhood home at the base of Steptoe Butte, just over the Washington state line. He later bought the land, turned it into a parkway in honor of his mother, and sought to donate it to the state of Idaho. The state wasn't too interested, but it finally took charge after McCroskey agreed to put up money for maintenance until his death. Since then, the park—or state reserve, as it's sometimes called—has remained undeveloped, but its 17 miles of road and 30 miles of trails afford many good views of the Palouse. You'll find a few picnic areas and primitive campsites scattered along the drive. The road isn't recommended for trailers of more than 25 feet in length.

Moscow, home to the University of Idaho, took its name not from the city in Russia but from a community in Pennsylvania. In its early years Moscow had an even more unusual name: Hog Heaven, so called because farmers saw their pigs munching merrily on the camas bulbs so prevalent in the area. In 1889 Moscow town was named the site of Idaho's federal land-grant college. It may seem odd that the state's namesake university is so far from Idaho's population center in Boise, but despite or perhaps even because of its remoteness, Moscow is the quintessential college town—a blend of funky charm and high-tech attitude and more liberal than anywhere else in the state, with the possible exception of Sun Valley/Ketchum.

The U of I is blessed with a beautiful campus that includes the nineteen-acre **Shattuck Arboretum,** one of the oldest university arboretums in the western United States. Planted from 1910 to 1917, the arboretum is a pleasant place for a stroll amid native Idaho trees, as well as those introduced from other regions. Just across Nez Perce Drive from Shattuck Arboretum, the sixty-three-acre University of Idaho Arboretum and Botanical Garden was planted during the 1980s. It showcases trees and shrubs from around the world grouped by their geographical origin. For self-guiding brochures to both arboretums, visit the campus information center on Pullman Road (State Highway 8) and Line Street. Guided tours may be arranged by calling (208) 885–6250.

Idaho's state horse, the Appaloosa, is best known by the spots on its rump. Learn everything you ever wanted to know about Appaloosas and more at the **Appaloosa Museum and Heritage Center** in Moscow. Exhibits recount the evolution of the Appaloosa, historical aspects of the breed, and its importance to the Nez Perce Indians. The museum is on Moscow's western edge at 2720 West Pullman Road, and it's open from 10:00 A.M. to 5:00 P.M. Tuesday through Friday and from 10:00 A.M. to 4:00 P.M. on Saturday year-round. Admission is free, but donations are welcome. Call (208) 882–5578 for more information.

Moscow's restaurant scene isn't on a par with many other college towns, but *Red Door,* at 215 South Main, is one of the more interesting eateries to emerge in recent years. Open for dinner Tuesday through Saturday, Red Door specializes in creative cuisine and a fun decor featuring framed post cards. Dishes include Indonesian pork tenderloin, coconut ginger shrimp, and Australian-style beef tenderloin. Call (208) 882–7830 for reservations for parties of five or more. If you're early, do some window shopping across the street at *Wild Women Traders,* an eclectic, locally owned store featuring all kinds of cool clothes and home accents at 210 South Main.

Moscow also has a good downtown coffeehouse scene. *Bucer's,* at 201 South Main Street, roasts its own coffee on the premises. The furnishings look like something out of a law office, with a wall of books and a big communal-style table in the center. Drop by at lunchtime for Italian-style panini sandwiches, or Friday or Saturday evening for live music. The phone number is (208) 882–5216. *BookPeople,* one of Idaho's best independent bookstores, doubles as an espresso joint in its new and larger location at 521 South Main. It also has a regular calendar of readings and other special events you can access at www.bookpeople.net.

On wooded acreage outside town, Solveig and Jon Miller welcome guests to *Paradise Ridge Bed & Breakfast.* The Palouse Suite features

Dig This

*I*daho is not the first place that comes to mind when you think about jazz. So fans of America's indigenous music are pleasantly surprised to learn that Idaho has a rich and growing jazz scene. In Moscow the University of Idaho is the setting for the annual **Lionel Hampton Jazz Festival,** one of the premier events of its kind. Held the last weekend each February in the university's Kibbie Dome, the festival has recently featured Ray Brown, Roy Hargrove, Jane Monheit, Lou Rawls, and dozens of other top jazz stars. Leonard Feather, jazz critic for the Los Angeles Times, *called it "the number one jazz festival in the world."* The festival also serves as a workshop for thousands of music students who travel to Moscow to play with the pros. For ticket and schedule information, call (800) 345–7402.

TOP ANNUAL EVENTS

Lionel Hampton Jazz Festival, Moscow (mid-February)

Dogwood Festival, Lewiston (late April)

Renaissance Faire, Moscow (early May)

Rendezvous in the Park, Moscow (early July)

Chief Looking Glass Days, Kamiah (mid-August)

Lumberjack Days, Orofino (mid-September)

a king-size bed, bath, vaulted wood ceilings, and a private deck along with a hide-a-bed for a third person. (Kids ten and older are welcome.) It rents for $105 single or double occupancy, $125 for three people. Two other rooms with a shared bath also are available for $75 each. The public areas include two hot tubs, and a short walk up a nearby ridge gives guests great views of the Palouse countryside and beyond. For information call (208) 882–5292 or write Paradise Ridge Bed & Breakfast, 2455 Blaine Road, Moscow 83843. Credit cards are not accepted.

Elk River, at the tail end of State Highway 8 east of Moscow, serves as the north gateway to Dworshak Reservoir. You can find a room or RV spot here at the **Huckleberry Heaven Lodge,** or rent snowmobiles, all-terrain vehicles, boats, skis, and fishing poles—just about any gear or guide needed to take advantage of nearby Elk Creek Reservoir and the surrounding country.

Before you leave Elk River, take a walk around town. It's the kind of place where every family has its members' names posted on the welcome sign. There's also a handsome old schoolhouse built in 1912, perched on a hill overlooking the town. It's no longer used, but a nearby church built the same year is still in operation. For a more vigorous workout, consider a hike up 5,824-foot Elk Butte, where a panoramic view awaits all who make it to the top.

Several other natural attractions are within easy drives of Elk River. Just west of town **Elk Creek Falls**—actually three separate falls—are reached via a set of short trails that run along what was once the old route to Orofino. If you have time to visit only one of the cascades, make it Middle Falls, at 90 feet the highest of the three. Along the way, hikers pass the site of Elk Creek Falls School, which operated between 1910 and 1930. The forest has reclaimed the building, but its gateposts still stand.

Some of Idaho's oldest and tallest trees may be seen north of Elk River. A giant Western red cedar, estimated at more than 3,000 years old, is accessed via Forest Road 4764, a branch off Road 382. At 177 feet tall and 18 feet in diameter, this is the largest tree in Idaho. Not far away, following Forest Roads 382 and 1969, is the Old Growth Cedar Grove. The eighty-acre stand is one of the few remaining old-growth cedar groves in Idaho, with trees estimated to be at least 500 years old.

The Dent Road leads from Elk River to Dworshak Dam and Reservoir. **Dworshak Dam** is notable because at 717 feet tall, it's the highest straight-axis, concrete gravity dam in the Western world and the largest ever built by the U.S. Army Corps of Engineers. A visitor center overlooks the dam; call (800) 321–3198 to check hours.

Dworshak Dam backs up the North Fork of the Clearwater River into a 53-mile-long reservoir. Among the recreation opportunities on the lake and its shores are dozens of primitive camping areas, known as minicamps, many of which are accessible by boat only. Each minicamp is outfitted with a grill, picnic table, tent pad, and access to a chemical rest room. In recent years the campsites have frequently been rendered inaccessible because of drawdowns aimed to help migrating salmon, but Northwest water policy is evolving and the situation may change. For information on the minicamps or water levels, call (208) 476–1255 or (800) 321–3198 for taped information. More traditional camping is available at Dworshak State Park.

Highway 12 west and southeast of Orofino is known as the **Northwest Passage Scenic Byway,** and it's here where the velvety brown hillsides of the Inland Northwest meet the mountains and forests of the Rockies, sometimes intercepted by vast plateaus and prairies. Take State Highway 11 east of Greer for a scenic drive across this changing landscape.

From Greer the highway climbs a dizzying grade onto the Weippe Prairie. Weippe, a town of about 500 people, has one of Idaho's best pizza parlors. **Weippe Pizza** at 118 North Main Street specializes in some unusual combinations with such toppings as German sausage, jalapeño peppers, and sauerkraut. Pizza tops the menu, but soup, sandwiches, and salads are all available, too. The restaurant is open for lunch and dinner Wednesday through Sunday. Call (208) 435–4823.

Backtrack to Greer, or use Weippe as a jumping-off spot for the North Fork Adventure Road—the backcountry route to Superior, Montana—or for Lolo Trail, the famous path trod first by Indians and later by Lewis and Clark on their trek across the continent. It was just outside Weippe, in fact, that the Corps of Discovery (as President Thomas Jefferson dubbed the Lewis and Clark party) met the Nez Perce, who were to become indispensable to the white men's survival.

The Lolo Trail

ewis and Clark had been told the Lolo Trail crossing could be made in five days, but it took the corps twice that time, and they almost froze and starved en route. An early snow blanketed the mountains, and—with no game to be found—the explorers were reduced to eating horse meat and candle wax. Finally, on September 20, 1805, Clark and an advance party of six other men dragged themselves out of the Bitterroot Mountains and onto the Weippe Prairie. Their route over the mountains can still be traced over the *Lolo Motorway,* accessible from the west via Weippe or Kamiah, or from the east via Forest Roads 569 (Parachute Hill) or 107 north from Highway 12. The Lolo Motorway—also known as Forest Road 500—is one of the roughest roads you'll encounter anywhere, but it's well worth the time and effort it takes to travel. The route is usually accessible only from mid-July through mid-September. Four-wheel drive isn't a must, but a vehicle with good clearance is essential. Before setting out, stop at the Forest Service office in Kooskia or Powell or the visitor center at Lolo Pass on the Idaho-Montana border for maps and a detailed brochure on the Lolo Motorway route, as well as information on current conditions. From 2002 through 2007, the Forest Service may require Lolo Motorway travelers to obtain a permit through a lottery system—they anticipate high usage during the Lewis and Clark Bicentennial. Details are to be announced each December, and people will have two months to apply for permits for the following summer's season. For updated information, see the Clearwater National Forest's Web page at www.fs.fed.us/r1/clearwater/, or call (208) 926–4274.

Castle Butte Lookout, a former working fire tower situated near the motorway, is a wonderful place to get away from civilization for a while. The lookout is about 15 feet square and is perched on a stone foundation

Author's Note

*I*n 2003–2006, the United States will mark the bicentennial of the Lewis and Clark Expedition. Interest in the expedition is already high in the wake of Ken Burns's PBS documentary on the explorers and Stephen Ambrose's best-selling Meriwether Lewis biography, Undaunted Courage. But to really understand Lewis and Clark, it's necessary to follow in their footsteps. Harlan and Barbara Opdahl of Pierce, Idaho, make that easy with their weeklong **Lewis and Clark** trips along the Lolo Trail. Participants ride horseback and hike along the route, visiting such landmarks as the Smoking Place and Spirit Revival Ridge. The cost is $1,575 per person. For more information call (208) 464–2349 or (208) 464–2761; write Triple "O" Outfitters, P.O. Box 217, Pierce 83546; or see the Web site at www.tripleo-outfitters.com.

Castle Butte Lookout

about 20 feet high. Visitors are treated to sweeping views in all directions, but especially to the south, where the Selway-Bitterroot Wilderness stretches beyond the Lochsa River and east into Montana. The river itself is barely visible thousands of feet below this ridge.

Castle Butte Lookout is furnished with a double bed, single cot, table with two chairs, propane stove, and several chests of drawers. It's a great place to read, write, nap, and daydream. Visitors also can amuse themselves by learning to use the firefinder (a device consisting of a map and a sighting instrument used to determine the location of a forest fire), exploring the local terrain, or rummaging through artifacts left by previous lookout tenants: a copy of *The Smokechaser,* a memoir by former fire lookout Carl A. Weholt; a deck of playing cards; old magazines; a Western novel. The lookout is available for rent from mid- to late summer; for information contact the Clearwater National Forest's Lochsa Ranger District Office, Route 1, Box 398, Kooskia 83539, or call (208) 926–4274.

Several Lolo Trail landmarks are a short hike or drive from Castle Butte. To the east are the Sinque Hole, where Lewis and Clark camped September 17, 1805, and the Smoking Place, where the returning explorers stopped in June 1806 to share a pipe with their Nez Perce guides. To the west, the dry camp of September 18, 1805, was where Captain Clark moved ahead with six hunters to look for game. And from nearby Sherman Peak, the captains first glimpsed the distant prairies. The corps called this spot Spirit Revival Ridge, realizing that their toilsome mountain travel was almost behind them.

Highway 12, the road the explorers' route paralleled, has many interesting sights of its own. Up near Lolo Pass, the ***Packer Meadows*** area is especially beautiful in mid-June when the purple camas are in bloom. Packer Meadows is also an excellent spot for cross-country skiing. The picnic area near milepost 165 on Highway 12 is known as the ***DeVoto Memorial Cedar Grove,*** named in honor of Bernard DeVoto, a noted writer and historian. Western red cedars tower here over the spot

DeVoto often camped at while editing the Lewis and Clark journals, well before Highway 12 was completed in 1961. DeVoto's ashes were sprinkled over the grove after his death in 1955.

Powell, a little outpost along the highway, is the last place to buy gas until Lowell, about 50 miles west. The **Lochsa Lodge,** built here in 1928, burned down in 2001, but its owners plan to rebuild. For now, a store and temporary restaurant provide fuel to hungry travelers. Call (208) 942–3405 to see when the new motel and cabins will open.

Colgate Licks and *Jerry Johnson Hot Springs,* both located near Highway 12 west of the Wendover-Whitehouse campgrounds, are among the most popular stops along Highway 12. At Colgate Licks, deer, elk, and other animals are attracted by the springs' saltiness. Take the loop trail from the parking lot to reach the springs. The Jerry Johnson site is accessed by a mile-long trail up Warm Springs Creek. *The Lochsa Historical Ranger Station,* with one of the West's best collections of Forest Service memorabilia, is also worth a stop. It's located across from the Wilderness Gateway campground, among the most pleasant along Highway 12.

At Lowell, Idaho, the Lochsa and Selway Rivers meet to form the Middle Fork of the Clearwater River. *Three Rivers Resort* sits at this confluence. Several lodging options exist here, including Old #1, a former ranger's cabin with modern amenities including a wood stove, hot tub on the front deck, full bathroom, kitchen, and a TV with VCR. The cabin is available April through mid-October, and nightly rates—about $100 double occupancy—include a bottle of champagne. For more information call

Three Rivers Resort

(208) 926–4430 or write Three Rivers Resort, HC 75 Box 61, Kooskia at Lowell 83539.

Of the 300 or so species of hummingbirds on the planet, three of them spend their springs and summers in the backyard of Ruth McCombs's home about 10 miles east of Kooskia. Stop by and you're likely to see as many as thirty of the little hummers flitting about the feeders McCombs lovingly keeps filled. McCombs calls her place **Hummingbird Haven,** and hundreds of bird fanciers stop by each year. She says the birds usually show up in mid-April and fly south for the winter about mid-August. McCombs charges no admission, and visitors are welcome to just drop by if they're in the area. Look for Hummingbird Haven at milepost 84 on U.S. Highway 12.

Land of the Nez Perce

The Nez Perce people—or Ne-Me-Poo, as they call themselves—have played a substantial role in the history of what is now Idaho, as well as that of the United States as a whole. For more than a century, history students have been moved by the words of Nez Perce leader Chief Joseph who, upon his tribe's capture in Montana, made his famous "I will fight no more forever . . ." speech. Those words, uttered just 42 miles short of refuge at the Canadian border, marked the end of a 1,000-mile march punctuated by the battles of the Nez Perce War.

The war was precipitated by the discovery of gold on the Nez Perce reservation, which—by the original treaty signed in 1855—included most of the tribe's traditional homeland. When the gold was found, however, the U.S. government redrew the reservation's boundaries to exclude the areas of mineral wealth. One Nez Perce leader known as Lawyer accepted the new boundaries and signed a new treaty. But other members of the tribe, led by Old Joseph, did not agree, and soon there were two bands of Nez Perce: the "treaty" and "nontreaty."

Soon after Lawyer signed the treaty in 1867, the government launched a campaign to move all Nez Perce to the new reservation. The nontreaty Nez Perce ignored the government's orders, and for a time they were able to live peaceably. But by 1877 the government was ready to force the nontreaty Nez Perce to move, and a June 14 deadline was set.

In the meantime Young Joseph had succeeded his father. He did not wish to move, nor did he wish to wage war, so he moved his followers toward the reservation. Before they made it, however, three young Nez Perce men—angry at the forced move and seeking revenge for the death of one of their fathers—killed four white settlers by noon on June 14. Over the next few days, other Nez Perce joined in and an additional fourteen or fifteen whites were slain. The Nez Perce War was on.

Although the Nez Perce trail crosses through several states, North Central Idaho and adjacent areas in Oregon and Washington comprise the tribe's ancestral homeland. For that reason the **Nez Perce National Historic Park** was established in the Gem State. Unlike most national park sites, however, the Nez Perce park isn't one specific place. Instead it includes thirty-eight sites scattered across this region. Two of the most interesting are located near Highway 12 on the way to Lewiston.

Just outside Kamiah, a basaltic formation known as the **Heart of the Monster** explains how the Nez Perce came to be. According to tribal legend, Coyote—a mythical figure central to much Native American literature—killed a great monster near here. The Nez Perce and other tribes were created, each as parts of the monster fell to the earth. An audio station at the site retells the legend, first in the Nez Perce's native tongue, then in English. Kamiah is also the site of the annual Chief Looking Glass Days festival held the third weekend of August. This traditional powwow features descendants of Chief Looking Glass, a Nez Perce leader, participating in dancing and other cultural activities. Call (208) 935–2525 for more information.

The Nez Perce National Historic Park headquarters are at Spalding, just east of Lewiston on Highway 95. This is where Henry and Eliza Spalding established their mission to the Nez Perce in the 1830s. A Presbyterian missionary, Spalding believed it was his duty to Christianize the Indians. "What is done for the poor Indians of this Western world must be done soon," he said. "The only thing that can save them from annihilation is the introduction of civilization."

The **Spalding Site,** as the headquarters are sometimes called, features an excellent visitor center that catalogs the changes—both good and bad—this philosophy wrought for the Nez Perce. Exhibits include a Book of Matthew printed in the Indians' language, a case full of beautiful beadwork, and a silk ribbon and silver friendship medal presented to the Nez Perce by Lewis and Clark. Another highlight is a 32-foot canoe made in 1837 from a single cottonwood log.

Lewiston is the largest city in North Central Idaho, and it has more than 15 miles of trails for joggers, cyclists, walkers, and strollers. Many of these paths are on the Lewiston Levee, which was constructed by the U.S. Army Corps of Engineers to protect Lewiston after the completion of Lower Granite Dam down the Snake River.

Visit the West End of Lewiston's charming downtown for one of the city's most interesting attractions. *Morgan's Alley* at 301 Main Street is a collection of specialty shops, restaurants, and a banquet facility. The "alley" is actually four old buildings linked together by thirteen stairways and seventeen brick arches.

Interspersed among the Alley's seventeen shops are numerous artifacts from area history. In the Country House, the front of the U.S. Postal Service substation came from the post office in Pomeroy, Washington, circa 1888. An old-fashioned gas pump marks the entrance to Bojacks, a steak-and-seafood eatery and cocktail lounge. Sets of doors came from the local sheriff's office and the Lewiston National Bank. And so on. *Shaggy's Cyber Cafe* in the lower level is a good place to check your e-mail.

Lewiston history is also the focus at the *Nez Perce County Museum,* at Third and C Streets. The museum sits on the site occupied by one of Lewiston's first buildings, the Luna House Hotel. After serving as a hotel, the building also functioned as a courthouse for a few years in the late 1880s. Today's museum is home to a collection of Nez Perce and pioneer artifacts, along with a striking trio of paintings by Dan Piel portraying the Indian leader Chief Joseph in his youth, maturity, and old age. The Luna House Museum is open from 10:00 A.M. to 4:00 P.M. Tuesday through Saturday, March through November. Admission is by donation. Call (208) 743–2535 for more information. Elsewhere downtown the *Lewis-Clark Center for Arts & History* at 415 Main Street has an interesting permanent exhibit, "Chinese at the Confluence," featuring artifacts from the city's nineteenth-century Chinese temple. Call (208) 799–2243 for hours or more information.

Do the Twist

*F*or a different perspective on Lewiston and environs, check out the famous **Spiral Highway** north of town. This twisting two-lane with sixty-four curves climbs 2,000 feet to the top of Lewiston Hill. It was completed in 1917 at a cost of $100,000— about twice the projected tab. Until 1979 the Spiral Highway was the only route from Lewiston to the Palouse region above. It's still open to traffic, but most motorists now use the newer four-lane section of U.S. Highway 95. Either way, stop at the overlook at the top of the hill for a great view of Lewiston, neighboring Clarkston, Washington, the confluence of the Clearwater and Snake Rivers, and the rolling farmland all around.

Lewiston has several interesting spots to get a meal or a quick snack. *BlackBird Java* at 326 Main Street is a comfortable spot to sip espresso and maybe enjoy a soup, sandwich, or pastry. There's eclectic live music several times a month, but if nothing's on when you visit, you can gaze at the local artwork and the pressed-tin ceiling. For fine dining, *Jonathan's* at 1516 Main Street is Lewiston's top choice, with steaks, seafood, pastas, and more. Nearly every entree is available in a smaller "eating light" version. Call (208) 746–3438 for reservations.

The *Hay Loft Bed & Breakfast,* located in the East Orchards area of town near the Lewiston Round-up Grounds, gears itself to horse-fancying visitors. Hosts Kipp and Lori Massey offer four guest rooms for people, plus box stalls and pastureland for travelers' equine pals. The rooms rent for $60 to $80 a night including a big country-style breakfast, with the horse facilities extra. For more details call (208) 746–2363 or write The Hay Loft, 2031 Powers Avenue, Lewiston 83501.

Lewiston spends much of the month of April celebrating the arrival of spring with the annual *Dogwood Festival,* named for the hundreds of dogwood trees and perennial plants that burst forth in bloom that time of year. Events typically include an invitational art show and sale at the Lewis-Clark Center for Arts & History; the Palouse Empire Dressage Show, featuring precision horseback riding; athletic competitions; food festivals; a children's parade; and a concert. Call (208) 799–2243 for information.

Lewiston is also the northern gateway for **Hells Canyon,** the deepest gorge in North America. Hells Canyon National Recreation Area straddles the Snake River south of Lewiston and includes parts of Oregon's Wallowa-Whitman National Forest and the Nez Perce and Payette National Forests of Idaho. More than thirty outfitters offer jet boat or rafting trips through the canyon. For a list contact the Hells Canyon National Recreation Area headquarters in Clarkston at (509) 758–0616. One of our favorites, *Snake River Adventures,* offers overnight accommodations, meals, and good fishing at its Kirby Creek Lodge, the only privately owned place to stay within the canyon's depths. For information, call (800) 262–8874 or see www.snakeriveradventures.com.

Private rafters and jet-boaters also may travel the river, but a Forest Service permit is required before launching. Many river trips leave from Hells Canyon Dam northwest of Cambridge, Idaho; see the Southwestern Idaho chapter for more details on those.

South of Lewiston, Highway 95 cuts across the Nez Perce Indian Reservation, with the aforementioned National Historic Park site and the tribal headquarters at Lapwai. Just outside Winchester, the tribe—in a partnership with the Wolf Education and Research Center (WERC)—has established a twenty-acre enclosure that is home to eleven wolves. The "Sawtooth Pack-Wolves of the Nez Perce," as they are known, originally lived north of Sun Valley, Idaho, under the care of WERC founder and photographer/filmmaker Jim Dutcher. The pack was relocated to Winchester in 1996 and serves as ambassadors for their wild cousins now being reintroduced in Idaho and elsewhere in the Rocky Mountain region.

The *Wolf Education and Research Visitor Center* is open from 9:00 A.M. to 5:00 P.M. Wednesday through Sunday from Memorial Day to mid-October. The small center features beautiful doors created by Nez Perce artist John Wilson, plus a small gift shop and exhibits. There's no charge for the center or for the viewing platform immediately outside, which overlooks the wolf enclosure, the main attraction. For $3.00 (children under twelve are free), visitors can take a short self-guided tour that ends at a closer viewing platform about 50 yards from the enclosure. Or visitors can plan to take a naturalist-guided tour, which goes inside the outer perimeter of the enclosure, where wolves can sometimes be seen within a few feet. Since early mornings or evenings are the best times to see wolves and hear them howl, these tours are scheduled Wednesday through Saturday at 7:30 A.M. and 7:00 P.M. Tours cost $10 for ages twelve and up; younger children are admitted free. Private tours can also be arranged in the off-season by calling (208) 924–6960.

The wolf center is near Winchester State Park, a popular place for camping and fishing in summer and cross-country skiing, ice fishing, and ice skating in winter. The park has three yurts available for rent year-round. Equipped with electricity and heat and big enough to sleep six, the yurts cost $35 per night for up to four people; up to two additional people cost $4.00 each. They can be reserved by calling Hells Gate State Park in Lewiston at (208) 799–5015. For more information on Winchester State Park, call (208) 924–7563 or visit their Web site at www.idahoparks.org/parks/winchester.html.

South of the Nez Perce reservation border on U.S. Highway 95, near the town of Cottonwood, you can't miss the sight of Sweet Willy, a 30-foot-high beagle looming over *Dog Bark Park.* Look closer and you'll see Sweet Willy actually doubles as a guest house that can comfortably sleep a family of four. The house has a queen bed, small kitchen, and bathroom in the main quarters and a loft for kids up in the dog's head. This clever idea was the brainchild of Dennis J. Sullivan, who with his wife Frances Conklin, has already found some measure of fame as a chain saw artist specializing in dogs. (A gift shop at the site features their work, and there's also a picnic area and visitor information center for passersby.) Sweet Willy can be rented for about $100 a night, including continental breakfast. For more information or a reservation, call (208) 962–DOGS.

Also near Cottonwood, the **Monastery of St. Gertrude** sits high on a hill overlooking the Camas Prairie. The monastery is well worth a visit for its stone chapel and a most impressive museum.

St. Gertrude's Chapel was built in 1920 of blue porphyry stone quarried nearby. Each stone was individually chiseled and placed by hand, with the nuns themselves doing much of the work. The resulting Roman-esque structure and its 97-foot twin towers may be seen for miles around. The tower's bells are rung daily to call the Benedictine sisters of St. Gertrude's to services, but they're also sounded at times of severe storms as a prayer for protection. The chapel's interior is equally striking, most notably the German altar at the front. In deference to the pain Jesus Christ felt when he was hung on the cross, not one nail was used to make the altar; each part was mortised and glued. A self-guiding tour brochure is available inside the chapel.

St. Gertrude's Museum is also quite a sight, particularly the Rhoades Emmanuel Memorial Wing added in 1988. This section houses the collection of Samuel Emmanuel, who gave the museum a treasure trove of artistic pieces ranging from Ming ceramics to a French cabinet that appeared in the 1892 World's Fair in Chicago to a Czechoslovakian chandelier with 160 crystals. This European finery may seem out of place on the prairies of Idaho, but plenty of local lore is represented, too, most notably an exhibit about the life of Polly Bemis. This fascinating Chinese woman was nineteen years old when she arrived in the Warren mining camps of Idaho, where she was sold into slavery. She wound up marrying saloon-keeper Charlie Bemis and running a boarding house.

St. Gertrude's Museum is open 9:30 A.M. to 4:30 P.M. Tuesday through Saturday year-round, as well as 1:30 to 4:30 P.M. Sunday May through September. Admission is $4.00 for adults and $1.00 for children ages seven to seventeen. The museum holds an annual Victorian tea the second Saturday in May and a raspberry festival the first Sunday of August. For more information or to arrange a group tour, call (208) 962–7123.

At the north entrance of Grangeville, it's worth a brief stop to check out the **mammoth exhibit** in Eimer's Park. In 1994, a heavy-equipment operator working at the bed of Tolo Lake 6 miles west of Grangeville

Author's Note

Quick: Name the deepest gorge in North America. If you said the Grand Canyon, you're wrong. The title actually goes to Hells Canyon on the Idaho-Oregon border. That's because the Snake River, flowing here near sea level, is bordered by the Seven Devils Mountains, which top 9,300 feet. The average depth of Hells Canyon works out to 6,600 feet. By contrast the Grand Canyon of the Colorado—although much longer and more expansive—is 4,000 to 5,500 feet deep from rim to river. Visit or call the Hells Canyon National Recreation Area office in Riggins for maps and detailed directions into the canyon. The phone number is (208) 628-3916. Also see the Southwestern Idaho chapter for information on trips from Hells Canyon Dam west of Cambridge.

discovered what turned out the be the thigh bone of a male Columbian mammoth. The Idaho Museum of Natural History from Pocatello led digs at the site in the summer of 1995 and found bones from at least nine mammoths. The glassed-in pavilion here in Grangeville features a full-size mammoth replica, as well as a mural by local artist Robert Thomas depicting what the Tolo Lake area may have looked like about 12,000 years ago when mammoths were on the scene. *Tolo Lake,* meanwhile, has refilled and is a popular spot for fishing and bird-watching.

When Grangeville got going back in 1876, the Grange Hall was the first building in town, which is how the city got its name. The hall later fell to fire, but a new building went up in 1909 and still stands on the northeast corner of Main and Hall Streets. The place is now home to **Oscar's Restaurant,** the best in town. Like many other Idaho eateries, Oscar's has walls decorated with various farm and ranching implements. But here, coupled with the high ceilings and the soft peach-and-green decor, the effect pays homage to the area's agricultural ties without dissolving into a tacky, haphazard mess. The classy ambience continues next door at Brodock's Saloon, where booths, tables, and even couches are grouped for easy conversation and where Albert Bierstadt prints and Thomas Moran artworks grace the walls.

All this would be for naught if the food faltered. But Oscar's menu succeeds, too, with wide variety and reasonable prices. At breakfast the "Egg-static" features eggs scrambled with diced ham and a pile of hash browns, while kids might want to order a "Teddy Cake" flapjack done up like a bear. For lunch there are homemade soups, salads, and fourteen sandwiches. Dinner choices include steak, prime rib, seafood, and chicken, with almost everything on the menu under $12. The dessert specialties include lemon meringue pie and Kentucky Pie, with chocolate chip filling. Espresso is available all day. Oscar's, at 101 East Main, is open 7:00 A.M. to 9:00 P.M. Monday through Saturday and 7:00 A.M. to 2:00 P.M. Sunday; hours are shorter in winter. The phone number is (208) 983-2106.

The town of Harpster, east of Grangeville on State Highway 13, serves as the gateway to another historic road way off the beaten path. The *Elk City Wagon Road* was developed in the late nineteenth century as a route to the gold mines of central Idaho. Earlier still, the Nez Perce on their seasonal rounds used the trail as a way from the Camas Prairie to the Bitterroot Valley in Montana. The 53-mile, mostly unpaved road doesn't appear much different now than it did a hundred years ago. Today, however, drivers can expect to traverse it in four to six hours instead of the two days (in summer) or five days (in winter) it took in the old days.

The Elk City Road is generally open June through September. To find it, look for Wall Creek Road by a group of mailboxes in Harpster and head east. Make sure your vehicle is in good condition, and fuel up before you go—there are no filling stations along the way, although gas and other services are available in Elk City. The return trip from Elk City to Harpster via State Highway 14, itself quite scenic, is 50 miles and takes about an hour and a half to drive. For more information on road conditions and a self-guiding brochure on the Elk City Wagon Road, stop at the Forest Service office in Grangeville or Elk City or call (208) 983–1963 or 842–2245.

Elk City also offers access to Dixie and Red River Hot Springs. The former is a sleepy former mining town once in the news as the nearest settlement to the contentious Cove-Mallard logging standoff; the latter is a year-round resort offering lodging, a cafe, and pools for swimming and soaking. For resort information call (208) 842–2589; write Red River Hot Springs, Elk City 83525; or see www.redriverhotsprings.com.

Back on Highway 95, the *White Bird Grade* south of Grangeville is one of Idaho's most notable highway achievements. Before it was completed in 1975, it took thirteen hours to drive from Boise to Grangeville—a distance of 197 miles. The grade replaced a tortuous old road that took 14 miles to climb 2,900 feet. (An Idaho historical marker overlooking the old road notes that if all the old route's curves and switchbacks were placed together, they'd make thirty-seven complete circles.) Yet the old White Bird Road was itself an engineering marvel, built from 1915 to 1921 at a cost of $400,000 to replace a wagon road. The old route—the only road linking Northern Idaho to the state capital—was finally paved in 1938. In 1974, the year before its replacement opened, the grade was added to the National Register of Historic Places.

The old White Bird Road is easily seen east of the present highway, which takes just over 7 miles to climb 3,000 feet. Stop at the pullout for a sweeping view of White Bird Canyon. This was the site of the opening battle in the Nez Perce War, described earlier. As you'll recall, several young nontreaty Nez Perce seeking revenge for the death of one of their fathers and angered by their forced move to the reservation killed a number of white settlers. In response General Oliver Otis Howard dispatched ninety-nine men led by Captain David Perry to confront the Indians at the Salmon River near here. Although they were poorly armed and outnumbered by the white men, the Nez Perce successfully turned back the Army while suffering no casualties of their own. From here the tribe started the three-and-a-half month, 1,000-mile retreat that finally ended with Chief Joseph's surrender in Montana.

The small towns of Lucile and Riggins serve as outfitting stops for the Salmon River as well as for treks into Hells Canyon National Recreation Area and the Hells Canyon Wilderness. For an inspiring, top-down look at the region, turn west off of Highway 95 onto Forest Road 517 for the 18-mile road to *Heaven's Gate.* This road, generally open from the Fourth of July until early October, can be managed by any passenger car (although trailers shouldn't make the climb). The first 8 miles are easily traversed; after that, the road gets washboarded, but the views make it all worthwhile. At Windy Saddle follow the signs for Heaven's Gate. A 350-yard trail climbs to a vista point at 8,429-feet elevation with dead-on views of the Seven Devils Range and the rest of the surrounding countryside. On a clear day you might see all the way into Montana. Unfortunately, the lookout at Heaven's Gate is only occasionally staffed by volunteers, and the interpretive signs could be better, but this is among the most memorable views in the Northwest.

River Odysseys West, one of Idaho's most established outfitters, runs trips on just about every major river in the state. One of their most popular offerings is the Salmon River Canyons Family Focus raft trip, which departs weekly in July and August. Traveling 35 to 53 miles over four to five days, the trips blend thrilling white-water action with lazy time on the lower Salmon's beautiful white-sand beaches. ROW owners Peter Grubb and Betsy Bowen have two children of their own, so they know how to please both parents (and grandparents) and kids. The cost for a five-day trip is about $1,300 for adults and $1,110 for children sixteen and under. For a complete brochure of ROW's trips—which also include runs on the Middle Fork, Lochsa, Selway, Owyhee, and Snake—call (800) 451–6034, visit their Web site at www.rowinc.com, or write River Odysseys West, P.O. Box 579, Coeur d'Alene 83816.

Highway 95 in Riggins is lined with businesses catering to the traveler, but it seems just as many locals as visitors wind down at the *Seven Devils Saloon & Steakhouse.* Dinner is served seven nights a week year-round, featuring such fare as barbecue shrimp stuffed with horseradish and wrapped in bacon; broiled salmon in a lemon-dill sauce; or the burrito-like chicken or rib-eye "P.H.A.T. Wraps." There's outdoor seating when the weather allows it. Seven Devils is at 312 South Main (Highway 95), and the phone number is (208) 628–3351.

Some of Idaho's most luxurious guest ranches can be found along the Salmon River east of Riggins. Ten miles from the highway on the south side of the river, *The Lodge at Riggins Hot Springs* is on a site revered by the Nez Perce for the water's healing properties. The resort features ten cushy rooms, fine dining, an impossibly beautiful pool, and a near-wilderness setting. High-season rates (from June through November) range from $265 to $350, double occupancy, which includes all meals and use of the facilities. Reservations are a must. For more information call (208) 628–3785; write The Lodge at Riggins Hot Springs, P.O. Box 1247, Riggins 83549; or see www.rhslodge.com.

Farther east you can't drive to the *Shepp Ranch* (located about 45 miles from Riggins), but they'll either send a jet boat to pick you up or arrange a charter flight from Boise. Once at Shepp Ranch, guests enjoy boating, rafting, trail riding, fishing, and hiking. Meals served family style feature the bounty of Idaho—trout, berries, vegetables from the ranch garden, and homemade bread, pies, and cakes. For more information call (208) 343–7729; write Shepp Ranch, P.O. Box 5446, Boise 83705; or see www.sheppranch.com.

A spur off Highway 95 south of Riggins leads to Pollock, a small community along the Little Salmon River. Pollock is the headquarters for *R&R Outdoors,* which, in addition to running one-to-six-day river trips, operates a comfortable lodge with river and mountain views. R&R also offers combination mountain biking-rafting trips, as well as romantic getaway packages. Call (800) 574–1224 for more information; write R&R Outdoors, HC 2 Box 500, Pollock 83547; or see www.rroutdoors.com.

Highway 95 continues along the Little Salmon clear to New Meadows. At that point, we've crossed over into what Idaho's tourism office calls Southwestern Idaho, but that's necessary to reach our final North Central Idaho destinations: the towns of Burgdorf and Warren.

At New Meadows, turn onto State Highway 55. Just before you reach Payette Lake and McCall, hang a left to head north on the Warren Wagon Road. The road is paved nearly to the Burgdorf turnoff (Forest Road 246, to the north), then it turns into gravel. Allow about an hour for travel to Warren, which sits about 44 miles from the highway. The route passes through a lot of timberland ravaged by forest fires in 1994, but signs of renewed forest growth can be seen, too.

Burgdorf Hot Springs, about 30 miles from McCall, is a popular soaking spot dating back to 1862. There are two pools: a large one, 5 feet deep, in which the temperature ranges from 98° to 104° F, and a small children's wading pool, plus several hot tubs. The pools look inviting enough, and the managers even have a supply of 300 extra bathing suits and 150 towels available for rent for anyone who came unprepared. But once you hear how they wash those suits and towels in a nearby stream, beating them with rocks to get 'em clean, you may wish you'd brought your own, home-laundered suit and towel. Pool admission is $5.00 for adults and $2.50 for children ages five to twelve.

The resort accommodates overnight visitors. Fourteen cabins, most built between the 1870s and 1930s, sleep from two to sixteen people. Rates (which include pool privileges) are $25.00 per adult per night and $5.00 per child ages five to twelve. The cabins come equipped with woodstoves, beds, kerosene lamps, and outhouses, but guests need to bring their own bedding, food, and utensils. No tents or RVs are allowed, but there are several Forest Service campgrounds nearby, one right next door. You can buy a few supplies (snacks, cold drinks, coffee, and a smattering of groceries) at Burgdorf, but it's wise to stock up ahead of time.

Although the road from McCall closes between November and mid-May, people come to Burgdorf all year long, usually by snowmobile, sometimes

In Plane View

*H*ere's how a Payette National Forest brochure tells it: On January 29, 1943, flying from Nevada back to Tacoma, Washington, a B-23 bomber made an emergency landing on frozen Loon Lake near Warren. The "Dragon Bomber" slid across the ice and 150 feet into the nearby trees, both its wings sheared off. All eight men aboard survived, with a broken kneecap the only injury.

But the crew had no radio, and they were stranded. After waiting five days for rescue, they decided to send three men for help. The trio, carrying a shotgun and chocolate, hiked about 42 miles over two weeks through waist-deep snow before reaching the Lake Fork Guard Station. Once there, they were able to contact the Forest Service in McCall, which sent assistance.

More than a half-century later, hikers can still see the **B-23 Dragon Bomber wreckage** near the south side of the lake. The Forest Service brochure gives detailed directions. For more information call (208) 634–0400 or write the McCall Ranger District, P.O. Box 1026, McCall 83638.

by cross-country skis. (There are 38 miles of groomed x-c trails in the area.) Year-round, this is an excellent spot to see wildlife: deer, elk, moose, and even the occasional black bear and mountain lion. For more information call (208) 636–3036 or write Burgdorf Hot Springs, McCall 83638.

Return to the Warren Wagon Road for the final 13 miles toward Warren. On the way the road passes through a community of private homes known as Secesh Meadows. "Secesh" is short for secessionist; seems there were quite a few Southern sympathizers among those mining here in the mid-nineteenth century. The Secesh Stage Stop sells gasoline, meals, and snacks to people passing through the area. Nearby, the Forest Service's Chinook Campground is a trailhead for the Secesh to Loon Lake Trail, part of the Idaho Centennial Trail. Aside from being a fairly easy trail, the path provides access to a fascinating and little-known artifact from Idaho history: the wreckage of a B-23 bomber. (See sidebar, page 48.)

Warren isn't literally the end of the road, but it's darn close. From here it's just a few bumpy miles to the edge of the Frank Church–River of No Return Wilderness, largest in the lower forty-eight United States. About a dozen people live year-round in Warren, maybe three times that number in summer. Once a year on the Fourth of July, they stage a "Spotted Owl Shoot" to raise money for community projects (the town water system is a recent beneficiary) and poke a bit of fun at environmentalists. No, they don't really shoot endangered wildlife—just targets. Warren has no electricity, but it did get phone lines in 1995.

Warren may not have many people, but it has plenty of history. Established in 1862 with the discovery of gold, this is one of Idaho's oldest towns. In its first boom, Warren had 2,000 people. By 1870 many of these first miners had left, but more than a thousand Chinese miners had moved in to try their luck. (Chinese mining artifacts can be seen at the Forest Service's Warren Guard Station and at the Winter Inn.) Warren had another population boom in the 1930s when dredging resumed. Although modern Warren was again threatened by a 1989 forest fire in the nearby Whangdoodle Creek drainage, the town survived, and many of the standing buildings are more than 100 years old. Stop by the Forest Service's Warren Guard Station for a Warren walking tour booklet.

For a memorable stay in Warren, you can't beat the **Backcountry B&B,** run by Betty and Leland Cavner on the far edge of town about a quarter-mile from the Forest Service compound. The Cavners, who had been visiting Warren since the 1950s, built this lodge themselves in the early 1990s, even logging and milling the logs. Models of self-sufficiency, the Cavners run their washing machine and television on solar power and heat their home with a huge stove made by Betty's father. Betty also made the quilts in the four guest rooms, and she's just as much a whiz in the kitchen, baking homemade bread and creating such luscious treats as nectarine cobbler and apple dumplings. She's a gifted decorator, too: Check out the shelf above the stairway, with its sweet collection of dolls, bears, and books, many from Betty's own childhood.

The downstairs living room is as welcoming as can be, both for its comfortable country furnishings and the Cavners' gift for making visitors feel immediately at home. Upstairs, travelers can relax with a game of pool or Scrabble, or even work out on the exercise equipment. The Cavners have built a wonderful second-story deck, too, perfect for viewing the deer, moose, and foxes that may happen by at sunrise or twilight.

Rooms at the Backcountry B&B go for $75 double occupancy including breakfast, $60 for one person. The four rooms share two baths. The inn is open year-round, though visitors must arrive by snowmobile or a long cross-country ski trek in wintertime. Smoking is allowed outdoors only. Children are welcome, and Betty adds, "If they're good kids, the price is reasonable. If they're bad, they pay full price." But chances are your kids—and you—will be enchanted by this house. For more information call (208) 636–6000 or write the Backcountry B&B, P.O. Box 77, Warren 83671.

PLACES TO STAY IN NORTH CENTRAL IDAHO

MOSCOW
Best Western University Inn, 1516 Pullman Road, (800) 325-8765

The Mark IV, 414 North Main, (208) 882-7557

Paradise Ridge Bed & Breakfast, 3377 Blaine Road, (208) 882-5292 (see text)

Peacock Hill Bed & Breakfast, 1015 Joyce Road, (208) 882-1423

ELK RIVER
Huckleberry Heaven Lodge, (208) 826-3405, fax: (208) 826-3284

Main Street Cabins, (208) 826-3689

OROFINO
Konkolville Motel, 2000 Konkolville Road, (208) 476-5584

Riverside Motel, 10560 Highway 12, (208) 476-5711

PIERCE
Pierce Motel, 509 Main Street, (208) 464-2324

LOWELL
Three Rivers Resort, (208) 926-4430, fax: (208) 926-7526 (see text)

KOOSKIA
Looking Glass Inn, Highway 12 east of town, (888) 926-0855

KAMIAH
Clearwater 12 Motel,
Highway 12 at Cedar,
(800) 935–2671

Lewis Clark Resort,
Highway 12 east of town,
(208) 935–2556,
fax: (208) 935–0366

LEWISTON
Comfort Inn,
2128 Eighth Avenue,
(800) 228–5150

Hay Loft Bed & Breakfast,
2031 Powers Avenue,
(208) 746–2363 (see text)

Kirby Creek Lodge
(in Hells Canyon),
(800) 262–8874

Red Lion Hotel,
Highway 12 and Twenty-
first Street, phone/fax:
(208) 799–1000

Riverview Inn,
1325 Main Street,
(800) 806–ROOM,
fax: (208) 746–7955

Sacajawea Select Inn,
1824 Main Street,
(800) 333–1393,
fax: (208) 743–3620

ELK CITY
Prospector Lodge and
Cabins,
(208) 842–2597

Red River Hot Springs,
(208) 842–2589

Cottonwood Bark
Dog Bark Park,
(208) 962–DOGS
(see text)

GRANGEVILLE
Downtowner Inn,
113 East North Street,
(208) 983–1110

Elkhorn Lodge,
822 Southwest First Street,
(208) 983–1500

Monty's Motel,
700 West Main Street,
(208) 983–2500

WHITE BIRD
Hoots Motel,
Highway 95,
(208) 839–2265

RIGGINS
Bruce Motel,
515 North Main Street,
(208) 628–3005

The Lodge Bed &
Breakfast, Highway 95,
(208) 628–3863 (This is
not The Lodge at Riggins
Hot Springs, which is 10
miles east of Riggins;
see text)

Riggins Motel,
615 South Highway 95,
(208) 628–3001

WARREN
Backcountry B&B,
(208) 636–6000 (see text)

Helpful Web sites

Regional tourism—*www.idahonwp.org*

Moscow community site—*www.moscow.com/*

Lewiston Morning Tribune—www.lmtribune.com/

Lewiston community site—*www.lewiston.com/*

Nez Perce National Historic Park—*www.nps.gov/nepe/*

Grangeville/Camas Prairie area—*www.camasnet.com*

Worth Seeing

McConnell Mansion—*Moscow*

Dworshak National Fish Hatchery—*Orofino*

Clearwater River Casino—*Lewiston*

Hells Gate State Park—*Lewiston*

Mecham Mills—*Lewiston*

Red River Hot Springs—*east of Elk City*

**PLACES TO EAT
IN NORTH CENTRAL IDAHO**

MOSCOW
Bucer's (coffee house
and light fare),
201 South Main Street,
(208) 882–5216

Gambino's Italian
Restaurant,
308 West Sixth Street,
(208) 882–4545

Red Door (eclectic),
(208) 882–7830
(see text)

WEIPPE
Weippe Pizza (American),
118 North Main Street,
(208) 435–4823 (see text)

LOWELL
Ryan's Wilderness Inn Cafe
(American), Highway 12,
(208) 926–4706

KOOSKIA
Idaho Backroads Cafe
(American),
118 South Main,
(208) 926–4304

KAMIAH
Jilinda's Family Dining
(American),
(208) 935–1158

Kamiah Cafe (American),
714 Third,
(208) 935–2563

OROFINO
Becky's Burgers (American),
105 Michigan Avenue,
(208) 476–7361

Ponderosa Restaurant
(American),
220 Michigan Avenue,
(208) 476–4818

LEWISTON
Bojack's Broiler Pit (steaks),
311 Main Street,
(208) 746–9532

Jonathan's
(steaks/seafood),
1516 Main Street,
(208) 746–3438

Meriwether's (American),
in the Red Lion Hotel,
(208) 799–1000

Rowdy's Texas Steakhouse
and Saloon (American),
1905 Nineteenth Avenue,
(208) 798–8712

Thai Taste (Thai),
1410 Twenty-first Street,
(208) 746–6192

Waffles N' More,
1421 Main,
(208) 743–5189

Zany's (American),
2006 Nineteenth Avenue,
(208) 746–8131

Many major fast-food
chains, mostly along
Twenty-first Street.

GRANGEVILLE
Camas Cafe (American),
123 West Main,
(208) 983–1019

Oscar's Restaurant and
Espresso (American),
101 East Main,
(208) 983–2106 (see text)

RIGGINS
Blackberry Patch Drive–In
(sandwiches/ice cream),
533 North Main,
(208) 628–3871

Seven Devils Saloon &
Steak House (American),
312 South Main,
(208) 628–3351 (see text)

WARREN
Winter Inn (American),
(208) 636–4393

Southwestern Idaho

outhwest Idaho is the Gem State's most varied region. It includes the fast-growing Boise metropolitan area of more than 430,000 people, yet it also contains several sprawling counties with fewer than 12,000 inhabitants. It is home to a thriving high-tech industry—again, in Boise, where Micron and Hewlett-Packard are among the corporate citizenry—but it also encompasses a few towns that didn't receive telephone service until the mid-1990s.

Because of this variety and the sheer sweep of backcountry, there is no one best way to explore Southwest Idaho, and it could easily take a week or more to cover the region. But here's one possibility, the option you'll see used in this chapter:

Start on the shores of Payette Lake near McCall and New Meadows, the region's most popular resort area. Head southwest on U.S. Highway 95 to Cambridge, then west to explore the Hells Canyon Scenic Byway and the upper reaches of North America's deepest gorge. After backtracking to Cambridge and New Meadows, you might want to head east from McCall into the wilderness areas near Yellow Pine and Warm Lake (and Burgdorf and Warren, covered in the North Central Idaho chapter but most accessible from McCall). After returning to State Highway 55, we'll veer off onto the back roads once again to survey the Boise Basin, rich in mining history. Adjacent to I–84 we'll visit the capital city of Boise, the Treasure Valley of farmland west of Boise, and the high desert outback of Owyhee and Elmore Counties.

For more Southwestern Idaho travel information, call (800) 635–5240 or write the Southwest Idaho Travel Association, P.O. Box 2106, Boise 83701.

Wilderness Gateways

cCall has been called Idaho's most complete resort town, and with a regionally noted ski area and a spacious lake at hand, it's difficult to challenge that assertion. Many who come to enjoy these recreational riches stay at the venerable *Hotel McCall* overlooking

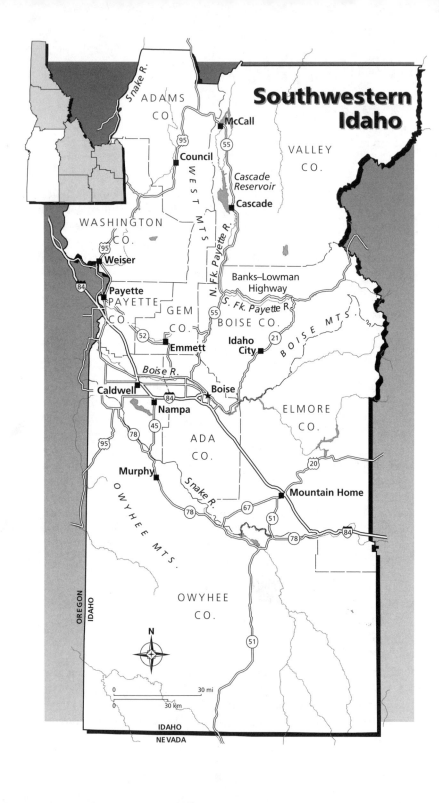

Southwestern Idaho

SOUTHWESTERN IDAHO

JULIE'S FAVORITES

Hells Canyon Scenic Byway—West of Cambridge

Hap and Florence Points Memorial Sleigh Rides—near Donnelly

Boise River Greenbelt—Boise

World Center for Birds of Prey—south of Boise

Bruneau Dunes State Park—near Hammett

Payette Lake. Opened in 1904, the inn offers many hospitable touches, including fresh flowers in each room, complimentary tea or wine each afternoon, and homemade cookies and milk each night before bedtime. A recreation room complete with games and a VCR is also at guests' disposal.

The hotel has thirty-six rooms, including several suites with lake views. A breakfast of granola, muffins, juice, and fresh fruit is served each morning at no extra charge. Rates range from $55 single or double occupancy for the lower-level rooms with shared bath to $350 for a two-bedroom condominium. Mention you're planning an anniversary or wedding celebration, and a chilled bottle of champagne will greet your arrival. For more information or reservations call (866) 800–1183 or write Hotel McCall, 1101 North Third Street, McCall 83638.

Restaurants come and go in McCall, but *The Mill Supper Club* is one of the oldest and most interesting spots in town. The menu includes steak, prime rib, and seafood, and the decor features lots of antiques and what may be the largest collection of beer taps anywhere in the United States—thousands of 'em displayed all over the restaurant and adjacent bar. Dinner is served seven nights a week starting at 5:30 P.M. The restaurant is at 324 North Third Street (Highway 55). Call (208) 634–7683 for reservations.

When MGM made its film *Northwest Passage* in the late 1930s, it built a home for the cast and crew at Crystal Beach on Payette Lake. That same home, later moved to a forested neighborhood a few blocks from downtown McCall, now serves as the *Northwest Passage Bed & Breakfast.* Choose from Spencer Tracy's quarters (Room 4) or Robert Young's lair (Room 3, now the honeymoon suite), or a stylish master suite where lead actress Ruth Hussey may have felt at home.

The guest rooms range in price from $70 to $100, single or double occupancy. Innkeeper Barbara Schott delights in decorating, and guests can have fun just looking at all her creative, whimsical touches throughout the home. A wraparound deck makes a great place to read while breathing the pine-scented air, while a well-stocked video collection (including *Northwest Passage,* of course) provides indoor entertainment. Each morning, cook-off winner Schott serves a hearty mountain breakfast that might feature such fare as eggs Benedict, hash browns, muffins, and huckleberry coffee. In the evenings guests often drink complimentary wine, relax, and talk around the large fireplace fashioned from Salmon River rock.

When you're ready to explore beyond the inn, Northwest Passage provides a thick binder labeled "Stuff to Do Around Here." The inn can accommodate up to six couples for reunions or retreats. No kids; no pets; smoking is allowed outdoors only. For reservations or more information, call (800) 597–6658 or write Northwest Passage Bed & Breakfast, 201 Rio Vista, McCall 83638.

The biggest winter event in North Central Idaho—possibly the entire state—is the *McCall Winter Carnival.* Each year the festival draws about 100,000 people. A snow-sculpting competition is the big attraction, and there are also fireworks, a full-moon cross-country ski tour, dogsled races, wine tasting, and more. Winter Carnival takes place in late January each year. For information phone the McCall Chamber of Commerce at (208) 634–7631.

Southwest of New Meadows, U.S. Highway 95 leads to Cambridge, gateway to the *Hells Canyon Scenic Byway,* the only canyon motor-access route generally open year-round. From Cambridge, State Highway 71 crosses into Oregon at Brownlee Dam and back into the Gem State at Oxbow Dam. From Oxbow Dam, the Hells Canyon Scenic Byway—an Idaho Power-owned road open to the public—runs north to its terminus (and back into Oregon) at Hells Canyon Dam. There's some fine camping along the reservoirs behind these dams. Sites are first come, first served. Call (800) 422–3143 for information.

Many boat trips launch from below Hells Canyon Dam. Choose from either a rafting expedition or, if your time and pocketbook are pressed, a jet-boat ride. For a raft trip of three to six days, choices include Hughes River Expeditions at (800) 262–1882, Northwest Voyagers at (800) 727–9977, or Mackay Wilderness River Trips at (800) 635–5336. Jet-boat trips ranging from two hours to two days (with an overnight in Lewiston) are run by Hells Canyon Adventures, which also does one-day white-water rafting/jet-boat combo trips. For a complete list of outfitters traveling in Hells Canyon, contact the Hells Canyon National Recreation Office at (509) 758–0616 or write P.O. Box 699, Clarkston, WA 99403.

Hells Canyon Adventures' two- and three-hour trips are just long enough to give riders a taste of the canyon's scenery and history; they're also good choices for families with young children who aren't yet ready to brave big white water on the rafts. (HCA is fond of saying even babies and grandmas enjoy these trips.) Highlights include an up-close, bottom-up view of Hells Canyon Dam; a stop at an area known for its Indian pictographs; and interpretation of early homestead life in Hells Canyon. A few of the stories you may hear verge on tall-tale territory—Lewis and Clark never made it into Hells Canyon, for example—but all in all, this is an enjoyable and scenic trip.

The two-hour trip begins at 2:00 P.M. Pacific time with a cost of $30 per adult, $10 per child under twelve, or a $90 family rate covering two adults and up to six kids. The three-hour ride, which includes lunch, starts at 10:00 A.M. Pacific time and costs $40 for adults and $15 for children under twelve. Allow about two and one-half hours for the winding, 64-mile drive from Cambridge to Hells Canyon Dam. For more information on these tours or other Hells Canyon Adventures, call (800) HCA–Flot; see their Web site at www.hellscanyonadventures.com; or write Hells Canyon Adventures, P.O. Box 159, Oxbow, OR 97840.

Aside from its role as Hells Canyon base camp, Cambridge is an interesting little town in its own right. Check out the **Cambridge Museum** at the junction of U.S. Highway 95 and State Highway 71 for fascinating

A Cambridge Classic

*I*f you plan to spend the night in Cambridge, bunk down at the **Hunters Inn Motel/Cambridge House Bed & Breakfast.** You can't miss it; just look for the 1962 stretch limo parked out front. This is clearly where the elite meet in Cambridge; the coffee shop brews Starbucks, a little blackboard displays a "word of the day," and innkeepers Jack and Aria Croly are engaging, attentive hosts. Yet despite the urbane touches, the inn remains an unpretentious place.

The B&B rooms, originally built in the twenties and priced at $65 double occupancy including breakfast, have been updated just enough to make guests feel at home. The motor-court motel rooms resemble small cabins inside and rent for $35–$45. With advance notice the night before, Jack Croly will make breakfast for motel guests at a cost of $7.50 per person. Four kitchenette units also are available for $60 per night. For more information or reservations, call (208) 257–3325 or write to Hunters Inn, P.O. Box 313, Cambridge 83610.

exhibits such as one detailing the journey of Edith Clegg, who went upriver through Hells Canyon in 1939. The museum is open May 15 through September 15 from 10:00 A.M. to 4:00 P.M. Wednesday through Saturday and 1:00 to 4:00 P.M. Sunday, or you can call (208) 257–3541 or 257–3485 for an appointment.

Two other scenic day trips out of the McCall area lead to some of Idaho's most cherished yet accessible backcountry destinations. North of McCall, the Warren Wagon Road leads to Burgdorf Hot Springs and the former mining town of Warren. (See the end of the North Central Idaho chapter for details on this route.) Another route leading east from McCall travels to Yellow Pine and Warm Lake before looping back to State Highway 55 at Cascade. The road from McCall to Yellow Pine, Forest Road 48, is a rough but scenic route passable by any vehicle in good condition driven by a motorist using care. The road runs alongside boulder fields and immense rock outcroppings, along with areas where extensive wildfire damage is visible; this region is among those most heavily damaged by forest fires in recent years.

A few spots along the way are worth noting. The **Duck Lake Trail,** just a mile long, is among the easier high-country paths you'll find in these rugged parts. It's not far east of Lick Creek Summit, and the trailhead is well signed. And near the junction of Road 48 and the Salmon River Road (Forest Road 674), there's an exhibit explaining the history of the Chinese miners who toiled in the area a century ago. From 1870 through 1900, in fact, the Chinese miners had a three-to-one majority among prospectors working the Warren mining district.

Yellow Pine, with a year-round population of about fifty, is surprisingly bustling despite its remote location. Yellow Pine folks also have a nifty sense of humor: Witness the University of Yellow Pine sign on the town's one-room schoolhouse. Most Idaho towns have an annual community bash or two, and Yellow Pine is no exception. The **Yellow Pine Harmonica Fest,** held the first full weekend of August, typically attracts between thirty and thirty-five contestants and about 1,200 spectators who crowd the tiny town for the mouth harp competition and other musical events, as well as barbecues, breakfasts, community potlucks, and a street fair. If you want to attend the festival, odds are you'll be camping out. The **Yellow Pine Lodge** has the only rooms in town, and it's not that big. If you do get in, however, you'll find reasonable prices ($35 a night double occupancy) and home-cooked meals. Innkeeper Darlene Rosenbaum will pack you a sack lunch if your plans for the day will keep you out of town over the noon hour. To reach the lodge call (208) 633–3377 or write P.O. Box 77, Yellow Pine 83677.

Nine miles south of Yellow Pine on Forest Road 413, the traveler discovers **Wapiti Meadow Ranch,** the oldest dude ranch in Idaho and one of the oldest in the Northwest. Long run by Lafe and Emma Cox, the ranch is now owned by Diana and Barry Bryant. Wapiti Meadow specializes in horseback riding and fly-fishing trips into the adjacent wilderness areas; hiking and cross-country skiing are popular, too. And Wapiti Meadow is no misnomer: Guests really are likely to see plenty of elk, especially in springtime, along with deer, moose, coyotes, and maybe a black bear.

The center of the ranch is its spacious stone and pine lodge, warmly furnished with antiques and comfortable furniture, like the big leather sofa sitting before the ample hearth. Four guest cabins plus two pondside suites in a log lodge are outfitted with living rooms as well as sleeping quarters. Each of the guest quarters has a woodstove (along with modern baseboard heating), and each comes graced with fresh flowers, a coffee maker, a refrigerator stocked with soft drinks, a fruit basket, and other snacks.

You might not have room for those goodies, however, once you've had your fill of Diana's cooking. The ranch specializes in "hearty gourmet" fare, and some guests have been known to book vacations at the ranch strictly for the food. The buffet-style breakfasts include such fare as mushroom and cheddar omelets and hot blueberry muffins. Breast of turkey on fresh croissants and homemade tomato bisque are among the luncheon selections. And dinners range from filet of beef served by candlelight to country ribs at a Western barbecue.

Wapiti Meadow offers a wide range of packages, depending on activities selected. Guided fly-fishing trips, available from mid-July through mid-September, are $1,750 per person for three days or $2,500 for six days. Riding vacations, offered June through September, cost $1,250 for three days and $1,750 for six days. Wapiti Meadow also has "bed-and-board" accommodations for $100 per person, per night in June, late September, and October, and at $200 per person, per night July through mid-September, with a three-night minimum stay. Chartered backcountry flights are available from Boise. For more information or reservations at Wapiti Meadow, call (208) 633–3217 or write to HC-72, Cascade 83611. You can also reach the lodge via fax at (208) 633–3219 or via E-mail at WapitiMR@aol.com. Wapiti Meadow's Web page is at www.guestranches.com/wapiti.htm.

Forest Road 413 continues south from Wapiti Meadow to Landmark, site of a Boise National Forest ranger station. From there a good paved road takes a steep and winding plunge through heavily timbered country to Warm Lake, a resort and summer home area.

The **Warm Lake Lodge** has been catering to backcountry adventurers since 1911. In summertime, fishing and hiking are big draws, while hunters pack the cabins come fall and snowmobilers and cross-country skiers arrive in winter. Warm Lake Lodge has nine cabins, some with cooking facilities, priced from about $30 to $160, based on double occupancy, with additional people a few extra bucks per night. The restaurant serves such fare as Idaho trout, breast of chicken, and homemade pies, and includes a lounge and a general store. If you're an angler, make sure to ask about Tule Lake, a trophy cutthroat fishery southwest of Warm Lake. Warm Lake Lodge is open year-round. Reservations may be made by calling (208) 632–3553 or writing Warm Lake Lodge, Warm Lake 83611. If this lodge is full, the nearby North Shore Lodge has similarly priced cabins and services in the summertime. There's also camping nearby.

The Warm Lake Road winds up back in Cascade, a recreation-oriented town at the south end of Cascade Reservoir and the scenic Long Valley. Summer or winter there's lots to do here. In the colder months check to see if the **Hap and Florence Points Memorial Sleigh Rides,** near Donnelly, are in operation.

The sleigh rides take place on the Points Ranch where, years ago, Hap Points started feeding the elk that came down to winter in the Goldfork River Valley. It was either that or see his cattle starve, since the elk would run the cows off and eat their hay. Hap just started setting out extra hay for the elk, and all the critters were happy.

Word soon got out that the elk were congregating on the Points Ranch, and folks came from miles around to see them feed. Unfortunately, that scared off the elk. These days, visitors can go along to feed the elk by reservation only, but that makes for a better experience. In fact the elk are so used to the horse-drawn sleds that they will come right up and eat off the hay bales on which the riders sit. This is one of only a few places

Molly's Tubs

in the West where it's possible to see bulls, cows, and calves all together.

The sleigh rides are now run by the Eld and Points families. They all know a lot about elk and can even relate stories about individual members of the herd. The sleigh ride season generally runs from December 20 through the end of March. Cost is $15.00 for adults, $10.00 for teens, and $5.00 for children twelve and under. For more information or reservations, call Vicki and Joe at (208) 325–8876.

Railroad buffs may want to schedule a trip with the **Thunder Mountain Line,** a historic railway that runs two routes along the Payette River. The "Cabarton Flyer" travels between Cascade and Smiths Ferry, and the "Horseshoe Bend Express" runs from its namesake town to Banks, with optional shuttle transportation available from Boise. Either excursion lasts two-and-a-half hours and costs $24.50 for adults, $23.00 for seniors age sixty and up, and $15.00 for children twelve and under. Some Horseshoe Bend trips include Wild West-style entertainment with a simulated train robbery and shoot-out; those runs cost a few dollars extra. Call (877) 432–7245 or (208) 793–4425 in the Boise area for reservations, or see www.thundermountainline.com for more details.

The Thunder Mountain Line also works in conjunction with **Idaho Whitewater Unlimited** to run summertime "Rivers and Rails" trips combining a train trek from Smiths Ferry to Cascade with a return raft trip down the Payette River. These cost $95 for adults, $90 for seniors, and $70 for children under twelve, including a Dutch oven lunch at the end of the float. For reservations or more information, call Idaho Whitewater Unlimited at (208) 462–1900.

South of Cascade, the Payette River can't help but command the traveler's attention, with plenty of handy pullouts for fishing, picnicking, or even taking a dip on a scorching summer day. Keep the camera handy, too: The graceful yet sturdy Rainbow Bridge south of Cascade is one of Idaho's most picturesque. Hang a left at Banks for a trip into the Boise Basin, a former mining hotbed still rich in scenic wealth.

The Boise Basin

East of Banks, the two-lane Banks-Lowman Highway leads through scenic Garden Valley. This road wasn't even paved until the early 1990s, but locals now say it's the best road in Boise County. It's no slouch on scenery either; the South Fork of the Payette, which had its headwaters near Grandjean, tumbles far below the road.

At Lowman, State Highway 21 treks north to Stanley and south to Idaho City. A short spur off the northern stretch leads to Grandjean. This tiny town on the western slope of the Sawtooth Mountains is literally within the Sawtooth Wilderness Area boundaries; although designated wilderness areas don't normally have roads (much less a resort), Grandjean was grandfathered in when the boundaries were drawn, which seems appropriate since the town was named for the Boise National Forest's "grandfather," Emile Grandjean, first supervisor of the forest from 1908 to 1919.

Grandjean is home to the **Sawtooth Lodge.** More accurately you could say the Sawtooth Lodge *is* Grandjean. The lodge serves meals from 8:00 A.M. to 6:00 P.M. (later by special request), with hearty mountain fare topping the bill. Log cabins sleep from two to four people at prices ranging from about $45 to $90 a night. Outdoors, guests are free to enjoy a warm mineral-water plunge pool, wildlife viewing, hiking, and fishing. RV and tent camping facilities are available, too, and it also should be noted that Grandjean makes an ideal vacation destination for folks with handicaps; one of the Sawtooth Lodge's cabins is outfitted for people with disabilities, and a mile-long nature trail is wheelchair accessible.

Sawtooth Lodge usually opens Memorial Day and closes around mid-October. For current rates, reservations, or other information, call (208) 259–3331 in Grandjean or (208) 344–2437 during the off-season. The mailing address is 130 North Haines, Boise 83712. Sawtooth Lodge also is home to **Sawtooth Wilderness Outfitters,** which provides horses and guides for trail rides and pack trips into the wilderness area. The outfitters' phone numbers are (208) 259– 3408 in summer or (208) 462–3416 in winter, with a mailing address of P.O. Box 81, Garden Valley 83622.

Although not as well known as the '49ers' rush to the California gold fields or the boom in the Yukon, Idaho miners had glory days all their own. During the 1860s more gold was mined from the mountains northeast of Boise than from all of Alaska. In fact, Idaho City was once the largest city in the Northwest, and like most mining towns, it had a reputation as a wild place. It's been reported that only 28 of the 200 people buried in the town's Boot Hill died a natural death. These days, however, it's much more calm—even peaceful—with a small selection of visitor services and abundant recreation nearby. The areas around Idaho City are justly famous for great hiking and cross-country skiing.

Stop by the town visitor center at the corner of Highway 21 and Main Street for a leaflet describing notable Idaho City buildings. Among them, the old 1867 post office now serves as the **Boise Basin Museum,** open daily from 11:00 A.M. to 4:00 P.M. Memorial Day through Labor Day. Museum visitors can buy a gold-panning kit or arrange a guided walking tour of Idaho City. (Tours also can be set up by calling Barbara Frentress at 208–392–4550 or 392–4447. Cost is $3.50 per person or $2.00 for seniors and kids six to twelve, with a $30.00 per-group minimum.)

For a meal in Idaho City, try **Trudy's Kitchen** at 419 Highway 21. This locally popular restaurant serves hearty breakfasts, bodacious hamburgers (eight varieties plus a veggie burger), and a house salad drizzled with huckleberry vinaigrette dressing. Sandwiches range in price from $3.95 to $6.50, with dinner entrees priced from $5.95 for the macaroni and cheese to $14.95 for a steak-and-prawn combo. Trudy's is open daily at 7:00 A.M., closing at 8:00 P.M. Sunday through Thursday and 9:00 P.M. Friday and Saturday. The phone number is (208) 392–4151.

The area around Idaho City is known for some of the best cross-country skiing in the state: Eighteen miles north of town on State Highway 21, the Whoop-Um-Up Park N' Ski area has 6.6 miles of marked trails, with sections suitable for all skier levels. Another 2 miles north, Gold Fork Park N' Ski accesses 21.4 miles of groomed trails, with terrain best for advanced beginners to serious skiers. Banner Ridge Park N' Ski, 3.5 miles from Gold Fork, has 22 miles of groomed trails for intermediate and expert skiers, plus off-trail bowl skiing. Gold Fork and Banner Ridge both have yurts available for rent. For more information, call the Idaho Department of Parks and Recreation at (208) 334–4199 or see www.idahoparks.org.

Another side trip off of State Highway 21 leads to **Atlanta,** a late bloomer among Idaho's mining districts and a scenic little town well worth the long drive. On one hand, several roads in the Boise Basin head toward Atlanta. On the other hand, none of them is easy—and some (notably Forest Road 126, the way from Rocky Bar) are sort of scary. The most popular routes are the heavily rutted, 68-mile Middle Fork Road (Forest Road 268) from Lucky Peak Reservoir near Boise and the 40-mile combination of the Edna Creek (384), North Fork Boise River (327), and Middle Fork Boise Roads. Check with the Forest Service office in Idaho City at (208) 392–6681 for information on road conditions. Logging trucks often work these highways, so monitor Channel 19 if you have a CB and always be an attentive, cautious driver.

There isn't a whole lot to do in Atlanta, but that seems to be the point. An "ATLANTA '96" sign outside the **Whistle Stop** tavern/cafe/convenience store is a souvenir from the Georgia Olympics, but it could just as easily be referring to this town's turn-of-the-nineteenth-century feel. Ask at the Whistle Stop for a key to the tiny local museum, housed out back in a former jail building. Its focal exhibit is a collection of photographs by Ella Gaetz, whose family moved from Buffalo, New York, to Atlanta in 1880, when Ella was five and Atlanta was having its first mining boom.

Two nearby hot springs beckon bathers. To find **Atlanta Hot Springs,** drive a mile east of town and look for the little parking area on the right-hand side of the road just past the big green pond. (No, the pond is not the hot spring!) The choice spot, **Chatanooga Hot Springs,** is much nicer, sitting below a waterfall in a rock pool on the Middle Fork of the Boise River. But it's also a bit harder to find—and to get there, you have to cross land owned by Pinnacle Peaks Sawtooth Lodge (see below), although the resort's current owners realize it is futile to keep bathers at bay. To get there, look for the spur road just west of Atlanta Hot Springs (but on the other side of the road) and follow it about 3/10 of a mile north. The road ends at the top of a bluff. Cross a small stream and hike down the bluff to the hot springs. The road leading to the bluff is marked PRIVATE PROPERTY, but locals say that if you stay on the road and refrain from rowdiness, you're OK.

There are two interesting accommodation options in Atlanta. The Boise National Forest maintains a rental cabin just down the hill from "central" Atlanta. It's among the Forest Service's more luxurious lodgings, with room for six people (in a double bed, sleeper sofa, and bunk beds), a propane oven/stovetop and fridge, a shower, and a woodstove. The house is available from May 31 through September 30 for just $45 a night. It must be reserved in advance by calling (208) 392–6681 or by writing the Idaho City Ranger District, P.O. Box 129, Idaho City 83631.

On the other end of the luxury scale, **Pinnacle Peaks Sawtooth Lodge** is Atlanta's secret showplace. Once the private playground of Herman Coors (of the Colorado brewing family), Pinnacle Peaks now caters to upscale vacationers and business retreats with its handsome 500-acre spread between the Middle Fork of the Boise River and the southernmost stretch of the Sawtooth Wilderness Area. With 9,317-foot Greylock Mountain as a backdrop, guests can ride horseback, swim or soak in the geothermally heated pool and hot tub, play tennis, fish, golf, hike, bike, or do nothing. Winter activities include cross-country skiing, ice skating, snowshoeing, and snowmobiling. Meals are ample and include lots of Idaho-grown produce. They are served indoors in the great room or outside when weather permits. Guests can bring their own alcohol, but smoking is allowed outdoors only.

Pinnacle Peaks has eighteen rooms with a variety of bed configurations. Rates range from $100 to $300 per person, per night, with all meals and many activities included. Minimum group sizes apply; call for details. For reservations or more information, call (208) 864–2168; write 416 North Greene Valley Lane, Atlanta, GA 83601; or see www. pinnaclepeaks.com.

From Atlanta, you can either backtrack along the Forest Service roads to Highway 21 or take the southern routes (Forest Service Roads 126 or 156) to Rocky Bar and the Featherville-Pine-Trinity Lakes area. (See the "Snake River Vistas" section later in this chapter for more information on this region.)

When Highway 21 intersects with I–84, it's just a few miles west to Boise. First, however, you might want to head east for a few miles to get your first look at Idaho's capital city as our forebears did, from **Bonneville Point.** This was the spot from which mountain men and Oregon Trail

Leave Your Watch at Home

*T*ime really does slow down in Atlanta, and it sometimes comes to a complete stop. On my arrival at the Forest Service rental cabin, I was surprised to see a clock on the kitchen wall. I soon realized it wasn't working, however, and that made me feel better. Who needs a clock in Atlanta?

Alas, my sleep was restless that night. The first time I awoke, I pulled on my pants and shoes and went outside to survey the stars. With no earthbound lights to compete, the heavens were magnificent, even by jaded Idaho standards. The Milky Way stood out like a gossamer scarf flung

across the sky, and the Pleiades glittered like a diamond bracelet. I did not look at my watch, but I knew it was well after midnight.

The next time I stirred, it seemed to be dawn. I reached for my watch on the bedside table, surprised to see it was only 2:40 A.M. How could this be, I wondered? Before long, I understood that my watch, like the kitchen clock, had stopped. Perhaps that is the message of Atlanta: Leave your watch at home. Time doesn't matter out here. You learn all you need to know by the angle of the sun, the still of the night, and the sound of your own heartbeat.

pioneers first spied the verdant Boise River valley below. Boise got its name, in fact, when a party of French trappers visited Bonneville Point in 1833. For weeks the trappers had seen nothing but lava and sage-brush. Now, far below but less than a day's walk, they saw a verdant river valley, the streambank lined with trees. "Les bois, les bois, voyez les bois" ("The trees, the trees, look at the trees"), the trappers cried in joy. The name stuck, and to this day Boise is known as the "City of Trees."

To find Bonneville Point, take exit 64 off of I–84 and follow the signs north. The Bureau of Land Management has placed an interpretive kiosk at the site, and a long stretch of wagon-wheel ruts may be seen nearby, along with a good look at Boise and its foothills. "When we arrived at the top we got a grand view of the Boise River Valley," emi-grant Cecilia E. M. Adams noted in her diary. The trees they saw, she added, were "the first we have seen in more than a month." Likewise, explorer John Fremont, who mapped the West, wrote of his joy in see-ing the Boise River, "a beautiful rapid stream, with clear mountain water" and noted he was "delighted this afternoon to make a pleasant camp under fine old trees again."

City of Trees

Boise is one of the nation's fastest-growing cities. Nevertheless, it remains wonderfully compact, with many of its most interesting sites within walking distance downtown. Looming over all is the **State Capitol,** which makes a logical spot to begin explorations. Although the Capitol itself isn't "off the beaten path," its interior harbors some little-known and fascinating lore.

For example, check out the replica of the Winged Victory of Samoth-race, a marble statue sculpted around 300 B.C. The original stands in the Louvre in Paris; in 1949 France gave a replica to each American state as a gesture of thanks following World War II, but Idaho's copy is supposedly the only one on public view in a statehouse. Then there's the one-of-a-kind statue of George Washington astride a horse on display just outside the attorney general's office on the second floor. The statue was created by Charles Ostner, a self-trained artist, Aus-trian immigrant, and Payette River ferry operator who worked for four years by candlelight to carve the statue from a single piece of yellow pine. No one is sure what the statue is worth, but the Smithson-ian Institution reportedly once sought—unsuccessfully—to add the work to its collections. Ostner presented the bronzed statue to the

Idaho territorial government in 1869, and it stood outside on the capitol grounds until 1934, when, weather damaged, it was brought indoors and re-covered with gold leaf.

The case in which Washington's statue stands also sports the only Idaho state seal of original design still left in the Capitol. The original seal, updated in 1957, was created in 1891 by Emma Edwards Green, winner of a national competition and the only woman to design a state seal in America. (Green placed just her initials on her entry, fearing the design would not be chosen if officials knew it was the work of a woman.) Another Idaho first: The state elected the nation's first Jewish governor, Moses Alexander, who served from 1915 through 1919. His portrait, along with those of other past chief executives, may be seen outside the present governor's office, also on the second floor. Duck inside the governor's suite to sign the guest book and pick up a free Idaho potato pin!

Self-guided Capitol tour brochures are available in the governor's office or at the travel information booth on the statehouse's main floor. Personal tours also are available weekdays, but it's best to call (208) 334–2470 to arrange one in advance (except during the state legislative session, generally January through March, when 208–334–2000 is the number to call).

Old Boise, the area just east of Capitol Boulevard, is chock-full of intriguing stores, restaurants, and other fine spots to explore. If you're feeling creative, check out *Ceramica,* a gallery and drop-in workshop in the Pioneer Building at Sixth and Main.

Former international money trader Jennifer Casey had dabbled in art for years when she decided the time might be right to establish a contemporary ceramics gallery and workshop in Boise. Patrons are invited to choose a ready-to-paint piece, with selections ranging from pots and plates to piggy banks, priced from $4.00 to $40.00, plus a $6.50 studio fee, which includes an unlimited selection of paints and glazes. After that they're seated at a table, given some instruction and advice, and encouraged to let their imaginations run wild. The price also includes firing, and patrons can typically pick up their completed piece the day after they paint.

Casey has been surprised at the varied clientele her studio attracts. One regular customer, an art major turned lawyer, says Ceramica helped him rediscover his creative roots. The shop is also a viable first-date alternative: Casey says it's amazing how much you can learn about a person from the way he or she approaches art. For example, "if you get someone painting skeletons, you know there may be a problem," she notes.

Ceramica operates on a no-appointment-necessary basis, but it also can be rented for parties and showers. (One bride-to-be had her friends paint a unique set of not-quite-matching plates.) The workshop is open from 10:00 A.M. to 9:00 P.M. Monday through Thursday, 10:00 A.M. to 10:00 P.M. Friday and Saturday, and noon to 5:00 P.M. Sunday. Call (208) 342–3822 for more information.

Idaho has the nation's highest percentage of people hailing from Euzkadi, or the Basque homeland that straddles the border of Spain and France. Although pockets of Basque culture can be found throughout the state, Boise, by virtue of its size, is probably the state's true Basque capital. A 1-block area of the capital's downtown is an especially rich site of Basque heritage and culture. Take a stroll down Grove Street between Sixth and Capitol for a look at what could be called Boise's *Basque Block.*

Starting from the block's east end and moving west, the *Basque Center* at 601 Grove was built in the late 1940s as a social club and gathering place, a role it continues to play today. The center is a popular site for wedding receptions, dinners, and dances, but it serves as an informal meeting spot, too, particularly for older Basques who enjoy drinking coffee, talking, and playing "mus," a Basque card game. At one time, the *Cyrus Jacobs–Uberuaga House* at 607 Grove housed the Basque Museum and Cultural Center (which has since moved next door). Built in 1864 this is the oldest brick building still standing in Boise, site of the city's first indoor bathtub and the wedding of Senator William Borah. The building served as a Basque boarding house for much of the twentieth century, and the local Basque community plans to renovate it to reflect that heritage.

At 611 Grove, the *Basque Museum and Cultural Center* has many fascinating exhibits on all aspects of Basque history and culture. Here you can learn, for example, about famous people of Basque heritage, including Simón Bolivar, Francisco Goya, Balboa, and Juan de la Cosa, who served as Columbus's navigator. Another Basque mariner was responsible for guiding Magellan's ship home after the explorer was killed in the Philippines following the first circumnavigation of the globe.

Visitors discover that most Idaho Basques trace their heritage to the province of Vizcaya in the northwest section of the Basque homeland. Here, too, are history lessons about Gernika, Boise's sister city and the ancient Vizcayan capital and spiritual homeland of the Basques. It was the bombings here during the Spanish Civil War of 1936–1939 that inspired Pablo Picasso's *Guernica* painting, one of his most famous. Gernika is also home to an oak tree that symbolizes Basque liberty; a model of the tree and its surroundings sits in the museum. The Basque Museum is open from 10:00 A.M. to 4:00 P.M. Tuesday through Friday and from 11:00 A.M. to 3:00 P.M. Saturday. Suggested donation is $1.00 for adults and 50 cents for children and senior citizens. Call (208) 343–2671 for more information.

The *Fronton Building* at 619 Grove was built in 1912 and, although it has housed businesses over the years, none has ever altered the fronton, or handball court, inside. It is the largest covered court of its kind in the Northwest, and it is still used by sporting Basques today. This building also served as a boarding house for a time.

Gernika Basque Pub and Eatery, at the corner of Grove and Capitol, was established in 1991. The menu here includes several Basque-inspired dishes, such as a Solomo sandwich (marinated pork loin topped with pimientos and served on a French roll) or a cheese plate accompanied with fresh bread and grapes. Espresso and microbrews are available, too. Gernika is open from 11:00 A.M. to 11:00 P.M. Monday; 11:00 A.M. to midnight Tuesday through Thursday; and 11:00 A.M. to 1:00 A.M. Friday and Saturday. The phone number is (208) 344–2175. Although it's not on the Basque Block, diners interested in Basque cuisine also may want to try **Onati** at 3544 Chinden Boulevard in nearby Garden City. There Basque chefs prepare meals of lamb, fish, steaks, shrimp, and prawns. Call (208) 343–6464 for reservations or more information.

Basque Center

Not far from the Basque Block, Julia Davis Park is home to the Boise Art Museum, the Idaho Historical Society, and now the *Idaho Black History Museum* at 508 Julia Davis Drive. Less than 1 percent of Idaho's population is African American, and visitors often wonder whether the state has any blacks at all, but this museum sets the record straight. Located in the former St. Paul's Baptist Church, the museum has featured exhibits on everything from Idaho's jazz heritage to the history of the state's African Americans in the military. From

June through September, the museum is open from 10:00 A.M. to 4:00 P.M. Tuesday through Saturday and 1:00 to 4:00 P.M. on Sunday. The rest of the year, it's open 11:00 A.M. to 4:00 P.M. Wednesday through Saturday. Admission is by donation. Special events at the museum include a Juneteenth festival to commemorate the Emancipation Proclamation. This is held the third Saturday of June and a gospel music workshop the first week of February. For more information, call (208) 433–0017 or see www.ibhm.org.

Another unusual museum, the *World Sports Humanitarian Hall of Fame,* includes tributes to such athletes as Roberto Clemente, Bonnie Blair, Arthur Ashe, Jackie Joyner Kersee, and David Robinson—jocks known as much for their philanthropic and community activities as for their sporting heroics. The fledgling hall of fame in the Eighth Street Marketplace, at 404 South Eighth Street, is open weekdays from 9:00 A.M. to 4:00 P.M. Admission is free, but donations are welcome. For more information, call (208) 343–7224 or E-mail hallfame@micron.net.

Boise visitors seeking a bed-and-breakfast stay should consider the *Idaho Heritage Inn* at 109 West Idaho, on the edge of the Warm Springs neighborhood of gracious old homes. Built in 1904 for Henry Falk, one of Boise's early merchants, the home was bought by Idaho Governor Chase Clark in 1943. Later, Clark's daughter, Bethine, and her husband,

Urban Oasis

*A*sk many Boiseans what they love most about their city, and chances are they'll mention the **Greenbelt.** More than 20 miles long, this network of paths reaches from Sandy Point Beach east of the city past Glenwood Street, with more mileage planned for the future.

On a warm weekend day, the Boise Greenbelt could hardly be considered off the beaten track since it sometimes seems half the city is out there walking, running, bicycling, or blading. Even then, however, it's possible to lose the crowds by venturing away from the crowded downtown corri-

dors (near the Boise State University campus and Julia Davis and Ann Morrison Parks) to less-traveled sections. The western stretch from Willow Lane to Americana Boulevard is a good bet, as is the area east of downtown.

A few Greenbelt sections are limited to pedestrian use only, including Kathryn Albertson Park and a stretch bordering the south banks of the Boise River just west of Barber Park. For more information on the Boise River Greenbelt, call (208) 384–4240 or write the Boise Parks & Recreation Department, 1104 Royal Boulevard, Boise 83706.

the beloved Senator Frank Church, used the home as their Idaho residence during Church's Senate tenure. The home remained in the Clark/Church family until 1987, when Tom and Phyllis Lupher bought it with an eye toward opening a bed-and-breakfast.

The Idaho Heritage Inn offers guests a choice of six rooms ranging in price from $65 to $105 for two. Each has a private bath and telephone, making this a good spot for business travelers. Room rates also include a breakfast featuring fresh-squeezed juice and fresh fruit in season along with an entree: Baked German pancakes, apricot cream cheese–stuffed French toast, and apple skillet cake are among past offerings. Call (208) 342–8066; write the Idaho Heritage Inn, 109 West Idaho, Boise 83702; or see www.idheritageinn.com for more information or reservations.

East of downtown on the opposite end of the Warm Springs district, the *Old Idaho Penitentiary* housed inmates from 1870 through 1973. More than 13,000 convicts did time behind its gates, including Harry Orchard, who killed former Idaho governor Frank Steunenberg in 1905 in the aftermath of mining unrest in North Idaho, and Lyda Southard, sentenced to the pen in 1921 after she killed her fourth husband (and maybe her previous spouses, too) with a slice of arsenic-laced apple pie. Visitors can tour the Old Pen on their own or with a guide; some guides earlier served as guards or inmates at the facility. The museum recently added exhibition space for the J. Curtis Earl Collection, a treasure trove of historic arms and military memorabilia. The collection, valued at $3 million, is among the largest of its kind.

The Old Pen is open seven days a week from 10:00 A.M. to 5:00 P.M. Memorial Day to Labor Day. It's open from noon to 5:00 P.M. the rest of the year, except state holidays. Admission is $4.00 for adults and teens and $3.00 for senior citizens and children ages six through twelve. (Kids under age six are admitted free.) For recorded information call (208) 368–6080.

Hyde Park in Boise's North End ranks among the city's other most stylish addresses. Centered at Thirteenth and Eastman Streets, this historic district has a good selection of restaurants and specialty shops. One of the most interesting, *Ten Thousand Villages,* sells crafts, toys, jewelry, and decorative items from around the world. Most of the goods are made by disadvantaged artisans from Third World nations—people who would otherwise be jobless or underemployed. All in all, a cool and fun place to shop. Ten Thousand Villages is at 1609 North Thirteenth Street and its phone number is (208) 333–0535. Hours are 11:00 A.M. to 5:00 P.M. Tuesday through Saturday.

Camel's Back Park, just north of the Hyde Park neighborhood, has one of Boise's best playgrounds. Past the park, Thirteenth Street veers into Hill Road, which soon intersects with Bogus Basin Road, the route to Boise's backyard ski resort of the same name. Near this intersection a nondescript building opposite the Bogus Basin Shopping Center might look like a dentist's office, but it's really home to **Harrison Hollow Brewhouse.** Quench your thirst with one of the beers brewed on-site, check out the collection of *Guitar Player* magazine covers dating back to the 1960s, and get some good grub, too; menu items include crab cakes, barley breadsticks, and the "mess-o-chops" (thinly sliced pork chops, lightly marinated and charbroiled). Harrison Hollow is open from 11:00 A.M. to 10:00 P.M. Monday through Thursday, 11:00 A.M. to 11:00 P.M. Friday and Saturday, and 11:00 A.M. to 9:00 P.M. Sunday, with extended hours at times during the ski season. Call (208) 343–6820 for more information.

The Treasure Valley

Picture a bright fall day. What do you think of? Piles of fat orange pumpkins? Baskets of tart, crisp apples? Roadside markets piled high with the harvest's bounty?

Southwestern Idaho is the state's fruit bowl. In autumn, many Idahoans take day trips on the roads linking such towns as Fruitland, Emmett, Payette, and Weiser to stock up on the season's produce and enjoy some of the state's loveliest fall foliage.

Any time of year, Weiser is the most interesting town in this neck of the woods. Weiser is best known as site of the annual **National Old-Time Fiddlers Contest.** As much a family reunion as a competition, the fiddle fests have been going on in Weiser since 1914. The town became host to the Northwest Mountain Fiddlers Contest in 1953, and the national championship was inaugurated in 1963, Idaho's territorial centennial. The contest is held the third full week of June, drawing about 300 contestants ages four to ninety and more than 10,000 spectators.

Year-round, Weiser is home to the **Fiddlers Hall of Fame,** located in the old Oregon Short Line depot at the end of State Street. Stop by to see photos of past champions, including noted bowman Mark O'Connor. If you miss the Old-Time Fiddlers Contest, try to time your Weiser visit to the second or fourth Thursday September through June, when local fiddlers come to jam. For more information call (208) 549–0452.

Down the block at 30 East Idaho Street, the Knights of Pythias built an impressive temple to Pythianhood back in 1904. Cross the street for a good view of the *Pythian Castle,* which was built for $9,000 using sandstone quarried on the nearby Weiser River. Inside, the building has a vaulted pressed-tin ceiling that may be the finest of its kind in the Northwest. The castle is open during special events, or it can be seen by appointment. To arrange a tour, call Steve Clausen at (208) 549–1844 or Tony Edmondson at (208) 549–0211.

Anyone allergic to chocolate or laughter should steer a wide berth around *Fawn's Classic Candies* at 449 State Street in Weiser. Fawn Olsen started her business in her home; today, it ships candies nationwide and even overseas. Fawn and her crew have a neat sense of humor, offering such confections as the "Chocolate Brady Gun" (labeled "Do Not Eat for Five Days") and "Kowpies" (chocolate fudge shaped into, well, you can imagine). But this is also a good place to learn about the serious business of candy-making. Stop by on a weekday to see the process in action. Each piece of candy is hand-dipped, and each has a subtle "signature" on the outside so the cooks can tell at a glance what kind of filling is inside.

In addition to its tempting candy counter, Fawn's serves muffins, bagels, coffee, ice cream, and deli-style lunches featuring a daily soup-and-sandwich special. The shop is open from 9:00 A.M. to 5:30 P.M. Monday through Friday and 10:00 A.M. to 5:00 P.M. Saturday. Call (208) 549–2850.

The small town of Parma, south of I–84 on U.S. Highway 20/26, is home to a replica of the Hudson's Bay Company's *Fort Boise,* built in 1834 and one of two nineteenth-century forts so named. (The town of Boise grew up around the other, a U.S. Army cavalry post erected in 1863.) The original Fort Boise was situated on the east bank of the Snake River about 8 miles north of the mouth of the Boise River. Although it was built as a fur-trading post, Fort Boise soon switched its emphasis to serving emigrants on the Oregon Trail, and it was a most welcome sight after 300 miles of dry and dusty travel from Fort Hall. An 1845 report on the fort told of "two acres under cultivation . . . 1,991 sheep, seventy-three pigs, seventeen horses, and twenty-seven meat cattle," but the pioneers frequently depleted the fort's stores of flour, tea, coffee, and other pantry staples.

Flooding extensively damaged Fort Boise in 1853, and historians believe any attempts to rebuild it were probably thwarted by increasingly hostile relationships with the Shoshone Indians. Tensions culminated with the 1854 Ward Massacre, in which eighteen emigrants (out of a party of twenty) died; a monument marking the event may be seen in a park south of Middleton, Idaho. Hudson's Bay Company abandoned Fort Boise two years later, and the land on which it originally stood is now a state wildlife management area.

The Fort Boise Replica in Parma sits 5 miles southeast of the original fort site. In addition to the emigrant story, the Fort Boise Replica has artifacts and displays from Southwestern Idaho history. One room features a desk built in 1891 by a boy whose family was traveling to Oregon when their money ran out and they decided to stay. Another exhibit tells how Parma is the only Idaho town to have produced two Gem State governors: Clarence Baldridge, a Republican, and Ben Ross, a Democrat. Visitors also may view a video on Fort Boise history.

A statue and historical marker on the Fort Boise grounds also are worth noting. They tell of Marie Dorian, an Iowa Indian who came to the area with Wilson Price Hunt's party of Astorians in 1811. Three years later, Marie and her two children were the sole survivors of a midwinter battle with Bannock Indians at a nearby fur-trading post. They set out with two horses on a 200-mile journey through deep snow and were finally rescued by a Columbia River band of Walla Walla Indians in April.

The Fort Boise Replica is open from 1:00 to 3:00 P.M. Friday, Saturday, and Sunday during June, July, and August, but if you want to see it during off-hours, you can call Jack Atkeson at (208) 722–7608 at least a day in advance to make arrangements. The park adjacent to the fort replica includes a small campground with showers and a dump station, as well as shady picnic spots, a playground, and a drive-in restaurant next door. Parma celebrates its role in pioneer history late each May with the Old Fort Boise Days celebration.

Nestled in a sheltered valley where State Highway 16 meets State Highway 52, Emmett is another town well known for its produce—although these days it's fast becoming more of a bedroom community for commuters who don't mind a scenic drive of up to an hour to their Boise workplaces. The foothills outside Emmett provide a striking location for **Frozen Dog Digs,** an oddly named bed-and-breakfast inn with equally unusual amenities. The inn, run by former English teacher and technical writer Jon Elsberry, may be the only one in Idaho with its own racquetball court. A major sports fan, Elsberry also has created a fun "sports bar" room featuring an overstuffed baseball mitt chair and lots of New York Yankees memorabilia. Another room resembles a one-room schoolhouse, complete with original Dick-and-Jane posters and desks salvaged from local classrooms. The newest addition is a bi-level suite complete with a kitchenette and jetted tub. The suite, decorated in an Asian motif, opens onto a Japanese garden. Throughout the house, Elsberry has made an effort to use local woods and other materials for the custom-built furnishings and decor.

Frozen Dog Digs' four guest rooms rent for $69 to $169 double occupancy, including breakfast. For reservations or more information, call (208) 365–7372 or write Frozen Dog Digs, 4325 Frozen Dog Road, Emmett, 83617.

Idaho is horse country, and the **R. C. Bean Saddlery** on the Star Road west of Meridian caters to the Western equestrian with beautiful handmade saddles and a wide selection of other tack. The Bean family has been in the ranching business since the 1950s, but R. C. "Rick" Bean started making saddles a bit more recently, around 1979. There's a two-year waiting list for his custom-made, hand-tooled models, which start at $2,500 and average about $3,000 in cost. Some particularly ornate saddles can command much more. Ask to see the bucking-horse saddle Rick made as a showpiece for the store. It's not for sale, but it gives customers a good idea of what Rick can do when money is no object. The Beans also stock more modest saddles made elsewhere, with prices starting at $700. It's worth a stop just to smell the leather. The shop is open from 9:00 A.M. to 6:00 P.M. Monday through Saturday. The phone number is (208) 286–7602.

Idaho's vineyards may never become as well known as those in California's Napa Valley, but the Gem State has a growing number of **wineries,** with the largest concentration in the state's southwestern region. Warm days, cool nights, and rich soil make valleys along the Snake River just right for growing wine grapes. Ste. Chapelle at 19348 Lowell Road near Caldwell is probably Idaho's best known winery, drawing many visitors for its summer jazz concert series. Other Treasure Valley vineyards worth a visit include Sawtooth Winery, at 13750 Surrey Lane south of Nampa, with its panoramic view and annual Mother's Day Wine and Food Festival, and Hells Canyon Winery, 18835 Symms Road, Caldwell. Ste. Chapelle is open daily for tours, and Sawtooth and Hells Canyon wineries welcome visitors on the weekends. You can pick up a brochure on Idaho wineries at many visitor centers and some finer restaurants, or get information online at www.idahowine.org.

If you're traveling along I–84 when the hungries hit, you could pull off almost any Treasure Valley exit into a wide selection of chain fast-food eateries. Or you could wander a bit farther from the freeway for the homemade fare served by Nampa's **Say You Say Me.** This cafe is famous for its eight-egg omelets, although the kitchen usually slips in as many as a dozen eggs. Prices are as low as the portions are huge. Say You Say Me, located at 820 Nampa-Caldwell Boulevard, is open from 6:00 A.M. to 9:00 P.M. Monday through Saturday and 6:00 A.M. to 3:00 P.M. Sunday. The phone number is (208) 466–2728.

Nampa also is well known for its Mexican restaurants. One of the most popular, *Tacos Jalisco,* draws a mixed Anglo-Hispanic crowd with authentic cuisine, reasonable prices, and friendly atmosphere. Look for the red-and-green tiled storefront at 219 Eleventh Avenue North.

Budget travelers, international vagabonds, and others who want inexpensive or nontraditional accommodations in the Boise metro area have cheered the recent opening of *Hostelling International-Nampa,* currently the only HI affiliate in southern Idaho. The hostel is in a rural setting at 17322 Can Ada Road, about 2 miles north of I–84 exit 38. Facilities include a kitchen, barbecue grill, common area, covered patio and big yard, and Internet access. Typical dorm-style hostel beds are $12 for HI members, $15 for nonmembers. One private room is available; it costs $27 for one person, $32 for two people, or $37 for three. Children under fourteen stay half-price; kids under age five stay free. Check-in is between 5:00 P.M. and 10:00 P.M., but once you've checked in, there's no curfew.

From the hostel, it's about a fifteen-minute drive to Boise. Travelers coming via Greyhound will want to get off the bus in Nampa, not Boise, and take a cab. Get more information by calling (208) 467–6858 or at www.hostelboise.com.

The Snake River Canyon in Southwestern Idaho is home to the world's largest concentration of nesting eagles, hawks, and prairie falcons. There are two ways to discover this raptor kingdom: Tour the *Snake River Birds of Prey Conservation Area* and visit the Peregrine Fund's *World Center for Birds of Prey* near Boise.

The conservation area encompasses more than 482,000 acres along 81 miles of the river, and it's best reached via the Swan Falls Road south of Kuna. The Bureau of Land Management has established an interpretive area near Swan Falls Dam, and visitors may catch a glimpse of raptors soaring through the canyon or nesting in its cracks, crevices, and ledges. Early morning and late afternoon mid-March through mid-June is the best time to visit. Bring binoculars, a bird field guide, water and food, sunscreen, a jacket, and a hat.

Because the raptors can be difficult to see, many visitors take a guided tour. *Whitewater Shop River Tours/Birds of Prey Expeditions* offers a variety of land and boat tours starting at about $50 per person. (The "Whitewater" name is a misnomer; people on the boat tours encounter no rapids.) Guides help participants identify bird species and locate the raptors' nesting areas. Every Saturday in May and June, tours are usually accompanied by Morley Nelson, who was instrumental in establishing the Birds of Prey Conservation Area. These full-day trips, which include lunch, cost about $100 per person. For more information or trip reservations, call (208) 327–8903; write WSRT/Birds of Prey Expeditions, 4519 North Mountain View Drive, Boise 83704; or see www.birds ofpreyexpeditions.com.

Scientists study raptors because, like humans, they are near the top of the food chain—and what happens to them could very well happen to us. Four decades ago the peregrine falcon (for which The Peregrine Fund is named) had almost been wiped out in the United States. Through research it was learned that falcons ate smaller birds that had in turn ingested insects exposed to DDT, and the chemical made the falcons' eggshells so thin that the baby birds could not survive.

DDT is now banned in the United States, and the peregrine falcon has made an impressive comeback on our continent. But the chemical remains legal in some other nations; that fact, coupled with other environmental woes, has endangered or threatened nearly a quarter of the world's 300 raptor species. So The Peregrine Fund continues to study birds of prey and their status as environmental indicators, and much of this work takes place at the World Center for Birds of Prey and its new Velma Morrison Interpretive Center sitting high on a windswept hill south of Boise. Take I–84 exit 50 and drive 6 miles south to 5668 West Flying Hawk Lane.

Visitors to the center can walk around on their own or join a guided tour. Through films, lectures, and displays visitors learn how The Peregrine Fund breeds raptors in captivity, then sets them free in their natural habitat. The odds against survival can be high: All peregrines, whether captive-bred or born in the wild, face a 50 percent mortality rate during their first year of life. Another 20 percent die in their second year. But those who survive two years usually go on to live an average of fifteen years. At the end of each tour, visitors are often treated to a visit with a live falcon. The World Center for Birds of Prey is open daily from 9:00 A.M. to 5:00 P.M. March through October and from 10:00 A.M. to 4:00 P.M. the rest of the year. Admission is $4.00 for adults, $3.00 for senior citizens ages sixty-two and up, and $2.00 for children ages four through sixteen. Call (208) 362–8687 for more information or see www.peregrinefund.org.

The Owyhee Outback

O wyhee County deserves its own section in any book about Idaho's lesser-known places, simply for its sheer size and remoteness. It isn't Idaho's biggest county—Idaho County takes that honor with 8,497 square miles. But Owyhee County, tucked into the state's corner, is mostly unexplored and unknown. At 7,643 square miles, it's larger than New Jersey, but with about one-eight-hundredth the population!

Nearly half the county's 10,650 residents live in the Homedale-Marsing area along the Snake River southwest of Caldwell. Lucky people, they can eat at the **Sandbar River House Restaurant** anytime they want. This classy yet casual eatery in Marsing attracts people from Boise and beyond in search of some of Idaho's best dining. House specialties include prime rib (served Friday, Saturday, and Sunday), pork chops, and beef en brochette. Seafood and chicken are also on the menu, and patrons are invited to make a combo dinner by adding such side orders as shrimp scampi, fresh mushroom topping, or a rock lobster tail to their main dish. A deck beckons for guests who want to dine outside overlooking the river. The Sandbar is open for lunch and dinner from 11:00 A.M. to 9:00 P.M. Tuesday, Wednesday, and Thursday and from 11:00 A.M. to 10:00 P.M. Friday and Saturday. Dinner only is served from noon to 8:00 P.M. Sunday, and the restaurant is closed Monday. Call (208) 896–4124 for reservations, which are recommended.

While in Marsing, look for **Lizard Butte,** the volcanic formation looming over town. Waterfall lovers may wish to travel west of Marsing to see **Jump Creek Falls.** The falls, a silver ribbon cascading into a placid pool, are part of the Bureau of Land Management's Jump Creek Special Recreation Management Area, an area of desert plateau and canyonlands. Look for the Jump Creek Road sign west of the intersection of Highways 55 and 95.

Givens Hot Springs, 12 miles from Marsing, got its start as a campground on the Oregon Trail. Pioneers frequently stopped here to wash their clothes; one emigrant said the water was "sufficiently hot to boil eggs." Before that, Native Americans used the area as a base camp. Milford and Martha Givens, pioneers themselves, had seen the springs on their way west. Once they got where they were going, however, they decided they liked Idaho better and came back.

The first Givens Hot Springs bathhouse was built way back in the 1890s, and a hotel stood on the grounds for a while as well. Givens Hot Springs is still a campground, with an enclosed year-round swimming pool, private baths, picnic grounds, softball and volleyball play areas, horseshoe pits, cabins, and RV camping. For more information call (208) 495–2000 or see www.givenshotsprings.com.

If you enjoy old mining towns but find most far too bustling for your tastes, don't miss **Silver City.** Although fairly well known, Silver, as the

Author's Note

Murphy, the seat of Owyhee County, has a sense of humor. Why else would there be a lone parking meter in front of the county courthouse? This town of about fifty people is also home to the **Owyhee County Museum,** *housed in a building that also includes the local library. The museum features varied displays of early county artifacts ranging from Indian tools to cowboy gear. Visitors also learn about life in the early mining towns, seen from several perspectives including that of the many Chinese miners who lived and worked in Idaho during the nineteenth century.*

The museum is open from 10:00 A.M. to 4:00 P.M. Wednesday through Friday year-round, as well as noon to 5:00 P.M. weekends May through Labor Day. There is a small admission charge. Call (208) 495–2319 for more information or current operating hours.

locals call it, is decidedly off the beaten path, an often rough and winding 23-mile drive southwest of Highway 78. Look for the sign and War Eagle Mines historical marker near milepost 34 east of Murphy, and drive carefully. The road is generally open from Memorial Day through late October.

Tucked away in the Owyhee Mountains, Silver was a rollicking place from 1864 through the early 1900s. Not only was it county seat for a vast reach of territorial southern Idaho, Silver was also home to the territory's first telegraph and the first daily newspaper. Telephones were in use by the 1880s, and the town was electrified in the 1890s. Silver City had its own doctors, lawyers, merchants . . . even a red-light district. During its heyday the town had a population of 2,500 people and seventy-five businesses, all made possible by the fabulous riches on War Eagle Mountain.

All this seems unlikely—even unbelievable— today. Silver City isn't technically a ghost town, since about sixty families maintain part-time residences in the vicinity. But there are just a handful of telephones to the outside world; within town, about two dozen more run on the town's magneto crank system, reportedly the last in Idaho. There's no local mail delivery and no electricity. It's not even the county seat anymore, since that honor went to Murphy in 1934. (The Idaho legislature finally made the change official in 1999.) Needless to say, there's no gas station, either.

Silver City's charm is that it has barely enough amenities to make an overnight or weekend stay possible, yet it hasn't become nearly as commercialized as many other Western "ghost towns." The best way to enjoy Silver is simply to walk its dusty streets, survey the many interesting buildings, and try to imagine what life was like here more than a hundred years ago. The second weekend after Labor Day marks the town's open house, when about ten buildings not normally open to the public may be seen for a nominal fee. Proceeds help pay the town watchman. The Fourth of July is another fun, but busy and crowded, time, with family activities including a parade and games. If you want solitude, you'd be better off visiting another time.

The *Idaho Hotel* serves as Silver City's focal point. Gorgeous antiques—an ice chest, slot machine, and pianos—vie for attention with whimsical signs and racks of guidebooks. The hotel was originally built in nearby Ruby City in 1863 and moved to Silver in 1866. After decades as a social and business center for the town, the hotel closed in 1942. Ed Jagels bought it in 1972 and reopened the historic hostelry. Although many visitors simply stop in for a cold drink, short-order meal, books, or postcards, it's still possible to stay overnight in the Idaho Hotel, and the current owners have welcomed guests from all over the world. Rates range from $25 to $50 per room. The hotel can also provide full family-style meals, with about a week's advance notice, to nonguests as well as guests.

The Empire Room may be the inn's finest. Used on occasion as a honeymoon suite, it is named for the style in which it is furnished, with some pieces dating back to the Late Empire era of the 1840s. For all the rooms, guests can bring their own linens or sleeping bags and towels, or the hotel can provide these for $7.00 per bed. Woodstoves provide heat, and kerosene and twelve-volt lamps shed light. The bedrooms are too small and historic to accommodate full baths, so there are toilets, sinks, and showers in other rooms down the hallways.

Rooms in the Idaho Hotel are available from Memorial Day until late October; after that, the city water system is turned off for the winter. Reservations are advised. For more information from May through October, call (208) 583–4104 or write The Idaho Hotel, P.O. Box 75, Murphy 83650-0075. (Call instead of writing if time is of the essence, since it often takes a week or more for mail to reach Silver City from Murphy.) The Bureau of Land Management also has a small campground at Silver City, and its sites are free.

Back on Highway 78 watch for the signs to Oreana. Located in a scenic valley 2 miles south of the highway, Oreana has a population of seven, maybe eight, according to the sign at the "city limits." It's also the setting for *Our Lady, Queen of Heaven Catholic Church,* a striking stone building that started life as a general store. Mike Hyde, an area rancher, built the store from native stone in the late 1800s. When only its walls were completed, word was heard around Oreana that a war party of Indians was on its way to the town. All the local folks reportedly took refuge behind the stone walls, expecting an attack. But the Boise-based militia arrived first, and the Indians were deterred.

The store served the Oreana area well into the twentieth century, but by 1961 it had been empty and unused for some time. That year,

Albert Black—on whose land it stood—gave the old building to the Catholic Diocese in Nampa. The diocese encouraged local Catholics to turn the store into a church, and Our Lady, Queen of Heaven, was the result. The small belfry atop the church houses the bell that originally hung at Our Lady of Tears in Silver City. The bell survived a 1943 flood and still rings to herald occasional services at the church. Unfortunately, the church is not open for tours, but it's still worth a look from the outside if you're in the area.

Snake River Vistas

For a pleasant riverside picnic or some good home cooking, consider a stop at Grand View, located at the intersection of Highways 78 and 67. The town's small park has fishing access, a nature trail, and several tables overlooking the Snake River. Grand View's small city center has an old-fashioned Western boardwalk. Stop in the ***Grand Owyhee Restaurant*** at 210 Main Street for an Owyhee Burger with beef, cheese, bacon, and ham with home fries and all the trimmings for $5.75 or chorizos (Basque sausage) and eggs, hashbrowns, and toast for $6.50. The Grand Owyhee also is known for its country-style chicken-fried steak, homemade soups, and milkshakes, along with prime rib every Saturday night. The restaurant is open from 7:00 A.M. to 9:00 P.M. during summer and from 7:00 A.M. to 8:00 P.M. the rest of the year. The phone number is (208) 834–2200.

Just outside Grandview, Jack and Belva Lawson have created one of the state's most unusual tourist attractions at ***Lawson's EMU-Z-Um.*** Here, on the land they've worked since 1967, the Lawsons have set up a replica of an 1860s town, complete with the contents of the Silver City Schoolhouse Museum. Visitors also see a silver mine replica, wood sculptures, pioneer and Native American artifacts, and one of the area's first hand-built automobiles.

EMU-Z-Um—it got its name from the emus the Lawsons raise—is open from 9:00 A.M. to 5:00 P.M. Friday, Saturday, and Sunday March 1 through October 15. Admission is $5.00 for ages thirteen and up and $2.50 for children ages six to twelve. To get there, look for the sign between mile markers 52 and 53 on State Highway 78. For more information, or to make an off-season appointment, call the Lawsons at (208) 834–2397.

Mountain Home, 23 miles from Grand View via Highway 67, is an Air Force town and a popular stop for travelers on I–84. Few visitors make it past the clot of gas stations and restaurants at exit 95, but those who do will find a few interesting places in town.

The military's presence is unmistakable in Mountain Home: Look no farther than **Carl Miller Park,** possibly the only place in the United States where you can picnic in the shadow of an F-111 fighter jet. The park was established in 1919 as a memorial for the first local soldier killed in World War I. This is also the site of Mountain Home's annual **Air Force Appreciation Day,** held the Saturday after Labor Day weekend each year. About 10,000 people turn out annually for the parade and free barbecue.

If you're not in town that weekend, **Rattlesnake Station Steakhouse** is a good bet. The family-run restaurant is overflowing with whimsical decor—pictures of "talking" cows; wildly painted floors, walls, and ceilings; historical photos and maps; graffiti from past patrons; and lots more. It's a good thing there's so much to look at because service can be slow. But the food is well prepared and worth the wait. You can get lunch specials for about $6.00 and dinner fare priced from about $8.00 to $20.00. Kids eat free Tuesday and Wednesday nights. Ask about sitting at one of the tables done up like old sheepherders' wagons. For reservations, which are a good idea on weekends, call (208) 587–3691. The restaurant is closed Sunday and Monday.

Mountain Home is the main gateway for trips to **Anderson Ranch Reservoir** and the **Trinity Lakes** area. Anderson Reservoir dams the South Fork of the Boise River, and while the man-made lake isn't especially scenic, it does have plenty of inlets and bays that provide visual relief from the high-and-dry hills all around. At one of the prettiest coves, **Fall Creek Resort and Marina** (on the reservoir's west side, 8 miles from the dam) offers eleven rooms priced at $50 and up double occupancy, which includes use of a sauna, hot tub, and exercise equipment. A restaurant and lounge serve up breakfast, lunch, dinner, and karaoke. Other amenities include swimming and fishing and an RV park. Call (208) 653–2242 for more information, or write the resort's office at 6633 Overland Road, Boise 83709. A few other little resorts dot Anderson Reservoir's east side near the settlements of Pine and Featherville.

From Fall Creek north it's 17 miles to Trinity Mountain. (Take Forest Service Roads 123 and 129. The steep, rough route is passable by most vehicles, but forget towing a trailer.) If the scenery was ho-hum around Anderson Reservoir, it is sublime here in the highlands. Stake a spot at one of four campgrounds, or rent one of two primitive Forest Service cabins, which sleep six for $25 per night. Cabins can be reserved by calling (877) 444–6777. For other information call (208) 587–7961 or write the Mountain Home Ranger District, 2180 American Legion Boulevard, Mountain Home 83647.

Not surprisingly the Trinity Lakes region is popular with hikers and other recreationists. The 4-mile, pedestrians-only ***Rainbow Basin Trail*** takes trekkers into a subalpine cirque basin dotted with nine lakes and populated by lots of critters including elk, deer, mountain lion, and black bear. From Trinity Mountain you can follow more forest roads over to Featherville or Atlanta (see the Boise Basin section), or turn around for the descent back to Mountain Home.

Southeast of Mountain Home, the top attraction is ***Bruneau Dunes State Park.*** Most sand dunes form at the edge of a natural basin, but these form at the center, making them unique in the Western Hemisphere. The Bruneau complex also includes the largest single structured sand dune in North America, with its peak 470 feet high. The combination of sand and a natural trap has caused sand to collect here for about 15,000 years, and the prevailing wind patterns—from the southeast 28 percent of the time and from the northwest 32 percent—ensure the dunes don't move far. The two prominent dunes cover about 600 acres.

Hiking, camping, and fishing are favorite activities at the Bruneau Dunes. Hiking to the top of a sand dune is an experience unlike any other. Once there, many hikers simply linger a while to savor the view before walking the crest of the dunes back to terra firma. Others use the dunes' inside bowl for sledding, sand skiing, or snowboarding. Bass and bluegill thrive in the small lakes at the foot of the dunes, and the campground—with one of the longest seasons in Idaho—has a steady stream of visitors March through late fall. Bruneau Dunes State Park has a good visitor center featuring displays of wildlife and natural history. There's also an observatory that features astronomy programs at dusk Friday and Saturday evenings, spring through fall. Take I–84 exit 95 or 112 to the dunes. A $3.00-per-vehicle park entrance fee is charged. For more information call (208) 366–7919; write Bruneau Dunes State Park, HC 85, Box 41, Mountain Home 83647; or see the Web site at www.idahoparks.org/parks/bruneaudunes.html.

At what is now ***Three Island Crossing State Park,*** pioneers traveling west on the Oregon Trail faced the most difficult river crossing of their 2,000-mile journey. Many chose not to ford the river and continued along the south bank of the Snake River through the same country we've just traversed. But about half the emigrants decided to brave the Snake to the shorter, easier route on the river's north side. It's still possible to see the islands used in the crossing, as well as scars worn by the wagon wheels.

The crossing is re-enacted in one of Idaho's most popular annual festivals, usually held the second Saturday each August. Although the Snake isn't as mighty as it once was, fording it remains dangerous. Wagons sometimes capsize, and livestock occasionally drown. It's hard for spectators to rest easy until every man, horse, and wagon has made it across safely. Once all have, however, everyone flocks to the festival's other attractions: food, arts and crafts booths, entertainment, and the park itself. If you can't make it at crossing time, you can still enjoy the park's year-round Oregon Trail History and Education Center and recreational activities, including camping, fishing, swimming, and picnicking. The park even rents tepees at a cost of $30 per night for up to five people. Three Island State Park is reached via exit 120 off of I–84. Drive south into Glenns Ferry and follow the signs to the park. For more information call (208) 366–2394 or visit the park Web site at www.idaho parks.org/parks/threeisland.html.

End your visit to Glenns Ferry with a stop at *Carmela Winery,* right next door to Three Island Crossing State Park. Located in a building that looks like a cross between a medieval castle and a French chateau, Carmela's tasting room is open daily, with tours available by request. The winery produces several varieties of riesling, chardonnay, merlot, cabernet, and blush. The wines also are featured in the on-site restaurant, with its panoramic view. The restaurant is open from 11:00 A.M. to 9:00 P.M. Monday through Saturday, and from 10:00 A.M. to 8:00 P.M. Sunday. It's closed Monday and Tuesday in winter. After your meal browse the adjacent gift shop's good selection of artwork, books, and Idaho products.

Carmela may very well be the only winery with a golf course right on the premises, too. Weekend summertime greens fees are $12 for nine holes and $20 for eighteen holes, with gas and pull carts available. If Three Island's campground is full, try the RV park adjacent to Carmela. For more information on the winery, call (208) 366–2313.

**PLACES TO STAY
IN SOUTHWESTERN IDAHO**

MCCALL
Bear Creek Lodge,
Highway 55,
(208) 634–3551,
fax: (208) 634–4299

Best Western McCall, ·
415 Third Street,
(800) 528–1234,
fax: (208) 634–2967

Hotel McCall,
1101 North Third Street,
(866) 800–1183 (see text)

Manchester at Payette Lake,
501 West Lake Street,
(208) 634–2244,
fax: (208) 634–7504

Northwest Passage
Bed & Breakfast,
201 Rio Vista Blvd.,
(800) 597–6658,
fax: (208) 634–4977
(see text)

Riverside Motel & Condo-
miniums, 400 West Lake,
(800) 326–5610

Scandia Inn Motel,
401 North Third Street,
(208) 634–7394

NEW MEADOWS
Hartland Inn & Motel,
Highways 55 and 95,
(208) 347–2114,
fax: (208) 347–2535

Meadows Motel,
Highway 95,
(208) 347–2175

CAMBRIDGE
Frontier Motel & RV Park,
(208) 257–3851

Hunters Inn/Cambridge
House Bed & Breakfast,
Highway 95,
(208) 257–3325 (see text)

COUNCIL
Starlite Motel,
102 North Dartmouth,
(208) 253–4868

YELLOW PINE
Yellow Pine Lodge,
(208) 633–3377 (see text)

WARM LAKE
North Shore Lodge,
(800) 933–3193

Warm Lake Lodge,
(208) 632–3553 (see text)

CASCADE
Chief High Country Inn,
112 North Main Street,
phone/fax: (208) 382–3315

Mountain View Motel,
(800) AOK–ROOM,
fax: (208) 382–4713

Pinewood Lodge
Motel & RV Park,
900 South Highway 95,
(208) 382–4948

LOWMAN
Sourdough Lodge & RV
Resort, (208) 259–3326

GRANDJEAN
Sawtooth Lodge,
(208) 259–3331 (see text)

IDAHO CITY
Idaho City Hotel/
Prospector Motel,
(208) 392–4290,
fax: (208) 392–4505

One Step Away Bed &
Breakfast, 112 Cottonwood
Street, phone/fax:
(208) 392–4938

ATLANTA
Beaver Lodge,
(208) 864–2132

Pinnacle Peaks
Sawtooth Lodge,
(208) 864–2168 (see text)

BOISE
Best Western Vista Inn,
2645 Airport Way,
(800) 727–5006, fax:
(208) 342–3060

Doubletree Club Hotel,
475 West ParkCenter
Boulevard,
(800) 222–8733,
fax: (208) 345–8345

Grove Hotel,
245 South Capitol
Boulevard,
(208) 333–8000,
fax: (208) 333–8800

Idaho Heritage Inn,
109 West Idaho,
(208) 342–8066 (see text)

J. J. Shaw House Bed &
Breakfast Inn,
1411 West Franklin Street,
(877) 344–8899

Motel 6,
2323 Airport Way,
(800) 466–8356

Owyhee Plaza Hotel,
1109 Main Street,
(800) 233–4611,
fax: (208) 381–0695

Plaza Suite Hotel,
409 South Cole Road,
(800) 376–3608,
fax: (208) 376–3608

Quality Inn Airport Suites,
2717 Vista Avenue,
(800) 228–5151,
fax: (208) 342–4319

Shilo Inn–Boise Riverside,
3031 Main Street,
(800) 222–2244

Super 8, 2773 Elder Street,
(800) 800–8000,
fax: (208) 344–8871

FRUITLAND
Elm Hollow
Bed & Breakfast,
4900 Highway 95,
(208) 452–6491

WEISER
Colonial Motel,
251 East Main Street,
(208) 549–0150

Indianhead Motel & RV
Park, 747 Highway 95,
(208) 549–0331

State Street Motel,
1279 State Street,
(208) 549–1390

EMMETT
Frozen Dog Digs Bed &
Breakfast, 4325 Frozen Dog
Road, (208) 365–7372
(see text)

Holiday Motel & RV Park,
1111 S. Washington
Avenue, (208) 365–4479

STAR
The Maples Bed & Break-
fast, 10600 West State
Street, (208) 286–7419

PARMA
The Court Motel,
712 Grove Street,
(208) 722–5579

NAMPA
Budget Inn,
908 Third Street South,
(208) 466–3594

Desert Inn,
115 Ninth Avenue South,
(208) 467–1161,
fax: (208) 467–5268

Hostelling International-
Nampa (Hostel Boise),
17322 Can Ada Road,
(208)467–6858 (see text)

Nampa Super 8,
624 Nampa Boulevard,
(800) 800–8000,
fax: (208) 467–2888

Helpful Web sites

Boise Convention & Visitors Bureau—
www.boise.org/

Boise-area entertainment/community site—
www.zidaho.com

Idaho Statesman (Boise daily newspaper)—
www.idahostatesman.com

McCall Area Chamber of Commerce—
www.mccall–idchamber.org/

Idaho Press–Tribune
(Nampa/Caldwell–area newspaper)—
www.idahopress.com/

Destination Northwest travel sites—
www.destinationnw.com/idaho/mccall.htm
www.destinationnw.com/idaho/boise.htm

Worth Seeing

Ponderosa State Park—*McCall*

Boise Art Museum

Idaho State Historical Museum—*Boise*

Zoo Boise

Discovery Center of Idaho—*Boise*

Morrison–Knudsen Nature Center—*Boise*

Warhawk Air Museum—*Caldwell*

Shilo Inn–Nampa Suites,
1401 Shilo Drive,
(800) 222-2244,
fax: (208) 465-5929

CALDWELL
Best Inn and Suites,
901 Specht Avenue,
(800) 237-8466,
fax: (208) 454-9334

Holiday Motel,
512 Frontage Road,
(208) 453-1056

Sundowner Motel,
1002 Arthur Street,
(208) 459-1585,
fax: (208) 454-9487

SILVER CITY
Idaho Hotel,
(208) 583-4104 (see text)

MOUNTAIN HOME
Best Western Foothills
Motor Inn, 1080 Highway
20, (800) 604-8477,
fax: (208) 587-5774

Motel Thunderbird,
910 Sunset Strip,
(208) 587-7927

Sleep Inn,
1180 Highway 20,
(800) 753-3746,
fax: (208) 587-7382

**ANDERSON RANCH
RESERVOIR AREA**
Deer Creek Lodge
(Pine–Featherville Road),
(208) 653-2454

Fall Creek Resort,
(208) 653-2242 (see text)

Featherville Motel
(Featherville),
(208) 653-2310

Nester's Mountain Motel
(Pine), (208) 653-2222

GLENNS FERRY
Great Basin Bed &
Breakfast,
319 East First Avenue,
(208) 366-7124

Redford Motel,
601 West First Avenue,
(208) 366-2421

**PLACES TO EAT
IN SOUTHWESTERN IDAHO**

MCCALL
Bev's Cottage Cafe
(sandwiches and pastries),
1133 East Lake Street,
(208) 634-3737

The Mill Supper Club
(American),
324 North Third Street,
(208) 634-7683 (see text)

Romano's Ristorante
(Italian/American),
downtown on the lake,
(208) 634-4396

NEW MEADOWS
High Meadows Cafe &
Pizza (American),
Highway 95,
(208) 347-2513

CAMBRIDGE
Bistro Espresso Coffee Shop
(coffee shop),
10 Superior Street,
(208) 257-3325

Bucky's Cafe (American),
Highway 95,
(208) 257-3330

Kay's Cafe (American),
Highway 95,
(208) 257-3561

COUNCIL
Norm's Corner
(American),
101 Michigan Avenue,
(208) 253-6014

YELLOW PINE
Yellow Pine Lodge
(American),
(208) 633-3377 (see text)

WARM LAKE
North Shore Lodge
(American),
(800) 933-3193

Warm Lake Lodge
(American),
(208) 632-3553 (see text)

CASCADE
Cascade Chef's Hut (family),
806 Highway 55 South,
(208) 382-4496

GRANDJEAN
Sawtooth Lodge
(American),
(208) 259-3331 (see text)

IDAHO CITY
Trudy's Kitchen
(American),
419 Highway 21,
(208) 392-4151 (see text)

ATLANTA
Beaver Lodge (American),
(208) 864-2132

BOISE
Brick Oven Bistro
(home-style cooking),
801 Main Street,
(208) 342–3456

Cottonwood Grille
(upscale),
913 West River Drive,
(208) 333–9800

Flying Pie Pizzaria (pizza),
6508 Fairview Avenue,
(208) 376–3454

Gernika Basque Pub &
Eatery, 202 South Capitol
Boulevard, (208) 344–2175
(see text)

Louie's (Italian),
620 West Idaho Street,
(208) 344–5200

Richard's Across the Street
(Pacific Northwest),
1520 North Thirteenth
Street, (208) 331–9855

Most major fast-food chain
restaurants, located mainly
along Broadway Avenue,
Fairview Avenue, Glenwood
Street, Milwaukee Street,
Orchard Street, Overland
Road, and Vista Avenue.

WEISER
Judy's Weiser In (American),
1800 East Sixth,
(208) 549–4962

McDonald's (fast food),
Highway 95,
(208) 549–8035

EMMETT
The Timbers (American),
300 Highway 16,
(208) 365–6915

NAMPA
Generations (American),
112 Third Street South,
(208) 467–4941

Say You Say Me
(American),
820 Nampa–Caldwell
Boulevard, (208) 466–2728
(see text)

Tacos Jalisco (Mexican),
219 Eleventh Avenue North,
(208) 465–5788 (see text)

Most major fast-food
chain restaurants, located
mainly along Nampa–
Caldwell Boulevard.

CALDWELL
The Armadillo (barbecue),
4808 East Cleveland
Boulevard,
(208) 459–1226

Tacos Michoacan
(Mexican), 605 North Fifth
Avenue, (208) 454–1583

MERIDIAN
Epi's Basque Restaurant
(Basque),
1115 East First Street,
(208) 884–0142

MARSING
Sandbar River House
Restaurant (American),
Highway 78,
(208) 896–4124 (see text)

GRAND VIEW
Grand Owyhee Restaurant
(American),
210 Main Street,
(208) 834–2200

MOUNTAIN HOME
Rattlesnake Station
Steakhouse (American),
135 Bitterbrush,
(208) 587–3691 (see text)

Top Hat Southern
Barbecue (barbecue),
145 North Second East,
(208) 587–9223

Several major fast-food
chain restaurants, located
at I–84 exit 95

**ANDERSON RANCH
RESERVOIR AREA**
Deer Creek Lodge
(American), Pine–
Featherville Road,
(208) 653–2454

Fall Creek Resort
(American),
(208) 653–2242 (see text)

GLENNS FERRY
Carmela Winery
(American),
(208) 366–2313 (see text)

South Central Idaho

To the casual traveler along I–84, South Central Idaho seems an arid, apparently barren expanse on the way to somewhere else—most likely Boise or Salt Lake City. To many visitors the best show seems to be in the sky, where clouds roll over wide vistas hemmed by distant mountain peaks.

This big landscape hides its treasures well, but they're not hard to find if you get off the freeway. U.S. Highway 30, a slower and more scenic alternative to I–84, crosses the region from Bliss east to Heyburn (near Burley) before returning to the freeway; Twin Falls, the region's largest city and crossroads to points north and south, is about midway, offering a good beginning and end to loop day-trips. From Twin Falls, U.S. Highway 93 drops south over high desert into Nevada, while Idaho Highway 75 climbs north over rugged lava fields to Sun Valley and the rest of mountainous Central Idaho. From these spokes, small byways and farm roads provide the passport to fertile farmland, abundant recreation, and one of the world's great canyons.

For more South Central Idaho travel information, call (800) 255–8946; write the South Central Idaho Tourism and Recreation and Development Association, P.O. Box 5155, Twin Falls 83303-5155; or see their Web site at www.rideidaho.com.

The Hagerman Valley

In many cases, South Central Idaho's best-kept secrets are just a few miles off the interstate. In the case of Malad Gorge, the highway literally passes right overhead.

At Malad Gorge, the Big Wood River becomes the Malad River, tumbling into a canyon 250 feet deep and just 140 feet wide. This area, called the Devil's Washbowl, is the centerpiece of **Malad Gorge State Park,** a wonderfully handy spot for a break from the interstate. To get there take exit 147 at Tuttle. *Malad* is French for sick, and Malad Gorge got its name when nineteenth-century fur trappers became ill after eating

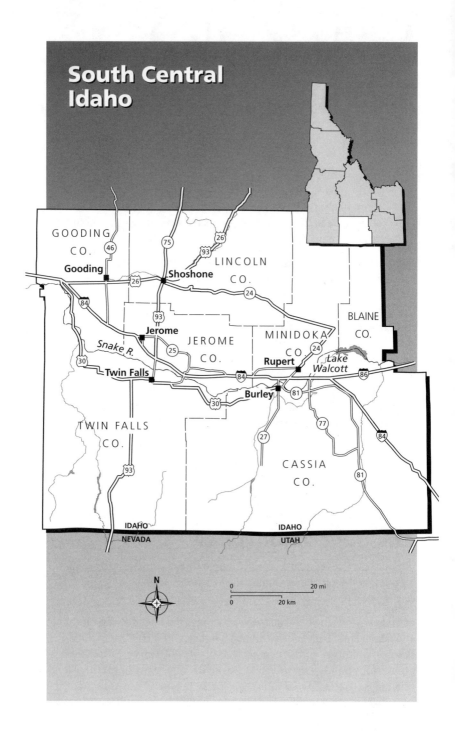

South Central
Idaho

beaver caught nearby. The Malad River itself is thought to be one of the world's shortest, running just 12 miles before being swallowed up by the mighty Snake River downstream. A short trail from the main parking area leads to a footbridge over the plunge. Wagon-wheel ruts from the Kelton Road, an old freight route from Utah to Idaho, may be seen nearby, as may traces of the old stage stop. Park staff discovered these several years ago while cleaning up a local garbage dump. Malad Gorge has facilities for hiking and picnicking, but no camping is permitted. The park's roads are excellent for walking, jogging, or bicycling; indeed this is the site of a popular annual run/walk event held the Saturday before each St. Patrick's Day. Most days, however, you'll likely have the place to yourself. For more information on Malad Gorge, call (208) 837–4505 or check the park Web site at www.idahoparks.org/parks/maladgorge.html.

From Malad Gorge, it's a short drive to the ***Gooding Hotel Bed & Breakfast.*** A historic inn built in Ketchum and moved to its current site in 1888, twenty years before the town of Gooding was even founded, the hotel is now owned by Dean Gooding, the great-great-nephew of former Idaho governor and U.S. Senator Frank Gooding, and Dean's wife, Judee. Gooding was an old railroad town, and the hotel is hard by the tracks. Then as now its location was ideal, within walking distance of restaurants, bars, and shops. Ten rooms are available, priced at $55 to $80 including breakfast. Most have their own bathroom. Ask about gift certificates and "pamper me" packages. The hotel also has a visitor information center. For more information or reservations, call (208) 934–4374 or (888) 260–6656. If you're in Gooding in midsummer, don't miss the annual Basque Picnic, usually served the third Sunday of July at West Park. The event includes a barbecue of lamb chops, chorizos (a highly seasoned pork sausage), beans, rice, and more, plus dancing, music, and games.

Northwest of town off of State Highway 46, the ***Gooding City of Rocks and Little City of Rocks*** offer panoramas of highly eroded canyon lands, Native American petroglyphs, and spring wildflowers. Both areas are located west off of Highway 46, and they're particularly appealing to kids, who will have a ball exploring the fantastic rock formations—but keep your eyes open for rattlesnakes and the elk herds who live on the high desert lands nearby. Highway 46 continues north to a sweeping vista of the Camas Prairie, its blue flowers usually in bloom shortly before Memorial Day.

South of Gooding the town of Wendell provides access to both sides of the Snake River Canyon and to the Hagerman Valley, where recreation and relaxation are a way of life. But since Snake River crossings are few and far between here, we'll first take a look at some north- and east-rim attractions that are best accessed from I–84.

An Idaho state park that is actually a satellite of Malad Gorge, **Niagara Springs State Park** has also been designated a National Natural Landmark. One of the last and largest remaining springs in an area that still bears the Thousand Springs name it received from Oregon-bound pioneers, Niagara Springs churns from the Snake River Canyon wall at 250 cubic feet per second.

Niagara Springs is a splendid spot for picnics and wildlife watching, especially waterfowl. Kids and senior citizens can fish for free at the nearby Crystal Springs Fish Hatchery, a commercial operation. To reach the Niagara Springs/Crystal Springs area, take I–84 exit 157 from Wendell and drive south on the Rex Leland Highway to the canyon rim. The steep, narrow road here drops 350 feet and is not suitable for large RVs or trailers. Incidentally, the fare at **The Farmhouse Restaurant** at exit 157 was voted the best food in the United States in a truckers' poll.

Not far west, The Nature Conservancy has established its **Thousand Springs Preserve** on Ritter Island in the Snake River. The seventy-acre island once was owned by Utah-based businesswoman Minnie Miller, who established what became one of the nation's top guernsey cattle herds right on this site. Today the preserve welcomes visitors who come to hike one of several easy trails, canoe around the island (it's a great spot for novice paddlers), or picnic at the adjacent Thousand Springs Power Plant Park. Tours of the grounds are offered most Saturdays during the summer, and an outstanding fine arts festival takes place in late September. Call (208) 536–6797 for a schedule and detailed directions to the preserve.

Hagerman itself is accessible via Highway 30 south from Bliss or north from Buhl and via the Vader Grade west from Wendell. With its year-round mild climate and abundant recreation, the Hagerman Valley offers many pleasures, and it's easy to enjoy several diversions on any given day. Fishing is a major lure, with some of the state's most productive waters— the Snake River, Billingsley Creek, Oster Lakes, and the Anderson Ponds—located nearby. Floating is another popular pastime, and rafters

TOP ANNUAL EVENTS

Western Days, Twin Falls
(late May/early June)

Idaho Regatta, Burley *(last weekend in June)*

Twin Falls City Band Concerts (each Thursday June through mid-August)

Sagebrush Days, Buhl
(Fourth of July week)

Gooding Basque Picnic (third Sunday in July)

Spud Art Contest/Art in the Park, Twin Falls *(last weekend of July)*

Twin Falls County Fair and Stampede, Filer *(six days ending Labor Day)*

Thousand Springs Festival of the Arts, Hagerman Valley *(late September)*

often can take to the Snake as early as April 1 (and as late as Halloween), with the area just below the Lower Salmon Falls Power Plant the most popular spot to put in. Many people navigate this stretch on their own, but at least three companies—*High Adventure River Tours* at (208) 837–9005; *Hagerman Valley Outfitters* at (208) 837–6100; and *Idaho Guide Service* at (208) 734–4998— offer guided white-water floats. *Thousand Springs Tours* specializes in scenic floats and dinner cruises on calmer waters in the area. Call (208) 837–9006 for information.

A float trip below Lower Salmon Falls is the best way to sneak a peak at *Teater's Knoll,* the only Idaho structure designed by Frank Lloyd Wright. The home and studio, which are perched high above the Snake, were built for Western artist Archie Teater and his wife, Patricia, who lived there part-time from the late 1950s through the 1970s. The home, later purchased and restored by modern-day Idaho architect Henry Whiting, is on the National Register of Historic Places. It is currently inaccessible to the public.

The Hagerman Valley continues to attract more than its share of creative people, bolstering the area's growing reputation as a center for the arts. One worthwhile stop is *Snake River Pottery,* just down the Old Bliss Grade west of the Malad River bridge. The pottery was started in 1947 by Drich and Di Bowler, self-taught artists who also traveled the state in a school bus performing classical dramas as the Antique Festival Theater. Di passed away in 1986, but her husband has kept the pottery in business with the help of younger artisans. Call (208) 837–6527 for more information.

For a good meal in Hagerman, try the *Snake River Grill* at State and Hagerman Streets. Meals include catfish, sturgeon, pasta, and wild game. Many locals and day-trippers drop in for the yummy catfish sandwiches, but classically trained Chef Kirt Martin also is known for creating specially prepared feasts with all sorts of wild game. (So now you know what to do with that venison or elk roast your brother-in-law brings over every hunting season. Call 208–837–6227 to make arrangements.)

As if all this wasn't enough to entice visitors to Hagerman, the town is host to one of the nation's newer National Parks units. The **Hagerman Fossil Beds National Monument** marks the spot where an area farmer discovered fossils that turned out to be those of the zebralike Hagerman Horse, now the official Idaho state fossil. In the 1930s the Smithsonian Institution sent several expeditions to collect specimens of the horse. Archaeologists unearthed 130 skulls and 15 skeletons of an early, zebra-like horse that dated back to the Pliocene Age, about 3.4 million years ago. Other fossils in the area preserved early forms of camel, peccary, beaver, turtle, and freshwater fish.

The monument has a visitor center at 221 North State Street in Hagerman, open daily late May through Labor Day and less often the rest of the year. Stop there to see the exhibits and get directions to other monument areas open to the public; opportunities include several hiking trails and interpretive areas. The monument also has a full summer slate of tours and special programs, mostly on Saturday. For more information or a schedule, call (208) 837–4793 or see www. nps. gov/hafo.

Hagerman celebrates **Fossil Days** each year over Memorial Day weekend. On Saturday of that weekend, there's a classic small-town parade, both provincial and poignant. In recent years a local nursing home's

Sage, Wind, and Stone

A few weeks after our daughter, Natalie, was born in 1994, my husband and I took a Sunday-afternoon drive to the Snake River between Hagerman and Bliss. We'd come to watch kayakers negotiate a new stretch of rapids created by a rock slide a year or so before.

We parked our car and walked the narrow dirt path down to the river, our child cradled in a baby carrier against my chest. Along the way, I picked a sprig of sagebrush and held it to Natalie's nose. Her tiny nostrils flared at the sweet, pungent scent. "This is what Idaho smells like," I told her.

At that moment, I realized my own Idaho walks have given me an intimate knowledge of the place where I live—things I would never know if I never left my car. What freshly picked sage smells like, for example, and how south winds blow much warmer than west winds, and how lava rock ranges from smooth and sinewy to rough and jagged. I have adopted this state, and so I came to this understanding as an adult. For my little native Idahoan, however, these facts will be the fabric of her childhood. No matter where she may live, Natalie will have immutable memories of sage, of wind, and of stone.

wheelchair drill team and a horse painted like the famous prehistoric zebra have been among the crowd-pleasing entries.

Thousand Springs

South of Hagerman, U.S. Highway 30 enters Twin Falls County. The highway here is known as the *Thousand Springs Scenic Route,* taking its name from the white cascades that gush from the black basalt of the Snake River Canyon. At one time there probably were truly a thousand springs, give or take a few. Today there are far fewer, but the sight remains impressive.

Where do the springs originate? Many have traveled underground from near Arco, where the Big Lost River and several other streams abruptly sink underground. From there the water moves ever so slowly, possibly just 10 feet a day, through the Snake River Aquifer before bursting forth from the canyon walls. In other words, the water you see here entered the aquifer about the year 1800 and has been making its way across the underground aquifer ever since.

Hot springs also are abundant in the area, and several resorts line Highway 30 between Hagerman and Buhl. Most feature swimming, camping, and picnic facilities; at least two *(Banbury Hot Springs* and *Miracle Hot Springs)* boast private VIP baths. *Sligar's 1000 Springs Resort* offers indoor swimming year-round in a spacious pool.

South Central Idaho produces a whopping 90 percent of the world's commercially raised trout, and *Clear Springs Foods*—by far the largest of the trout processors—provides a glimpse of the fish business at its visitor center north of Buhl on the Snake River. Little kids in particular love to press their noses against the underground fish-viewing window, where trout swim by within inches and huge sturgeon can be seen dwelling in the murkier depths. The center has good picnicking grounds, too.

In Buhl itself, the little coffeehouse/bookstore *Cosmic Jolt* at 120 South Broadway provides a taste of the metaphysical in this unlikely farm-town setting. Check out the cool decoupaged tables, each with a different theme, where you can enjoy a latte or luscious muffin. *Smith's Dairy,* another local institution at 205 South Broadway, scoops up ice-cream cones. Enjoy one in the gazebo outside.

South Central Idaho's cultural scene got a big boost in 1999 with the opening of the Buhl Arts Council's new headquarters at the *Eighth Street Center.* Set in a beautifully renovated landmark building, the center has outstanding programming that goes well beyond the arts to include such fare as labyrinth walks (the third Sunday afternoon of each month), intimate concerts, and classes in everything from yoga to taxidermy to French cooking. For more information or a list of upcoming programs, call (208) 543–2888 or write the Buhl Arts Council, 200 North Eighth Street, Buhl 83316.

A short drive southwest of Buhl leads to *Balanced Rock,* a curious geological formation that appears poised like a giant mushroom (or maybe a question mark?) against the blue Idaho sky. The landmark is just a few miles west of Castleford, and a nearby small county park along Salmon Falls Creek provides another perfect spot for a picnic. To get there follow the signs out of Buhl for 16 miles.

Clover, a small farming community due east of Castleford, is the setting for one of Idaho's most beautiful country churches. *Clover Lutheran Church* has long served the families of the area, and the parishioners have given back to the church in equal measure, most notably through the stained-glass windows that grace the north and south sides of the sanctuary. These windows, done in traditional leaded stained-glass style, were made entirely by members of the congregation. The windows on the south side depict the local farming community, including sprigs of clover; those on the north are rich in Christian symbolism. The church also has its original ceiling of embossed tin.

Sunday mornings would be the best time to see Clover Lutheran, hear its pipe organ, and visit with the congregation. But the church is worth a stop at any time. If no one's in the office on the building's northwest side, check at the parsonage, located at the ranch house just to the north. The church cemetery also is notable for its headstones, some of which are in the native German of the people who settled Clover. The oldest graves are in the cemetery's southwest corner.

Just east of Filer, U.S. Highway 93 swings south from Highway 30 for the Nevada border some 40 miles away. Just over the Nevada line, *Jackpot* serves as the gambling

Balanced Rock

hub for Idaho (and, judging from license plates in the casino parking lots, for revelers from as far away as Montana, Manitoba, and Saskatchewan, too). The town's biggest draw is **Cactus Pete's,** a full-fledged resort with comfortable rooms, abundant dining options (including the Plateau Room, possibly the classiest restaurant in a 100-mile radius), and semi-big-name entertainment. But some folks prefer the down-home, distinctly non-Vegas atmosphere of the town's smaller casinos, especially **Barton's Club 93.**

Highway 93 is also the best jumping-off spot for the Jarbidge country, one of the West's most wild and remote areas, located about 60 miles southwest of Rogerson. (All but the last 17 miles are paved.) Although on the Nevada border like Jackpot, Jarbidge's main attraction isn't gambling but natural splendor: The **Jarbidge Mountains** boast eight peaks higher than 10,000 feet, the highest concentration in Nevada; and campers, hikers, and horseback riders will swear they've found paradise. The town itself has about three dozen homes, a couple of cafes, and the **Tsawhawbitts Ranch Bed & Breakfast,** a retreat originally built by New York City publishing magnate Roscoe Fawcett in the 1970s. The main house has several rooms whose rates are about $60 to $70 double occupancy; there also are private cabins—one sleeps four people for $150, and two sleep up to eight people for $230. All rates include breakfast. Call (775) 488–2338 for more information or reservations (a must). The ranch is also the meeting spot for guests of outfitter Lowell Prunty, whose Jarbidge Wilderness Guide & Packing offers horse packing, backpacking, and hunting trips. For more information, call (208) 857–2270 or see www.jarbidge.com. Have a look at *Nevada: Off the Beaten Path* for more ideas on seeing the Silver State.

*Filer is home to the **Twin Falls County Fair,** which the* Los Angeles Times *named one of the top ten rural county fairs in the United States. The "Filer Fair," as it's known locally, runs the six days up to and including Labor Day. It's big enough to draw top-name country singers and rodeo cowboys, yet small enough to retain a real down-home feel. For many Southern Idahoans, the fair recalls a reunion, high time to get caught up on gossip and marvel at how much the kids have grown.*

The fair also provides a ready excuse to forget your diet for a while: For some of the most unusual fare, check out the Job's Daughters' elephant-ear scones (deep-fried dough topped with cinnamon sugar), the one-of-a-kind troutburgers served up by the Buhl Catholic Church, or the tater pigs—a link sausage stuffed inside an Idaho baked potato—offered by the Magichords, a local barbershop singing group. You'll also find everything from cotton candy and ice cream to home-made pies and gyros. Just remember to visit the carnival rides before you eat, not after!

The Magic Valley

ack on Highway 30, the traveler reaches Twin Falls, the largest city in South Central Idaho, with a population of about 35,000. Highway 30 becomes Addison Avenue within the city; at Blue Lakes Boulevard you can either turn left (north) for the city's crowded commercial strip or south (onto Shoshone Street) to find charming downtown Twin Falls.

Twin Falls is as Midwestern a town as you'll find anywhere in the western United States. The city throws a big **Western Days** celebration each spring, but make no mistake: This is a Jimmy Stewart sort of place, complete with a tree-lined downtown, open-air band concerts every Thursday night June through mid-August, and neat neighborhoods of mostly modest homes. But like the rest of Idaho, Twin Falls is growing, and the city's personality has started to mirror the new diversity with new culinary and cultural options.

Most of Twin Falls' best dining bets are found in and around downtown. **Rock Creek** is a first-class spot for steaks and seafood, though it's easy to miss amid the gas stations and motels along Addison Avenue West. (It's at 200 Addison Avenue West.) Unlikely as it seems, Twin Falls has a sizable population of refugees from Eastern Europe, many of whom regard the **Balkan Cafe** at 900 Main Avenue North a home away from home. In downtown proper, **Dunken's Draught House,** a friendly, well-lit tavern at the intersection of Main Avenue and Shoshone Street, is the local version of Cheers, but with a decidedly Idaho flavor. Dunken's offers an excellent selection of beers and ales from the Northwest and beyond, and the walls—a veritable capsule history of Twin Falls—are a sight to see.

The Uptown Bistro at 117 Main Avenue East has interesting theme dinners and a regular menu specializing in Cajun and Creole specialties, with sidewalk dining in season. **Metropolis Bakery Cafe** at 125 Main Avenue East is a good spot to sip espresso, read a magazine, check your E-mail, or view changing art displays. Weekdays about noon, the Metropolis is a favorite with hungry downtown workers. The menu is small—usually only three or four selections including soup, salad, and pizza—but all are creative, tasty, and reasonably priced.

To the south of downtown Twin Falls, the city's long neglected **Old Towne** district is undergoing a revival. New development is centered at the corner of Second Street South and Sixth Avenue South, where

Muggers Brewpub anchors a block that also includes a steakhouse, nightclub, movie theater, and unusual home furnishings shop. Since its opening in 1996, Muggers has drawn raves as one of inland Northwest's most handsome brewpubs. The building—an abandoned hovel before owner Rick Beus renovated it as the home for his new Twin Falls Brewing Company—includes a fifty-barrel copper brew kettle used in Chicago before Prohibition; an antique spiral staircase from the True Blue Brewing Company in North Hampton, Pennsylvania; and a spit-polished 1890s backbar from New York City.

In addition to handcrafted ales and lagers made on the premises, Muggers' menu includes traditional pub grub daily and finer dining on the weekends. An outdoor patio complete with sand volleyball court, a reading room popular with cigar aficionados, old-time dart games, and an eclectic entertainment calendar all help make Muggers one of the livelier spots in Twin Falls. The brewpub is open daily at 11:00 A.M., closing at 10:00 P.M. Sunday through Wednesday and 1:00 A.M. Thursday through Saturday. Tours of the brewery are available from 11:00 A.M. to 2:00 P.M. Saturday or by appointment. Muggers is located at 516 Second Street South, and the phone number is (208) 733–2322.

Twin Falls has an unusually high number of movie screens for a city of its size—a whopping twenty-six if you include its two drive-ins and four screens in the neighboring town of Jerome. All are owned by one company save for the *Lamphouse Theatre* at 223 Fifth Avenue South in Old Towne. The Lamphouse is run by Dave and Tris Woodhead, a couple who really love movies. Aside from screening the latest independent and foreign films, the Lamphouse rents movies and serves a light menu of soup, wraps, and desserts, plus beer and wine. Call (208) 736–8600 or see www.lamphousetheatre.com to see what's showing.

Twin Falls is the home of the College of Southern Idaho, a rapidly growing junior college known for its fearsome women's volleyball team (seven-time national champs in the 1990s), an outstanding midwinter Blues & Jazz Summit (call 733–9554 ext. 2750 for exact dates), and the *Herrett Center for Arts and Science.* The Herrett has a remarkable collection of pre-Columbian art and tools from Central and South America, but it's now best known as home to the largest planetarium in the Northwest. The Faulkner Planetarium's state-of-the-art Digistar II projection system beams an ever-changing array of astronomy spectacles onto the planetarium's 50-foot dome; show times are generally Tuesday and Friday evenings and Saturday afternoon and evening, with additional shows added during peak periods. The Herrett also has galleries featuring contemporary art and natural history along with a great rain forest exhibit featuring some live critters. The center is open from 9:30 A.M. to 9:00 P.M. Tuesday and Friday, from 9:30 A.M. to 4:30 P.M. Wednesday and Thursday and 1:00 to 9:00 P.M. Saturday. Memorial Day through Labor Day it's open 1:00 to 9:00 P.M. Tuesday through Saturday. Museum admission is free; admission is charged for planetarium shows. Outdoor star-viewing parties are held monthly, usually on the second Saturday. For more information or a planetarium update, call (208) 736–3059.

Few towns can match Twin Falls for an impressive "front door," in this case, the majestic **Snake River Canyon.** The canyon was created by the Bonneville Flood, which came roaring from prehistoric Lake Bonneville through Southeastern Idaho's Red Rock Pass about 15,000 years ago. At its peak the flood spewed 15 million cubic feet of water per second, or three times the flow of the Amazon River, carving the massive canyon that now serves as Twin Falls's welcome mat. The gorge is spanned by the **Perrine Bridge,** a 1,500-foot-long engineering marvel standing 486 feet above the river. When the first Perrine bridge was completed in 1927, it was the highest cantilever bridge for its length in the world. The present span was completed in 1976, and visitors can view the canyon from overlooks on either rim or from a walkway on the bridge itself.

The **Buzz Langdon Visitor Center** on the south rim is staffed by helpful senior citizen volunteers who can guide you to local attrac-

Evel Knievel Jumped Here

*S*eptember 8, 1974, is arguably the most notable date in the history of South Central Idaho. On that day, in an event televised worldwide, motorcycle daredevil Evel Knievel attempted to leap the Snake River Canyon at Twin Falls on his rocket-powered Sky-Cycle X-2. After weeks of hype, the stunt proved a dud: Knievel's parachute malfunctioned and he plunged into the river, everything—even his monumental ego—surviving unscathed.

The Great Snake River Canyon Jump

went awry, but few people have forgotten it. That's why most visitors to Twin Falls are only too happy to gape upriver from the Perrine Bridge at the dirt remains of **Evel Knievel's launch site** on the south rim, and why boaters scan the canyon's north wall for Knievel's supposed "target," still visible just below the rim. Robbie Knievel once sought permission to avenge his father's most spectacular failure, but local officials—memories of 15,000 marauding Knievel fans still fresh in their minds—were reluctant to let Knievel Jr. take a flying leap.

tions. Also visible from the Perrine Bridge are two of America's prettiest golf courses: *Canyon Springs Golf Course* (which is open to the public) and *Blue Lakes Country Club* (which is private). Twin Falls is a great golfing and tennis town, with links and courts accessible nearly year-round.

The *Idaho Farm and Ranch Museum,* along U.S. Highway 93 north of Twin Falls at the I–84 interchange, is a good place to explore the history of high-desert farming. Southern Idaho is one of the most productive agricultural areas in the United States, but it would be little more than a sagebrush flat were it not for the Snake River. Several massive irrigation projects fostered early in the twentieth century turned the desert's dry but fertile soil into rich agricultural land, just like "magic." That's how this part of Idaho, known as the Magic Valley, got its nickname. The Farm and Ranch Museum is still a work in progress, but plans call for the eventual additions of a pioneer town Main Street, a petting zoo for children, and a nature trail. A wide variety of old-time agricultural implements, a 1909 settler's "prove-up" shack, and barracks from the nearby World War II-era Hunt Camp Japanese internment facility are already on display. A Live History Day held the second Saturday each June is the best time to stop by for pioneer skills demonstrations and wagon rides. Set up a tour other times of the year by calling (208) 324–5641.

Before you leave this area, consider a trip a few miles farther up Highway 93 to *Spanbauer Barn,* 2½ miles north of I–84 on the left side of the road. Longtime Idaho ranchers John and Marie Spanbauer are the hosts for old-time Western barn dances held every Saturday night year-round. Dusty Sheets and the Nomads get the music under way at 8:00 P.M., and the 2,000-square-foot dance floor fills up faster than a bronc bucks its rider. The price is right, too: just $7.00 a head, and kids under thirteen get in free. For more information call the Spanbauers at (208) 324–7366.

A few miles east of Twin Falls, *Shoshone Falls* ranks among Idaho's most impressive sights. Sometimes called the Niagara of the West, this cataract is actually 212 feet tall, or nearly 40 feet higher than Niagara Falls. Shoshone Falls' main viewpoint is a fine one, but if you'd like a seldom-seen vista, head up the steep trail on the opposite end of the viewpoint parking lot. Up the hill the trail meets a road (now closed to traffic) that becomes a path to several other viewpoints. These spots are undeveloped and unfenced, so use caution, but they'll give you a chance to enjoy the falls in solitude.

Shoshone Falls is best seen in springtime before much of the Snake

Author's Note

*When most people think about **Snake River floats,** they picture raft trips in the shadows of the Grand Tetons in Wyoming. But the Snake River near Twin Falls is becoming the destination of choice for many serious white-water junkies. In years of heavy snowfall, the resulting spring runoff turns the Snake's 14-mile Murtaugh Section (just downstream from Caldron Linn) into a thrill fest for expert kayakers, and several other nearby stretches are nearly as challenging.*

These advanced-level river runs shouldn't be taken lightly. Inquire locally on conditions and precautions before you set out. Better yet, get on a guided trip. Area chambers of commerce and sporting goods stores can recommend a good outfitter; Olin and Shelley Gardner of Idaho Guide Service at (208) 734–4998 are among the most experienced in these waters, and they also run canoe trips to the base of Shoshone Falls when water levels allow it. The IGS Web site at www.idahoguideservice.com has cool pictures of what you can expect.

River's runoff is diverted for the aforementioned agricultural irrigation. But the falls and adjacent Dierkes Lake Park are well worth visitors' attention any time of year. Swimming, fishing, rock climbing, picnicking, and boating are among the available activities, and an easy hike back to Dierkes's "Hidden Lakes" is pleasant (at least if you overlook the behemoth homes rising above the canyon wall). If you ever happen to be here on New Year's Day, be sure to stop by the impoundment above Shoshone Falls to watch crazy water skiers raise funds for local charities in the "Freeze on Skis" event.

South Central Idaho is Oregon Trail country, and one trading post used by the emigrants—the ***Rock Creek Stage Station***—can still be seen 5 miles south of Hansen. (Follow the signs off of Highway 30 east of Twin Falls.) Built in 1865 by James Bascom, the log store at the site is the oldest building in South Central Idaho. Interpretive signs tell how the site (also called Stricker Ranch, after a later owner) served the pioneers at the intersection of the Oregon Trail, Ben Holladay's Overland Stage route, and the Kelton Road from Utah. The old Stricker House, also on the grounds, is open Sundays April through October. Shaded picnic facilities are available. Poke around on your own, or arrange a tour April through October by calling (208) 423–4000.

The road south from Hansen continues along Rock Creek into the Twin Falls district of the Sawtooth National Forest, known locally as the ***South Hills.*** Long considered a private playground by Twin Falls–area residents, the South Hills offer good trails for hiking, horseback riding, cross-country skiing, mountain biking, all-terrain vehicle sports, and snowmobiling. Facilities include several campgrounds and picnic areas, along with the small, family-run ***Magic Mountain Ski Area.*** The new Pike Mountain overlook makes a fitting turnaround for anyone on a scenic drive. Call the Forest Service office at (208) 737–3200 for more information.

Rock Creek Stage Station

During World War II more than 110,000 American citizens of Japanese descent were rounded up from the West Coast and incarcerated farther inland. Many from the Seattle area were transported to the Minidoka War Relocation Center, or **Hunt Camp,** as it came to be known. At one time nearly 10,000 people lived at Hunt, making it Idaho's eighth-largest city. Conditions in the camp were less than ideal. People lived in cramped tar-paper shacks. Guards were posted and prisoners told they would be shot if they moved too close to the barbed-wire fences. Despite the hardship and indignities, about one in ten camp residents wound up serving in the U.S. Armed Forces during World War II.

Little remains of the camp, but it was recently designated for protection under the National Park Service. Currently, visitors can see the waiting room and guard station, both made of lava. A plaque nearby pays tribute to residents who died in the war, and another shows the layout of the camp. Of particular note are the half-dozen or so ball diamonds—the prisoners found some solace and entertainment in pick-up baseball games—and the fields where evacuees grew various crops for the war effort. The camp site is located a little more than 2 miles north of State Highway 25, seven miles west of Eden. A pair of Idaho highway historical signs—one on Hunt, the other on Prehistoric Man—marks the turn.

The Prehistoric Man sign refers to nearby **Wilson Butte Cave,** an archaeological site of great importance. Artifacts from Wilson Butte Cave near Eden have been carbon dated at 14,500 years old, making them among the oldest findings in the New World. There are no interpretive displays at the cave, but it can be found by driving 2 miles north of the Hunt Camp, then 3⁷/₁₀ miles west. Here the road turns to dirt and, in 2 more miles, crosses a canal. A sign another half-mile or so down the road points the way to the cave, still 2 miles away.

Shoshone Falls gets all the publicity, but **Caldron Linn**—or Star Falls, as it's sometimes called—merits its own mighty place in the Snake River Hall of Fame. It was here the 1811 Wilson Price Hunt fur-trapping expedition gave up the river after losing one of its most valuable members, Canadian boatman Antoine Clappine, in the rapids nearby. A year later, according to Cort Conley's *Idaho for the Curious,* Robert Stuart returned to the scene and made this journal entry: "In one place at the Caldron Linn the whole body of the river is confined between two ledges of rock somewhat less than 40 feet apart and here indeed its terrific appearance beggars all description—Hectate's caldron was never half so agitated when vomiting even the most diabolical spells, as is this Linn in a low stage of water."

Caldron Linn can be reached from I–84 by taking Valley Road south of exit 188. After about 3 miles, the road swings east and hits Murtaugh Road a mile east. Follow Murtaugh Road to the canyon and watch for the signs. If you cross the Murtaugh Bridge over the Snake River, you've gone too far. Also keep an eye on kids and pets near Caldron Linn. It's still a nasty, turbulent piece of river real estate.

Lava is the dominant feature of the landscape north of the Snake River Canyon. North and east of Shoshone, the Lincoln County seat, the roadways are rimmed with rugged lava flows that rolled over the land between 2,000 and 15,000 years ago. Some are lava tubes, created when a shell formed around a still-flowing river of lava. When the lava moved on, the shell remained. Some of these **lava tubes** may be explored; the Shoshone office of the Bureau of Land Management at (208) 886–2206 can provide information on locations and necessary equipment.

For another fascinating look at the area's geology, stop by the **Black Magic Canyon** wayside exhibit just south of the Lincoln-Blaine county line at the junction of Highway 75 and West Magic Road. This small but impressive canyon, full of potholes and weirdly sculpted boulders, was carved when pebbles and cobbles from nearby mountain ranges were swept along by melting glacial waters from the last ice age. The best time to explore the canyon is late fall or winter; stay out if there's water in the channel.

Shoshone has seen a bit of a building boom in recent years as people get priced out of Sun Valley 60 miles to the north and even Twin Falls 25 miles to the south. With light traffic and a good supply of audio books, locals have no problem making these distant commutes over the desert. Visitors also have discovered Shoshone's advantages as a base camp, so there's more lodging now, too. The *Governors Mansion Bed & Breakfast* on Highway 75 has a variety of accommodations ranging from the Pink Room, suitable for a special occasion, to a basement bunkhouse, which is able to sleep six people at $20 per bed. Call (208) 886–2858 for more information or reservations.

Banana splits and bargain movies are the double feature at the *Sundae Matinee Ice Cream and Pizza Parlor* and the *Shoshone Showhouse,* both at 125 South Rail Street West. Second-run films are shown on weekends at just $2.50 a seat (a dollar for senior citizens). Call (208) 886–2332 for movie information. *The Manhattan Cafe* a few doors down at 133 South Rail Street West has a basic but extensive menu and daily specials.

Mini-Cassia Land

Word is getting out about *Lake Walcott State Park,* a high-desert oasis situated along the portion of the Snake River stopped short by Minidoka Dam. The park, one of Idaho's newest, is located within the Minidoka National Wildlife Refuge, where migratory waterfowl including ducks, geese, and tundra swans stop on their fall and spring journeys. Recent improvements at the site have helped Lake Walcott better cater to campers, horseback riders, picnickers, and growing ranks of windsurfers. There's also an 18-hole flying disc golf course, so bring your Frisbees. The park is located 10 miles northeast of Rupert on State Highway 24.

Minidoka Dam itself also is worth a look. Built starting in 1904 the dam became the first federal hydroelectric power project in the Northwest. Along with Milner Dam near Murtaugh, Minidoka Dam made possible the irrigation and settlement of southern Idaho's fertile but dry soil.

Rupert, the Minidoka County seat, has a charming town square that's listed on the National Register of Historic Places. Each year on the day after Thanksgiving, Rupert holds a *Christmas City USA* celebration with Santa's arrival, holiday lighting, fireworks, and a chili feed. The *Minidoka County Historical Society Museum,* 100 East Baseline Road, is open 1:00 to 5:00 P.M. Monday through Saturday year-round, with admission by donation. Call (208) 436–0336 if you need more information.

Burley is best known for the *Idaho Regatta,* a major powerboating event held annually in late June; call (208) 679–4793 for dates and information. Lesser known and a lot more quiet, but just as fascinating, is the *Cassia County Historical Museum* at East Main Street and Highland Avenue, where a large map documents the area's many pioneer trails. Other exhibits tell of Idaho's farming, ranching, mining, and logging history. The museum is open 10:00 A.M. to 5:00 P.M. Tuesday through Saturday, April through October. Call (208) 678–7172 for more information. Burley has a fair variety of dining for a small town. *Price's Cafe* is clear on the opposite end of Burley from the interstate at 2444 Overland, but it's been a favorite among local folks since 1932—except on Sunday, when it's not open.

Overland Avenue turns into State Highway 27, which heads south on a loop drive that takes the traveler back in time to one of the West's best-preserved Victorian towns, mountain scenery, and a world-class rock climbing area. Seventeen miles south of Burley, the community of *Oakley* was settled around 1878 by Mormon pioneers and is famous for its

"Diamondfield" Jack Davis

*O*f all the characters in South Central Idaho lore, "Diamondfield" Jack Davis has had an unusually tenacious hold on the region's imagination for his role in the sheepmen vs. cattle owner wars of the 1890s. Hired by cattle magnate John Sparks to keep the rangeland near Oakley free from sheep, Davis earned a reputation as a scrappy fighter—so he was naturally fingered as the prime suspect when two sheepmen were found dead.

The 1897 Davis trial in Albion, then the Cassia County seat, might have been an ordinary one had it not been for the cast of supporting players. Davis' boss, John Sparks, hired James Hawley—the veteran of more than 300 murder cases and a future Idaho governor—to defend his watchman. The prosecution was mounted by William Borah, a young Boise lawyer who went on to become one of Idaho's most famous U.S. senators. The jury

swiftly found Davis guilty and sentenced him to hang. A year later, area ranchers Jim Bower and Jeff Gray confessed to the killings—yet Davis remained on death row, a requested pardon denied.

Other legal maneuverings ensued, with papers filed all the way up to the U.S. Supreme Court. Bower and Gray, tried for the murders, were acquitted on grounds of self-defense. Hawley sought a new trial for Davis, but his motion was denied—and Davis once again was ordered to the gallows. Many stays of execution later, Davis—by then jailed at the Idaho Penitentiary in Boise—was finally pardoned and set free in 1902. His first act on leaving the pen in Boise was stopping for a drink with the city's new mayor, Jim Hawley. Davis moved to Nevada, where he became a successful miner, only to squander his wealth and die in 1949 after being hit by a Las Vegas taxicab.

impressive collection of fine historic buildings. In fact all of Oakley has been designated a National Historic District, with particularly notable landmarks including the Marcus Funk residence (on Center Avenue between Poplar and Main), the Oakley Co-op (at Main and Center), and Howells Castle (at Blaine and Poplar). Benjamin Howells, an early settler and judge, also built Howells Opera House, where the Oakley Valley Arts Council continues to present musical performances several times each year. (Call 208–677–ARTS for information.) A tour of the Oakley's notable homes is held every year on the third Saturday in June. For more information call (208) 862–3493 or 862–3495.

The peaks rising to Oakley's east are the Albion Mountains, the loftiest in South Central Idaho. Inquire locally or call the Sawtooth National Forest's Burley Ranger District at (208) 678–0430 for directions into the high country. Day hikers and backpackers alike will enjoy a trek to **Independence Lakes,** four tiny blue gems tucked against 10,339-foot Cache Peak. **Lake Cleveland,** another locally popular outdoor playground atop adjacent Mount Harrison, may be accessed by motor vehicle. Camping, picnicking, and fishing are favorite pastimes here. **Pomerelle,** a family-friendly ski area featuring about two dozen runs and the region's only nighttime skiing, also is located on Mount Harrison. Call (208) 673–5555 for recorded information including the ski report.

Southeast of Oakley, Emery Canyon Road provides access to the **City of Rocks National Reserve.** This 14,300-acre area was named by California Trail pioneers passing through in the mid-nineteenth century, some of whom marked their names in axle grease on the ancient granite formations. "During the afternoon, we passed through a stone village composed of huge, isolated rocks of various and singular shapes, some resembling cottages, others steeples and domes," wrote Margaret Frink, who visited in 1850. "It is called City of Rocks, but I think the name Pyramid City more suitable. It is a sublime, strange, and wonderful scene—one of nature's most interesting works." The City of Rocks' hoodoos, arches, caves, and monoliths are the result of erosion, not earthquakes or volcanic activity as some visitors suppose. Most of the rock is part of the Almo Pluton formation, about 25 million years old, while some is part of the 2.5-billion-year-old Green Creek Complex, among the oldest rock in the continental United States. Both kinds can easily be seen at the Twin Sisters formation. The darker "twin" is the older rock, the lighter is from the younger formation.

Today's City of Rocks is in a state of steady development, much of it prompted by the legions of rock climbers who come here to scale the

City's challenging spires, some sixty to seventy stories high. In addition to climbers and history buffs, the City beckons stargazers (who value the pitch-black sky), campers, mountain bikers, cross-country skiers, and sightseers. For more information call (208) 824–5519, visit the reserve's Web site at www.nps.gov/ciro/, or stop by the reserve office in nearby Almo, the City's eastern gateway.

For an extended stay in the area, consider the wagon and horseback trips led by Ken Jafek of **War Eagle Outfitters and Guides** in nearby Malta. Jafek's trips travel from Massacre Rocks to City of Rocks along the Raft River Valley, crossing the California Trail in several locations. He also offers hunting, fishing, and camping trips. For information call (208) 645–2455.

From Almo, the Cassia County loop and State Highway 77 resume at the crossroads town of Connor. Head north 11 miles to Albion, notable as the former home of the **Albion State Normal School,** one of Idaho's leading teacher-training colleges. The school's beautiful campus later housed a Christian college; today, local residents are trying mightily to preserve the grounds.

The **Mountain Manor Bed & Breakfast** at 249 West North Street in Albion has three comfortable guest rooms and a sunny indoor garden room. Room rates at the B&B range from $40 to $50. For reservations or more information, call (208) 673–6642 or (208) 645–2235. From Albion, State Highway 77 leads back to I–84 via either Declo to the north or Malta to the southeast.

**PLACES TO STAY
IN SOUTH CENTRAL IDAHO**

GOODING
Gooding Hotel Bed & Breakfast, 112 Main Street, (208) 934–4374 (see text)

Skyler Inn,
1331 South Main Street,
(208) 934–4055,
fax: (208) 934–0974

WENDELL
Hub City Inn,
115 South Idaho Street,
(208) 536–2326

HAGERMAN
Hagerman Valley Inn,
State and Hagerman
streets, (208) 837–6196

Rock Lodge Resort,
1 mile north on
Highway 30,
(208) 837–4822

BUHL
Oregon Trail Motel,
510 Broadway Avenue
South (U.S. Highway 30),
(208) 534–8814

TWIN FALLS
Ameritel Inn,
1377 Blue Lakes Boulevard
North, (800) 822–TWIN,
fax: (208) 734–7777

Best Western Apollo
Motor Inn, 296 Addison
Avenue West,
(800) 528–1234

Comfort Inn,
1893 Canyon Springs Road,
(800) 228–5150

Monterey Motor Inn,
433 Addison Avenue West,
(208) 733–5151

Shilo Inn,
1586 Blue Lakes Boulevard
North,
(800) 222–2244

Twin Falls Motel,
2152 Kimberly Road,
(208) 733–8620

West Coast Twin Falls
Hotel, 1357 Blue Lakes
Boulevard North,
(800) 325–4000

JEROME
Best Western Sawtooth Inn,
2653 South Lincoln Street,
(800) 528–1234

Sleep Inn,
I–84 exit 173,
(800) 753–3746

SHOSHONE
Governor's Mansion Bed
& Breakfast,
315 South Greenwood,
(208) 886–2858 (see text)

Shoshone Inn,
403 South Rail Street West,
(208) 886–2042

BURLEY
Best Western Burley Inn,
800 North Overland,
(800) 599–1849

Budget Motel,
900 North Overland
Avenue,
(800) 635–4952

Parish Motel,
721 East Main Street,
(208) 678–5505

OAKLEY
Poulton's Bed & Breakfast,
200 East Main Street,
(208) 862–3649

ALBION
Marsh Creek Inn,
on Highway 77,
(208) 673–6259

Mountain Manor Bed &
Breakfast, 249 West North
Street, (208) 673–6642
(see text)

Helpful Web sites

Hagerman Fossil Beds National Monument—
www.nps.gov/hafo

South Central Idaho Tourism Information—
www.rideidaho.com

Twin Falls Area Chamber of Commerce—
www.twinfallschamber.com

Destination Northwest travel site—
www.destinationnw.com/idaho/twinfalls.htm

The Times-News (Twin Falls newspaper)—
www.magicvalley.com

City of Rocks National Reserve—
www.nps.gov/ciro

Mini-Cassia Chamber of Commerce—
www.minicassiachamber.com

Worth Seeing

Twin Falls County Historical Museum—
west of Twin Falls

Magic Valley Speedway—*south of Twin Falls*

Nat–Soo–Pah Hot Springs—*Hollister*

Idaho's Mammoth Cave—*north of Shoshone*

Shoshone Ice Caves—*north of Shoshone*

**PLACES TO EAT
IN SOUTH CENTRAL IDAHO**

BLISS
Oxbow Cafe (American),
199 East U.S. Highway 30,
(208) 352–4250

GOODING
Main Street Pub & Grill
(American),
227 Main Street,
(208) 934–8003

Wyant's Family Cookhouse
(American),
222 Fourth Avenue East,
(208) 934–9903

WENDELL
Cavazos Mexican Food
(Mexican),
287 West Avenue H,
(208) 536–9921

Farmhouse Restaurant
(American), I–84 exit 157,
(208) 536–6688 (see text)

HAGERMAN
Larry & Mary's Cafe
(American),
141 North State Street,
(208) 837–6475

Snake River Grill
(eclectic), State and
Hagerman Streets,
(208) 837–6227 (see text)

Sportsman River Resort
(American),
18678 Highway 30,
(208) 837–6364

BUHL
Arctic Circle (fast food),
606 Broadway Avenue
South, (208) 543–5321

Linda's Family Dining
(American), 631 Broadway
Avenue South,
(208) 543–2060

TWIN FALLS
Balkan Cafe (European),
600 Main Avenue North,
(208) 737–0632 (see text)

Creekside (steak/seafood),
233 Fifth Avenue South,
(208) 733–1511

La Casita (Mexican),
111 South Park Avenue
West, (208) 734–7974

Peking Restaurant
(Chinese), 824 Blue Lakes
Boulevard North,
(208) 733–4813

Rock Creek (steak/seafood;
dinner only), 200 Addison
Avenue West,
(208) 734–4154 (see text)

Uptown Bistro (eclectic),
117 Main Avenue East,
(208) 733–0900

Most major fast-food chain
restaurants, located mainly
along Blue Lakes Boulevard.

JEROME
El Sombrero (Mexican),
143 West Main Street,
(208) 324–7238

Jerome Cafe (American),
628 South Lincoln Street,
(208) 324–5861

McDonald's (fast food),
2661 South Lincoln Street,
(208) 324–5505

Pizza Hut (fast food),
1210 South Lincoln Street,
(208) 324–3932

SHOSHONE
Manhattan Cafe
(American),
133 South Rail Street West,
(208) 886–2142 (see text)

Sage Berry House
Restaurant (American),
103 East B Street,
(208) 886–2892

Shoshone Snack Bar
(fast food), Highway 75,
(208) 886–2294

EDEN
Traveler's Oasis Restaurant
(American), I–84 exit 182,
(208) 825–4147

RUPERT
Connor's Cafe (American),
I–84 exit 208,
(208) 678–9367

The Pancake House
(American),
Fifth Street and Scott
Avenue, (208) 436–3660

HEYBURN
Stevo's (American),
290 South 600 West,
(208) 679–3887

BURLEY
Cancun Mexican Restau-
rant (Mexican),
262 Overland Avenue,
(208) 678–8695

Price's Cafe (American),
2444 Overland Avenue,
(208) 878–5149 (see text)

Shon Hing (Chinese),
109 East Main Street,
(208) 678–4950

Many major fast-food
chain restaurants, located
mainly along Overland
Avenue.

Southeastern Idaho

Southeastern Idaho serves as a microcosm of the history of American westward expansion. It was here that pioneers had to decide whether to jump off onto the California Trail for the gold country. It was here many others came north from Utah, following their Mormon leaders' orders to farm the land and settle new towns. And it was here many pressed on toward Oregon, pausing briefly for supplies and rest before crossing the rugged Snake River Plain.

I–86 enters Southeastern Idaho from the west, making a lonely crossing of Power County and part of the Fort Hall Indian Reservation before reaching Pocatello, the region's major city. At Pocatello, I–15 heads north and south; 25 miles south of town, travelers can hop off on U.S. Highway 30 to make a loop around the region via U.S. Highway 89, State Highway 34 or 36, and U.S. Highway 91. Drivers may want to extend their explorations of Southeastern Idaho into Utah, since the border between these two states is blurrier than most, as we shall see.

For Southeastern Idaho travel information, call (888) 201–1063, see www.seidaho.org, or write the Pioneer Country Travel Council, P.O. Box 669, Lava Hot Springs 83246.

Trails and Rails

Crossing Power County it's easy to get the feeling you're alone. Most travelers veer off the interstate either east of Burley, where I–84 runs southeast to Utah, or at I–15 at Pocatello. It's not hard to imagine what it might have been like for the pioneer wagon trains crossing the same stretch 150 years ago.

Most of those emigrants traversed southern Idaho without trouble from the Indians. But as traffic along the trail increased, the native peoples grew ever more resentful of the whites invading their land. This may have been the impetus for an August 1862 incident that led to the deaths of ten westward-bound emigrants and an unknown number of Shoshones in two days of fighting amid the lava outcroppings along the

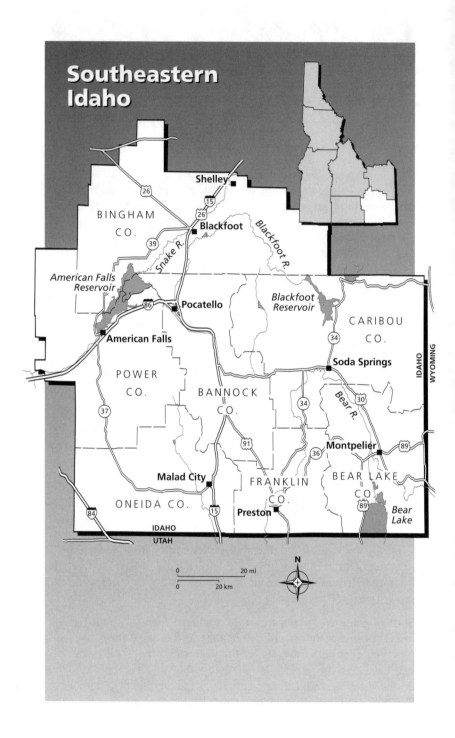

Southeastern Idaho

Shelley

BINGHAM CO.

Blackfoot

Snake R.

Blackfoot R.

American Falls
Reservoir

Blackfoot
Reservoir

Pocatello

American Falls

CARIBOU CO.

Soda Springs

POWER CO.

BANNOCK CO.

Bear R.

IDAHO

WYOMING

Malad City

Montpelier

FRANKLIN CO.

BEAR LAKE CO.

ONEIDA CO.

Preston

Bear
Lake

IDAHO

UTAH

0   20 mi

0   20 km

N

SOUTHEASTERN IDAHO

JULIE'S FAVORITES

Idaho's World Potato Exposition—*Blackfoot*

Lava Hot Pools— *Lava Hot Springs*

Bear Lake—*on the Idaho/Utah border*

National Oregon/ California Trail Center— *Montpelier*

Deer Cliff Inn/Cub River Canyon—*near Preston*

Snake River. During the emigrant era, the area became known as the Gate of Death or Devil's Gate because of a narrow, rocky passage through which the wagons rolled (now gone as a result of blasting for the construction of I–86). But stories of the 1862 battles eventually led the locals to dub the area Massacre Rocks.

Massacre Rocks State Park, situated on a narrow strip of land between I–86 and the Snake River, has made the most of its location. Hikers can trace history or see more than 200 species of birds and 300 varieties of desert plants along nearly 7 miles of trails. The park also has notable geologic features, many the result of extensive volcanic activity, others created by the massive Bonneville Flood, the second-largest flood in world geologic history. But things are quieter today. In addition to hiking, fishing, boating, and searching out the local flora and fauna, visitors can spend a peaceful respite in the park's campground, where nightly campfire programs are held each summer. Those making a brief stop in the area can combine a hike with a stop in the visitor center. Exhibits include the diary of Jane A. Gould, who traveled from Iowa to California in 1862 along the Oregon Trail and was in the area at the time of the skirmish with the Shoshones. For more information on Massacre Rocks, call (208) 548–2672 or see the Web site at www.idahoparks.org/parks/massacre.html.

Register Rock, located a few miles west of Massacre Rocks, was a favorite campground along the Oregon Trail, and many visiting emigrants signed their names on a large basalt boulder that is now the centerpiece of a small park. Some signatures date from as early as 1849, and many are still legible. On a smaller rock nearby, J. J. Hansen, a seven-year-old emigrant boy, carved an Indian's head in 1866. Nearly five decades later, after he had become a professional sculptor, Hansen returned and dated the rock again. Register Rock's shady picnic area offers welcome relief from the searing Idaho summer.

For an interesting detour off the interstate between American Falls and Blackfoot, consider taking State Highway 39. This 55-mile route (as opposed to 47 miles via the interstate) offers a pleasant two-lane alternative through several small towns and a lot of pretty potato country on the north side of ***American Falls Reservoir.*** Watch for the signs showing access to fishing on the man-made lake.

South and east of the reservoir, many Native Americans from the Shoshone and Bannock Tribes live on the 544,000-acre ***Fort Hall***

Indian Reservation, which stretches across much of Power, Bannock, and Bingham Counties. Fort Hall is the most populous of Idaho's four reservations, with about 3,200 people living within its boundaries.

The *Shoshone-Bannock Indian Festival* and *All-Indian Rodeos* are held the second week of each August, and the tribes also operate a number of small businesses, including a truck stop and trading post complex at exit 80 off of I–15. Browse at the *Clothes Horse Trading Post,* which features a good selection of Indian beadwork, craft items, and cassette tapes by Native American musicians. Visit the tribal museum, which showcases exhibits on the Shoshone and Bannock people's past. Play a little bingo at the tribe's gaming hall. Or eat at *Melina's,* where the specialties include buffalo burgers, buffalo steaks, eggs and buffalo sausage, buffalo stew, and fry bread. The restaurant is open daily from 6:00 A.M. to 10:00 P.M. Its phone number is (208) 237–0472.

The Oregon Trail really did pass through what is now the Fort Hall Reservation—and there truly was a Fort Hall on what is now reservation land, too. Nathaniel Wyeth established the outpost near the banks of the Snake River in 1834, selling it to the British Hudson's Bay Company three years later. It was a busy place, teeming first with fur trappers and traders and later with emigrants through the mid-1850s. There is nothing left of the original Fort Hall, but there are wagon ruts, emigrant grave sites, and other traces of the fort's history scattered across what is now known as the *Fort Hall Bottoms.* Because the sites are on tribal land, they are not generally open to the public. But if you'd like to have a look, contact Shoshone-Bannock tribal member Red Perry Sr., who leads personal tours through the bottomlands. Perry often can be found at the Fort Hall Museum. If not, call (208) 238–0097 or write Oregon Trail Tours, Route 6 Box 666, Pocatello 83202.

Shelley, up Highway 91 from Blackfoot, is best known for its annual *Idaho Spud Day* celebration and as the headquarters of *Cox Honey Farms.* The Coxes have been in business since the 1930s, keeping bees all over Southeastern Idaho and even into Wyoming. No tours are available, but you can stop by their little storefront at 456 South State in Shelley anytime between 7:00 A.M. and 4:00 P.M. weekdays to pick up gift boxes and a handy brochure listing honey recipes and uses for beeswax (fish bait, mosquito repellent, and lip balm among them). The Coxes also ship gifts throughout the United States. Call (208) 357–3226 for more information.

North of Blackfoot on I–15, meanwhile, travelers will notice the vast lava beds to the west. *Hell's Half Acre Lava Field,* located midway between Blackfoot and Idaho Falls, is a 180-square-mile flow that has been desig-

TOP ANNUAL EVENTS

Dodge National Circuit Finals Rodeo, Pocatello (*mid-March*)

Massacre Rock Rendezvous, Massacre Rocks State Park (*early June*)

Shoshone-Bannock Festival, Fort Hall (*early August*)

Eastern Idaho State Fair, Blackfoot (*late August/early September*)

Idaho Spud Day, Shelley (*mid-September*)

Festival of Lights, Preston (*Thanksgiving through Christmas*)

nated a National Natural Landmark. This is a relatively young lava field, with the last eruptions probably taking place about 2,000 years ago (although the flows near the interstate are probably twice that old). Hikers have two options here: a short educational loop trail (marked by blue-topped poles) that takes about a half-hour to traverse, or a 4½-mile route that leads to the vent, or source, of the lava flow. The way to the vent is marked by red-topped poles, and the hike takes a full day. Be sure to wear boots with sturdy soles and carry plenty of water.

Pocatello, Idaho's second-largest city, apparently took its name from that of Pocataro, a Shoshone chief, but it owes its prominence—and a lot of its character—to railroading. The Utah and Northern narrow-gauge and Oregon Short Line railways, both part of the Union Pacific system, intersected at Pocatello, and railroad activity spurred settlement and construction. By World War II, more than 4,500 railroad cars passed through Pocatello each day. Rail fans may want to pay a visit to the old *Oregon Short Line Depot* on West Bonneville Street. President William Taft attended the dedication of this building, erected in 1915. The *Yellowstone Hotel,* frequently used by rail passengers, is just across the street from the old depot. Also downtown, the *Pocatello Model Railroad and Historical Society* operates out of Union Pacific Building B-59 southwest of the Union Pacific depot. The public can come see the trains run during open houses that take place from 10:00 A.M. to 2:00 P.M. the third Saturday of each month. The club is especially well known for its holiday train displays, which are open every Saturday late November through the last Saturday before Christmas. It's always seeking donations of old railroad items, too. For more information, write the Pocatello Model Railroad and Historical Society, P.O. Box 2902, Pocatello 83201.

Perhaps because of its railroad links, perhaps because it is home to a university, Pocatello has a different feel than Idaho's other large towns: more transient, a bit scruffy, but not without a charm of its own. Like all good-sized American towns, Pocatello has its "on-the-beaten-path" commercial strips and its soul—its downtown. *Simplot Square* is the heart of what's called Old Town Pocatello, and despite its corporate name (the J. R. Simplot Company is a huge force in Idaho agribusiness), the plaza is a calm and thought-provoking place. A striking fountain flows into a long pool, symbolic of both the area's river heritage and the way individuals from many cultures have congregated in Pocatello's melting pot. Benches and grassy knolls surround the water, and live music happens on the third Thursday evening of each summer month. The square is bordered by West Center Street and Arthur Avenue, 1 block west of Main Street.

The Continental Bistro at 140 South Main Street is widely considered the best restaurant in town, and it's unbeatable in the warmer months. On a fine summer day, it's possible to peer through the bistro's windows and see the place look abandoned. That's because most patrons favor the restaurant's spacious rear patio, which recalls an Italian formal garden. At lunchtime the bistro offers a good variety of salads, sandwiches, and pasta dishes, most in the $5.95 to $6.95 price range. Try the Cobb Sandwich: honey-cured turkey, bacon, lettuce, tomato, avocado, and shaved bleu cheese on foccacia bread.

At dinner, the Bistro serves up a varied menu, featuring such dishes as garlic-rubbed veal chops ($18.95 for a half rack), grilled sirloin mari-

Spuds Aplenty

*B*lackfoot, located just north of the reservation, narrowly lost an 1880 bid to replace Boise as capital of the Idaho Territory. Instead Blackfoot has become the Potato Capital of Idaho and probably the world. Potatoes have long been synonymous with Idaho, and Blackfoot is the seat and largest town in Bingham County, the state's top spud-producing region. Small wonder, then, that Blackfoot's top attraction is **Idaho's World Potato Exposition,** dedicated to "fun and educational exhibits about the world's most popular vegetable." The world's largest potato chip—of the Pringles variety, 25 inches by 14 inches, the equivalent of eighty regular chips—is on display, as is a photo of Marilyn Monroe modeling an Idaho potato sack. The center also offers "Free

Taters for Out-of-Staters," one free baked Idaho potato to eat after touring the exhibits. A snack bar offers such treats as potato cookies and potato fudge. Picnic grounds are available.

The Potato Expo is located in downtown Blackfoot at 130 Northwest Main Street in the old train depot. (Watch for the Burma Shave–style roadside signs extolling the Expo and the potato's many virtues as you approach the Blackfoot exits on I–15!) The Expo is open daily Memorial Day through Labor Day and by appointment the rest of the year. Admission is $3.00 for adults, $2.50 for seniors over age fifty-five, and $1.00 for children ages six through twelve. For more information call (208) 785–2517.

nated in ginger, lime, and honey ($12.50), and roast vegetable lasagna ($9.95). The restaurant has won a *Wine Spectator* magazine award two years running and has a list of about 200 selections. The Continental Bistro also has a lounge featuring sixteen microbrews on tap and live jazz each Wednesday night in the summer. (Wednesday evening is also "inexpensive beer night," with all micros priced at $1.50 apiece starting at 4:00 P.M.) The Continental Bistro is open for dining from 11:00 A.M. to 10:00 P.M. Monday through Saturday, with the patio generally open May through October. The lounge is open until 1:00 A.M. nightly except Sunday. For more information or reservations call (208) 233–4433.

Pocatello has some beautiful architecture in its central core. Stroll along *Garfield Avenue* 2 blocks west of Main Street to see some fine examples. The church at 309 North Garfield, shared by the local Congregationalists and Unitarian Universalists, dates back to 1904. The *Standrod House* at 648 North Garfield was built in 1901, its light gray and red sandstone quarried in nearby McCammon and hauled to the site by horse-drawn wagons. The city of Pocatello acquired and renovated the Standrod House in the 1970s and for a time it regained its status as community center. Now, however, it houses an upscale furniture store.

For a look around the rest of the city, try the *Pocatello Centennial Street Car,* which runs weather permitting and boards at the city transit center, 215 West Bonneville (at Main). The trolleys keep somewhat irregular schedules, though one usually leaves the downtown center at about seven minutes after the hour in the afternoon. Call (208) 234–2287 for updated schedule information. Fare is 60 cents for adults and 30 cents for students. Stops on the route include such high spots as the Idaho State University campus (with its Idaho Museum of Natural History), the Pine Ridge Mall, and Ross Park (summers only). The latter is the site of our next destination.

Even if you've taken the Sho-Ban tour of the original Fort Hall site (see page 115), the *Fort Hall Replica* in Pocatello's Ross Park is worth a visit. Exhibits at the replica include a blacksmith's shop and extensive displays on Indian lifestyles. A videotape on Fort Hall's history may be viewed on request. The Fort Hall replica is open daily from 10:00 A.M. to 6:00 P.M. from Memorial Day through Labor Day; from 10:00 A.M. to 2:00 P.M. from after Labor Day through the end of September; and from 10:00 A.M. to 2:00 P.M. Tuesday through Saturday during April and May. Admission is $2.50 for adults, $1.75 for seniors and youth ages twelve to eighteen, and $1.00 for children ages six through eleven. Ross Park also

Fort Hall Replica

includes a pool, rose garden, picnic areas, a playground, and a fenced field in which deer and antelope play and elk and bison roam. For more information call (208) 234–1795.

Fort Hall admission includes entrance to the ***Bannock County Historical Museum,*** also located in Ross Park. This is a good place to learn more about Pocatello's railroading past; other exhibits include war memorabilia, Indian artifacts, a restored stagecoach, and rooms that offer glimpses into how early Pocatello lived and worked. The museum is open from 10:00 A.M. to 6:00 P.M. daily Memorial Day weekend through Labor Day and 10:00 A.M. to 2:00 P.M. Tuesday through Saturday the rest of the year. The phone number is (208) 233–0434.

Hot Baths and Pioneer Paths

The entire state of Idaho is justly famous for its hot springs. But perhaps no other town has been so blessed with wondrous thermal activity as ***Lava Hot Springs,*** situated along Highway 30 and the Portneuf River 35 miles southeast of Pocatello.

Tucked in a mile-high mountain valley near the north edge of the Wasatch Range, Lava Hot Springs once served as a winter campground for the Bannock and Shoshone Indian tribes, who thought the local springs held healing powers. Geologists believe the springs have been a consistent 110 degrees for at least fifty million years. The springs are rich with minerals—calcium carbonate, sodium chloride, and magnesium carbonate being most prevalent—but have no sulfur and, therefore, none of the nose-wrinkling odor typical of many hot springs.

The town has two main attractions, both operated by a state-run foundation: an **Olympic Swimming Complex** on the west side and the **Lava Hot Pools** on the east end. The huge free-form Olympic pool has one-third of an acre of water surface, 50-meter racing lanes, a 10-meter diving tower, and a surrounding carpet of green grass for sunbathing; another 25-meter pool nearby meets Amateur Athletic Union standards. Both are open Memorial Day through Labor Day from 11:00 A.M. to 9:00 P.M. weekdays and from 10:00 A.M. to 9:00 P.M. Saturday, Sunday, and holidays. The four hot pools—open every day of the year except Thanksgiving and Christmas—are set amid the sunken gardens of an extinct volcano and range in temperature from 102° to 110° F. A private indoor tub also is available for an extra charge. Hours at the hot pools are 8:00 A.M. to 11:00 P.M. April through September and 9:00 A.M. to 10:00 P.M. October through March, except on Friday and Saturday evenings, when they remain open until 11:00 P.M. An $8.00 fee buys all-day admission to both the pools and the hot baths; single admission to either runs $4.50 for adults and youth ages twelve and up and $4.00 for seniors and children ages four through eleven. An $11 family pass, available Monday through Thursday except holidays, admits everyone in an immediate family to all the pools. Suits, towels, and lockers may be rented, and group rates are available. Call (800) 423–8597 for more information.

The pools, hot baths, and Portneuf River tubing have made Lava Hot Springs justly popular, so quite a few other tourist-oriented businesses have sprung up to serve visitors. Motel rates are very reasonable for a resort area; many rooms (some including private hot mineral baths) go for less than $50 a night. The most expensive places in town top out at about $100, the going rate for the Jacuzzi rooms at the **Lava Hot Springs Inn,** a European-style bed-and-breakfast supposedly complete with its own ghost. Lava Hot Springs Inn has accommodations priced from $65 to $185 (for a family suite that can sleep eight), including a full breakfast. There's also a massage therapist on-site and an 80-foot-long year-round therapy pool. For more information call (208) 776–5830 or write Lava Hot Springs Inn, 95 East Portneuf Avenue, Lava Hot Springs 83246.

Lava Hot Springs has a full calendar of summer special events, including a big **Classic Car and Truck Show** the last weekend in June and a mountain man rendezvous and **Pioneer Days** celebration in mid-July. But autumn may be the best time of all to visit; room rates dip even lower at some establishments, and the surrounding hills are ablaze with some of

Idaho's most colorful fall foliage. If you're a fan of Thai food, be sure to have a meal at the **Riverwalk Cafe,** 79 West Portneuf. This small, family-run restaurant serves authentic, inexpensive fare in a slightly ramshackle building every day but Monday. Call (208) 776–5872. For more information on Lava Hot Springs, call (800) 548–5282.

Back on Highway 30 heading east from Lava Hot Springs, consider one of two short side trips to Black Canyon or the ghost town of Chesterfield. **Black Canyon** is one of Idaho's hidden geological gems. The gorge gets its start just downstream of the town of Grace, which is located about 5 miles south of Highway 30 via State Highway 34. Turn west on Center Street in town (Turner Road) and pause at the bridge to see the chasm opening up. As the Bear River rolls across the farmland surrounding Grace, it quickly widens and deepens into a canyon rivaling those on the Snake River. Sadly, however, there's no public access to the rim along the deepest parts, and a modest fishing access spot near the Utah Power plant southwest of Grace just doesn't do the canyon justice. But take a peek where you can—some farmers along the Black Canyon Lane southwest of Grace via Turner and Hegstrom Roads might let you look if you ask permission. East of Grace there are interesting interpretive signs detailing how the Last Chance Canal Company struggled to provide irrigation to this region.

Most extinct Western towns owed their existence to mining, but **Chesterfield** had its roots in agriculture. Mormon pioneers settled the town in 1880 along the old Oregon Trail. The town reached its peak in the 1920s with a population of about 500 people. After that, however, Chesterfield slowly shrunk. After World War II few local boys came home, and the town lost its post office a few years later.

No one lives year-round in Chesterfield today, but the town's memory remains remarkably well preserved. About two dozen buildings still stand, with plans to rebuild a few others. The most notable remaining structure is the old Chesterfield LDS Ward meetinghouse, which the Daughters of Utah Pioneers have preserved as a museum. Daffodils and a manicured lawn greet visitors, while exhibits inside the handsome brick building include photos of many early settlers, an old pump organ, and a tribute to the prolific Western novelist Frank Robertson, a local boy who grew up to write 128 books (including eight each in 1935 and 1936).

The museum may be toured May through October by checking with the caretaker couple who live nearby at 3111 Moses Lane. (Look for signs giving directions.) Many descendants of early Chesterfield residents come back each Memorial Day for a luncheon and reunion. Nearby Chesterfield

Reservoir is a good fishing spot, too. Chesterfield is located 10 miles north of the town of Bancroft and 15 miles north of U.S. Route 30.

Continuing east on Highway 30, the traveler reaches Soda Springs, Caribou County's seat and largest town. The area was another major point along the Oregon Trail, with many emigrants stopping to camp and sample the water from the area's abundant natural springs. Most are gone now, but evidence remains of two of the most famous. One pioneer spring is preserved under a small pavilion in **Hooper Springs Park,** located 2 miles north of the center of town. DRINK DEEPLY OF NATURE'S BEST BEVERAGE, a plaque advises. Hooper Springs is named for W. H. Hooper, who was a leading Salt Lake City banker, Utah congressman, and president of the Zion's Cooperative Mercantile Institution (still going strong as ZCMI, the Intermountain region's major home-grown department store chain). He had a summer home in Soda Springs and helped the town's soda water reach international markets.

Another spring regularly gave off a sound like that of a steamboat. It's now drowned beneath Alexander Reservoir, but **Steamboat Spring** has not disappeared altogether; on a clear day it can still be viewed puffing and percolating beneath the water's surface. The best way to see evidence of the spring is to play a round on the **Oregon Trail Golf Course.** Look south to the reservoir from either the No. 1 green or the No. 8 tee. From those vantage points you also can see what are probably the only Oregon Trail wagon ruts on a golf course, a phenomenon that was once featured in *National Geographic*. Traces of the wagons' wheels cut across the No. 9 fairway and skirt the No. 1 green before traveling across the No. 8 fairway. Still another famous local spring tasted almost exactly like beer—and produced similar effects once drunk—but it, unfortunately, has vanished completely.

Author's Note

Two miles west of Lava Hot Springs on Highway 30, would-be Robin Hoods and Maid Marians can't help but be intrigued by the small sign for SOMERVILLE MANOR—MEDIEVAL LIVING HISTORY. Here at the start of the twenty-first century, husband and wife Steve and Linda Simmons have created a living history farm that offers visitors a chance to experience sword fighting, Shakespeare, and other ways of life from the Middle Ages.

Steve Simmons was a teacher for many years before he and Linda, both longtime medieval enthusiasts, moved to rural Idaho to open Somerville Manor. The manor presents a variety of events including a Medieval Faire, Christmas feasts, and a Midsummer's Eve celebration. In addition to the special dates, visitors are welcome to stop by anytime between 10:00 A.M. and 10:00 P.M. Tuesday through Saturday Memorial Day through Labor Day or by appointment during the rest of the year. For a brochure detailing activities and events, call (208) 776-5429; write Somerville Manor, 8890 Maughan Road, Lava Hot Springs 83246; or see www.somervillemanor.org.

Several other Soda Springs attractions are of particular note. The town has the world's only captive geyser, the centerpiece of the aptly named *Geyser Park.* The gusher was discovered in 1937 as the town attempted to find a hot-water source for its swimming pool. The drill hit the geyser, which was later capped and controlled by a timer. These days it erupts every half-hour in the summer and every hour on the hour in the winter (unless strong west winds are blowing, which would send the 150-foot-high spray cascading over nearby businesses). The surrounding park offers a pleasant place to rest while waiting for the next "show."

North of town, The Nature Conservancy has established a preserve at *Formation Springs.* Here visitors see crystal-clear pools amid a wetlands area at the base of the Aspen Mountains. The springs that feed the pools and nearby creek system deposit high concentrations of calcium carbonate, giving the site its unusual geology. Formation Cave, about 20 feet tall and 1,000 feet long, is among the impressive features, and abundant wildlife may be seen.

Bear Lake Country

Two designated scenic routes traverse the state's extreme southeastern corner, intersecting in Soda Springs. The *Pioneer Historic Byway* follows State Highway 34 northeast to Wyoming, skirting the shores of Blackfoot Reservoir and Grays Lake, and the south to Preston and Franklin, two of Idaho's oldest towns. The *Bear Lake–Caribou Scenic Byway* follows U.S. Highways 30 and 89 through Montpelier and south to Bear Lake, a 20-mile-long recreational paradise straddling the Idaho-Utah border. We'll look at the region following a clockwise direction southeast from Soda Springs and back north toward Pocatello.

Settled in 1864 by Mormon families, Montpelier was named for the capital of Brigham Young's home state, Vermont. Outlaw Butch Cassidy visited here in 1896, joining with two other men in robbing the local bank of $7,165. The bank they supposedly robbed is gone now, but the building in which it stood remains on Washington Street downtown.

Montpelier also is home to the *National Oregon/California Trail Center,* built at the junction of Highways 30 and 89 at the site known in the 1850s as Clover Creek, a popular emigrant rest stop. Through living history, artwork, and exhibits, the center explains how early travelers made it over the "Big Hill," a nearby ridge that many pioneers considered among the roughest obstacles on the way west; how they lived in the wagon trains; and how they encountered such characters as Thomas "Peg Leg" Smith, a

Geyser Park

nineteenth-century mountain man who had to amputate his own leg. Smith opened a trading post at what is now Dingle, Idaho, and reportedly made $100 a day catering to the emigrants' needs. The center is open daily in the summer from 10:00 A.M. to 5:00 P.M. and by reservation the rest of the year. Admission is $6.00 for ages thirteen and up and $4.00 for youngsters ages six through twelve. (Children five and under get in free.) For more information call (208) 847–3800 or see www.oregontrailcenter.org.

Although southeast Idaho is geographically and politically part of the Gem State, spiritually the region is closely aligned with Utah and Mormonism. Nowhere is this more true than in the towns and counties bordering the Beehive State. In fact the 1863 settlers who arrived in what was to become Paris, Idaho, thought they were in Utah until an 1872 boundary survey set the record straight.

The imposing and beautiful ***Paris Stake Tabernacle*** was a labor of love for the local Mormon settlers, who spent half a decade building the Romanesque-style church, completed in 1889. A "stake" is the term used by the Church of Jesus Christ of Latter-day Saints to describe a geographical area; the Paris, Idaho, stake was the first organized outside the Utah territory, and the tabernacle was built to serve the Mormon communities and congregations that sprung up within a 50-mile radius of the town.

Author's Note

*With all the lava in Idaho, you wouldn't think people would pay much heed to another pile of the stuff. Ah, but when it's a **man-made lava flow** bubbling over the landscape before your eyes—well, that's enough to generate interest. And that's just what happens north of Soda Springs at the Monsanto Chemical Company.*

Monsanto, which produces elemental phosphorous—a substance used in laundry detergents, soft drinks, toothpaste, and other products—dumps the resulting slag from its electric furnaces. The slag, 1,400° F. hot, fills trucks bearing special cast-steel pots. The trucks then pour the molten rock onto the slag pile five times each hour, twenty-four hours a day. You can almost imagine the local kids asking each other, "Whaddya wanna do tonight, watch MTV, cruise Highway 30, or go to the slag heap?"

The tabernacle—designed by Joseph Young, a son of Brigham—was built from red sandstone hauled by horse- and ox-drawn wagons from a canyon 18 miles away. In the winter the rock was pulled by sled over frozen Bear Lake. A former shipbuilder crafted the ceiling, using pine harvested in nearby forests. Tours are offered daily through the summer; arrive mid-day and you may be treated to music from the tabernacle's Austin pipe organ.

A monument on the tabernacle grounds honors Charles Coulson Rich, the man sent by Brigham Young to settle the Bear Lake Valley. It was Rich who, on one of his many missions for the church, went to Europe to find the skilled craftsmen recruited by the Mormons to help build their new churches and towns in the American West. Rich had six wives and fifty children and ultimately became an apostle in his church. Despite his contributions, Paris was named not for Rich but for Frederick Perris, who platted the town site. One of the first settler cabins, built in 1863 by Thomas Sleight and Charles Atkins, is still standing and may be seen in a park near the tabernacle.

Several intriguing side canyons south of Paris beckon independent-minded motorists from well-traveled Highway 89. *Bloomington Canyon,* west of the tiny town of the same name, leads to a pristine little lake and meadows filled with wildflowers. *Minnetonka Cave,* located west of St. Charles, is the largest developed limestone cave in Idaho and among the state's more spectacular underground wonderlands. Ninety-minute tours weave through a half-mile of fantastic formations and fossils of preserved tropical plant and marine life in nine separate chambers, the largest of which is about 300 feet around and 90 feet high.

In the late 1930s the federal government began development of Minnetonka Cave via the Works Progress Administration, constructing a trail from St. Charles Canyon and installing interior paths, steps, and railings. But the cave was open only for a couple of years before World War II began, halting efforts at improvement. After the war the Paris Lions Club operated the cave for a time. It is now managed by the U.S. Forest Service as part of the Cache National Forest. Tours of Minnetonka Cave are given every half-hour from 10:30 A.M. to 5:00 P.M. each day from Memorial Day through Labor Day. The cost is $4.00 for adults, $3.00 for children ages six through fifteen, or $18.00 for a family pass. Children ages five and under get in free. Visitors should be prepared for lots of steps and cool temperatures; good walking shoes and a jacket are recommended. Several campgrounds are available up St. Charles Canyon. For more information on the cave or surrounding forest, call (208) 847–0375.

St. Charles serves as gateway to *Bear Lake,* one of the bluest bodies of water in North America. Explanations for its turquoise tint vary, but it's usually credited to a high concentration of soluble carbonates.

Bear Lake also is unique because it boasts several species of fish found nowhere else. In addition to the rainbow and cutthroat trout so plentiful throughout the Rockies, Bear Lake is home to the Bonneville cisco, a sardinelike whitefish that spawns each January and is popular year-round for bait. Check with the Idaho Department of Fish and Game at (800) 635–7820 for regulations on angling for cisco or other fish; information and licenses also are available at sporting goods dealers throughout the state. Bear Lake State Park is on the Internet at www.idahoparks.org/parks/bear.html.

In addition to fish, Bear Lake Country is thick with animals and birds. The Bear Lake National Wildlife Refuge at the lake's north end draws Canada geese; sandhill and whooping cranes; redhead, canvasback, and mallard ducks; and the nation's largest nesting population of white-face ibis. Deer, moose, and smaller mammals are also known to wander through the refuge's nearly 18,000 acres. Check with the refuge office in Montpelier or call (208) 847–1757 for information on waterfowl hunting, boating, and hiking opportunities.

The Utah end of Bear Lake is far more commercially developed than Idaho's shores. Bear Lake Boulevard in and near Garden City, Utah, is lined with resorts and restaurants, but there are very few visitor services north of the border. That's one reason Esther Harrison's *Bear Lake Bed & Breakfast* stands out—that and the fact the inn sits high on a hill overlooking the lake. The "Carriage House," as it's also known, is a good base for summer lake activities, but it's also popular with winter sports enthusiasts, with a 380-mile network of snowmobile trails starting just outside the door. Six guest rooms (two with private baths, one with a fireplace) rent for $80 to $90, with winter discounts available if visitors rent the whole house. For more information call (208) 945–2688 or write Bear Lake Bed & Breakfast, 500 Loveland Lane, Fish Haven 83287.

Southwest of Bear Lake, U.S. Highway 89 makes a scenic 45-mile swing through the Wasatch National Forest and Logan Canyon before meeting U.S. Highway 91 at Logan. From there it's a short drive back north into Idaho, where our explorations continue at Franklin. (For more information on the Beehive State, check out *Utah: Off the Beaten Path*.)

Franklin, founded in 1860, beats out Paris for the title of Idaho's oldest settled town by three years. But like the pioneers at Paris, Franklin's early townsfolk thought they were part of Utah until the 1872 survey confirmed the town's location in what was to become the state of Idaho. Franklin's museum is called **The Relic Hall,** and it houses many artifacts and photos of pioneer life. A park complete with picnic grounds and a fireplace now surrounds the hall. Two of Franklin's most interesting sights are located just outside of town on the Old Yellowstone Highway. (Turn west at the Daughters of the Utah Pioneers marker north of town.) The ruins on the north side of the road are those of what is likely the **oldest flour mill** in the state of Idaho. And just across the road, the **Yellowstone Rock** shows the old route to the nation's first national

Idaho's "Loch Ness"

*P*hotographers find Bear Lake at its most beautiful at sunrise, when the water frequently glints pink, red, and gold as it catches the waking orb's rays. But locals say sunset visitors are more likely to spy the **Bear Lake Monster,** a serpentlike creature said to live underwater along the lake's east shore. Rumors of the beast have circulated for centuries, first by Native Americans and mountain men, later by Joseph Rich (a son of Mormon pioneer Charles Coulson Rich), who reported his findings in an 1868 article for the Desert News of Salt Lake City. Sightings were especially prevalent around 1900, when people reported strange creatures of up to 90 feet long that could move as fast as running horses.

According to a local tourism brochure, for a long time no one could find a bottom to Bear Lake. People thought perhaps Bear Lake was connected to Scotland by underground tunnels and that the Bear Lake monster was actually the famous Loch Ness monster. Today Bear Lake–area folks speculate the "creature" could be anything from ice formations or a cloud on the water to a large school of fish or elk swimming across the lake. "No one is willing to say if it is real or not," the pamphlet adds. "That is up to you to decide. But be on the lookout for the monster, and please report any sightings."

park. After Yellowstone received its national park designation, large boulders with arrows pointing the way were placed along what was then the main road to the park to help travelers find their way. This may be the last such marker still in existence.

The scenic **Cub River Canyon** east of Highway 91 between Franklin and Preston is home to the **Deer Cliff Inn,** which bills itself as "The Most Romantic Spot in the West." Family-run since 1940, this retreat offers rustic cabins and a restaurant featuring seasonal streamside patio dining. Menu items range from $6.75 to $16.25 and include steaks, chicken, shrimp, trout, halibut, and lobster. The restaurant is open from 5:00 P.M. Monday through Saturday during June, July, and August and from 5:00 P.M. Thursday through Saturday during May, September, and October (except on holidays May through September, when it opens at noon). Live entertainment is on hand most Friday and Saturday nights. For more information call (208) 852–0643. Drive on up the canyon for beautiful Wasatch Mountain scenery, especially in fall when the maples turn a dazzling red—an autumn color all too rare elsewhere in Idaho.

Brigham Young, the Mormon leader, urged his followers to heed the golden rule when dealing with Native Americans. "Treat them in all respects as you would like to be treated," he said in an 1852 speech. Indeed the Mormons who settled Idaho early on made pacts with the local Indian chiefs to share crops and live together peacefully. Still there were tensions, and they boiled over in January 1863 in the **Battle of Bear River** 2½ miles north of Preston. More Indians died in this little-known incident than in any other; there were more casualties—as many as 400 men, women, and children killed—than at Wounded Knee, Sand Creek, or Little Big Horn. The battle was triggered by the death of a miner on Bear River during an Indian attack; Colonel Patrick Connor of the Third California Infantry, stationed at Fort Douglas near Salt Lake City, used the incident as an excuse to make war. William Hull, a local pioneer who witnessed the battle, gave this account of its after-math: "Never will I forget the scene, dead bodies were everywhere. I counted eight deep in one place and in several places they were three to five deep. In all we counted nearly 400; two-thirds of this number being women and children." A monument along the east side of Highway 91 north of Preston makes note of the battle, and the actual battle site was nearby along aptly named Battle Creek. Not far north of the Battle of Bear River site, another wayside commemorates **Red Rock Pass.** It was through here that prehistoric Bonneville Lake breached its shores about 14,500 years ago, unleashing one of history's greatest floods.

Malad City, the seat of Oneida County, is more on the beaten path (I–15) than off, but it has a few spots to recommend a stop. The **Iron Door Playhouse** offers a full theatrical menu of about six productions each year including Broadway fare, youth-oriented shows, dinner theater, cowboy poetry, and melodramas. The playhouse is located at 59 North Main Street in what was once one of the nation's first JC Penney stores, since remodeled into a modern theater. Call (208) 766–4705 for reservations or information on upcoming events.

And what about that "Iron Door" name? *Malad* is French for "sick," and—like the Malad Gorge and Malad River in South Central Idaho—Malad City and its nearby (and much longer) Malad River reportedly earned their names when a party of trappers became sick after drinking from the stream. But those early trappers probably didn't feel nearly as sick as did Glispie Waldron, who, in 1890, may have blown his chance at finding a buried treasure.

It seems that during the 1860s and 1870s, Malad City was a major stop for freight wagons taking supplies from Utah north to the mines of Idaho and Montana, as well as those returning with gold. This traffic also made Malad a favorite target of robbers and other ne'er-do-wells, one group of which reportedly hid the loot from a stagecoach hold-up somewhere in the Samaria Mountains located southwest of town, planning to retrieve it later. Waldron was traveling in the area in 1890 when he reportedly spied an iron door covering a cave. He tied his coat to a nearby tree to mark the spot, intending to return. But he didn't make it back for a couple of years, and by then, his coat was gone. To this day treasure seekers are still searching for the fabled iron door and the riches that may lie behind it. If you're interested in trying your own luck, stop by the Oneida County **Pioneer Museum** at 27 Bannock Street in Malad City for tips on where to look.

If you haven't had your fill of Southeastern Idaho water recreation by now, check out **Downata Hot Springs Resort,** located near the town of Downey. Aside from a pool and water slides, this year-round resort offers everything from RV and tent camping and indoor lodging to water aerobics classes. Downey is on Highway 91, 6 miles south of its junction with I–15. Call (208) 897–5736 for more information or see www.downatahotsprings.com.

PLACES TO STAY
IN SOUTHEASTERN IDAHO

AMERICAN FALLS
American Motel,
2814 Pocatello Avenue,
(208) 226–7271

Hillview Motel,
2799 Lakeview Road,
(208) 226–5151

BLACKFOOT
Best Western
Blackfoot Inn,
750 Jensen Grove Drive,
(208) 785–4144,
fax: (208) 785–4304

Western Riverside Inn,
I–15 exit 93,
(208) 785–5000

POCATELLO/CHUBBUCK
Ameritel Inn,
1440 Bench Road
(Pocatello),
(800) 600–6001,
fax: (208) 234–0000

Black Swan Inn,
746 East Center
(Pocatello),
(208) 233–3051

Holiday Inn,
1399 Bench Road
(Pocatello),
(800) 200–8944,
fax: (208) 238–0225

Motel 6,
291 West Burnside Avenue
(Chubbuck),
(800) 466–8356

Pine Ridge Inn,
4333 Yellowstone Avenue
(Chubbuck),
(208) 237–3100

West Coast Pocatello Hotel,
1555 Pocatello Creek Road
(Pocatello),
(208) 233–2200,
fax: (208) 234–4524

LAVA HOT SPRINGS
Lava Hot Springs Inn &
Spa, 94 East Portneuf,
(208) 776–5830 (see text)

Riverside Inn & Hot
Springs, 255 East Portneuf,
(208) 776–5504

SODA SPRINGS
Caribou Lodge,
110 Highway 30,
(208) 547–3377,
fax: (208) 547–2663

J–R Inn,
179 Highway 30,
(208) 547–3366

Trail Motel,
213 East 200 South,
(208) 547–0240

MONTPELIER
Best Western Clover Creek
Inn, 243 North Fourth
Street, (800) 528–1234,
fax: (208) 847–3519

Three Sisters Motel,
112 South Sixth Street,
(208) 847–2324

FISH HAVEN
Bear Lake Bed & Breakfast,
Milepost 2 U.S. Highway 89,
(208) 945–2688 (see text)

PRESTON
Deer Cliff Inn,
up Cub River Canyon,
(208) 852–0643 (see text)

Plaza Motel,
427 South Highway 91,
(208) 852–2020

PLACES TO EAT
IN SOUTHEASTERN IDAHO

AMERICAN FALLS
Melody Lanes Cafe
(American),
152 Harrison,
(208) 226–2815

Pizza Hut (fast food),
2840 Pocatello Avenue,
(208) 226–5707

BLACKFOOT
Betty's Cafe (American),
Riverside Plaza,
(208) 785–6423

POCATELLO
Buddy's (pizza/ISU
favorite), 626 East Lewis,
(208) 233–1172

Continental Bistro
(fine dining),
140 South Main,
(208) 233–4433 (see text)

Food for Thought
(salads/sandwiches),
504 East Center,
(208) 233–7267

Mama Inez (Mexican),
390 Yellowstone Avenue,
(208) 234–7674

Portneuf River Grille
(American),
230 West Bonneville,
(208) 478–8418

Remo's (American),
160 West Cedar,
(208) 233–1710

Most major fast-food
chains, mainly along
Yellowstone Avenue in
Pocatello/Chubbuck

LAVA HOT SPRINGS
Duke's Fine Dining
(eclectic),
255 East Portneuf,
(208) 776–5504

Riverwalk Cafe (Thai),
79 West Portneuf,
(208) 776–5872
(see text)

SODA SPRINGS
Betty's Cafe (American),
Highway 30 west of town,
(208) 547–4802

Cedar View Supper Club
(American),
2525 Highway 30,
(208) 547–3301

MONTPELIER
Butch Cassidy's Restaurant
& Saloon (American),
260 North Fourth,
(208) 847–3501

Ranch Hand Truck Stop
(American),
23200 Highway 30,
(208) 847–1180

PRESTON
Deer Cliff Inn (American),
up Cub River Canyon,
(208) 852–0643 (see text)

The Main Street Grill
(eclectic), 96 South State,
(208) 852–1447

The Udder Place Cafe &
Creamery (American),
101 North State Street,
(208) 852–0332

MALAD CITY
Me 'n' Lou's Diner
(American),
75 South 300 East,
(208) 766–2919

Helpful Web sites

City of Pocatello—
www.ci.pocatello.id.us/

Greater Pocatello Chamber of Commerce—
www.pocatelloidaho.com

Idaho State Journal (Pocatello newspaper)—
www.journalnet.com

Worth Seeing

American Falls Reservoir—
north of American Falls

Bingham County Historical Museum—
Blackfoot

Idaho Museum of Natural History—
Pocatello

Pebble Creek Ski Area—*Pocatello*

Rails and Trails Museum—*Montpelier*

Grays Lake National Wildlife Refuge—
north of Soda Springs

Eastern Idaho

n Eastern Idaho the outdoors are never far away. This is the western gateway to two of America's premiere national parks, as well as to swift-running rivers and backcountry byways. Mountain peaks and massive buttes rim every horizon, shadowing the fertile, irrigated fields.

Eastern Idaho is defined by three routes: I-15, busy around Idaho Falls, then rather lonely on its trek north to Montana; U.S. Highway 20, which carries traffic to West Yellowstone, one of Yellowstone National Park's major entrances; and U.S. Highway 26, a popular route to Jackson Hole and Grand Teton National Park. As might be expected, summertime traffic is thick on Highways 20 and 26. Fortunately, several possible alternatives give travelers the chance to break away from the pack or make a loop tour of the region. The most popular of these, the Teton Scenic Byway and adjacent Mesa Falls Scenic Byway, are still well traveled—yet on these routes, you'll complete your trip feeling you've at least seen something other than the bumper of the vehicle in front of you.

For additional Eastern Idaho travel information, call (800) 634–3246 outside Idaho or (208) 523–1010 in-state; write the Yellowstone/Teton Visitor & Convention Bureau, P. O. Box 50498, Idaho Falls 83405-0498; or see www.yellowstoneteton.org.

The Upper Snake River

ven within the city limits of the region's biggest city, Idaho Falls, nature makes her presence known. Unlike Twin Falls, where a set of Snake River cascades gave the town its name, Idaho Falls got its name before any falls really existed. The town started life as Eagle Rock, taking that name from a ferry built in 1863 by Bill Hickman and Harry Rickards. (The ferry was positioned near a small rock island on which bald eagles frequently nested in a juniper tree.) In its early days Eagle Rock served as a major fording point for miners heading to the riches of central and western Idaho; the community also was known as Taylor's Crossing or Taylor's Bridge for the early

Eastern Idaho

EASTERN IDAHO

JULIE'S FAVORITES

Willard Arts Center—
Idaho Falls

Tautphaus Park Zoo—
Idaho Falls

Jefferson County TV &
Pioneer Museum—Rigby

Idaho Centennial
Carousel—Rexburg

Mesa Falls Scenic Byway—
near Ashton

Harriman State Park—
near Island Park

span built by James "Matt" Taylor. Later, Eagle Rock served as the center of railroad activity in the new Idaho Territory, but all that changed in 1887 when the Union Pacific moved its headquarters south to Pocatello and Eagle Rock's population plummeted. By 1891 a team of Chicago developers—Charles N. Lee, W. G. Emerson, D. W. Higbee, J. B. Holmes, and Bernard McCaffery—had descended on Eagle Rock. Seeing the rapids on the Snake River, they encouraged the locals to change the town's name to Idaho Falls. But it was not until 1911 that man-made falls were completed, giving the city legitimate claim to its name.

Since then Idaho Falls has made good use of its riverside location. The 2½-mile **Idaho Falls Greenbelt** runs between the falls area and downtown, offering office and shop workers a pleasant place to spend the lunch hour. On weekends local residents flock to the greenbelt to enjoy a picnic, often sharing their food with the numerous ducks and geese who call the area home. Joggers, cyclists, strollers, and in-line skaters also enjoy the greenbelt's picturesque view. Another good outdoor destination, especially with children, is the **Tautphaus Park Zoo.** This once-decrepit facility has improved vastly over the past few years. Exhibits include an Australian outback area, a bi-level otter home, penguins, zebras, a chidren's petting zoo, and a great pond filled with Idaho waterfowl. An "Asian Adventure" exhibit with red pandas and sloth bears is set to open sometime in 2002; call (208) 528–5552 or see www.idahofallszoo.org for updates. Zoo admission is $3.50 for age thirteen and up, $1.75 for children ages four through twelve, and $2.25 for seniors age sixty-two and up. Children age three and under get in free. Hours are 9:00 A.M. to 6:30 P.M. daily Memorial Day through Labor Day, 9:00 A.M. to 4:30 P.M. daily in May and after Labor Day in September, 9:00 A.M. to 4:30 P.M. Saturday and Sunday in April, October, and November. Tautphaus Park is between Rollandet Avenue and South Boulevard east of Yellowstone Avenue in south Idaho Falls.

The Idaho Falls Arts Council has its headquarters in the **Miles and Virginia Willard Arts Center,** a $4.2 million project that includes the renovated Colonial Theater. Recent performers have included Riders in the Sky, Pancho Sanchez Latin Jazz Band, and Manhattan Transfer. The center also has a regular menu of arts classes for children and adults. For information on upcoming events, call (208) 522–0471;

write the Idaho Falls Arts Council, 498 A Street, Idaho Falls 83402; or see www.idahofallsarts.org.

Next door to the arts center, **D.D. Mudd** has some of the best coffee in town, along with weekend breakfasts and special dinners. The restaurant at 401 Park Avenue is open daily from 6:30 A.M. to 10:00 P.M. except Sundays, when it's open 9:00 A.M. to 3:00 P.M. For details of upcoming events, call (208) 535–9088.

Idaho Falls has an abundance of interesting architecture. The city's landmark structure is the **Idaho Falls Temple** of the Church of Jesus Christ of Latter-day Saints, located along the Snake River at 1000 Memorial Drive, its spire visible for miles. The temple's visitor center is open daily from 9:00 A.M. to 9:00 P.M. Free tours are available, and exhibits highlight Mormon history, art, and culture.

Elsewhere in the city, the Idaho Falls Historic Preservation Committee has prepared several informative pamphlets detailing walking tours. For example, the **Ridge Avenue Historic District** has sixty-seven notable buildings, with styles ranging from Queen Anne to craftsman to colonial revival. One of the most auspicious structures on the tour is the **First Presbyterian Church** at 325 Elm Street, a neoclassical building complete with Roman dome and Ionic portico. History buffs will enjoy a stop at the **Bonneville County Historical Museum,** located at 200 North Eastern Avenue in a former Carnegie library. After passing through the museum's art deco entrance, visitors are treated to exhibits ranging from pioneer life to the atomic age, along with a replica of the original Eagle Rock town site. The museum is open from 10:00 A.M. to 5:00 P.M. Monday through Friday and 1:00 to 5:00 P.M. Saturday; closed Sunday and holidays. Admission is $2.00, or 50 cents for children under eighteen. Guided tours are available; for more information call (208) 522–1400. Watch for a major expansion at the museum in 2003.

Highway 26, the road from Idaho Falls to Grand Teton National Park, isn't exactly off the beaten path. Sometimes in our hurry to get somewhere else, however, we miss seeing something interesting right along our way. Such is the case with the big, unusual looking building at 4523 Highway 26, a few miles north of Idaho Falls. For years I drove by wondering: Was it a school? A barn? Actually, it was both: a school built in 1899 and a barn erected shortly thereafter. Both structures now sit on the same site and serve as home to the **Country Store Boutique,** a fascinating antiques and gift emporium run by Eric and Melanie Seneff.

The Country Store Boutique boasts 15,000 square feet of the old, new, and unusual. Unlike many shops featuring antiques and collectibles,

Top Annual Events

Teton Valley Hot Air Balloon Festival, Driggs (early July)

Idaho Falls Padres baseball (June-September)

Fourth of July Events, Idaho Falls

Grand Targhee Bluegrass Music, Grand Targhee (mid-August)

Idaho International Folk Dance Festival, Rexburg (late July-early August) (see text)

the Country Store Boutique doesn't feel musty and overstuffed. There's room to move around amid the solid old wood furniture, the antique glassware, and the Indian pottery and jewelry. The boutique also carries quilts, rugs, baskets, arrowheads, sheet music, folk art, and more. It's a great place to shop for a gift or for your home. The store is open from 10:00 A.M. to 6:00 P.M. Monday through Saturday. Call (208) 522–8450 for more information.

Do you watch television? If so, you may want to make a pilgrimage to Rigby, hometown of **Philo T. Farnsworth,** who invented the cathode-ray tube and made TV possible. No couch potato, Farnsworth was a natural whiz at all things mechanical.

Born in Utah in 1906, he moved to a farm near Rigby when he was a boy. Fascinated by electricity, he played violin in a dance orchestra to earn money for books on the topic. Farnsworth was fourteen years old when he got the idea for TV while plowing a field, and one day he sketched out his ideas on a blackboard at Rigby High School. By 1927 Farnsworth—then living in California—was able to prove his idea worked by transmitting a single horizontal line from a camera in one room to a receiving screen in another. He was just twenty-one.

In 1930 electronics giant RCA offered to buy Farnsworth's invention for a cool $200,000 and give him a job, but the inventor—preferring to preserve his independence—turned them down flat. That refusal apparently triggered the patent war between Farnsworth and RCA, which claimed one of its own employees, Vladimir Zworykin, had actually invented television. Zworykin had been tinkering with TV, but it wasn't until he visited Farnsworth's lab and saw the Idaho native's invention that he was able to duplicate Philo's principles and work. RCA eventually filed suit against Farnsworth, but the inventor prevailed, especially after his former high-school science teacher produced a 1922 sketch of Philo's television theory.

Farnsworth never finished high school, yet by the time he died in 1971 he had earned 300 patents and an honorary doctorate from Brigham Young University. His other notable inventions included the baby incubator, and at the time of his death, he was working on the theory of nuclear fission. Zworykin still sometimes gets credit for Farnsworth's television invention, but the truth is coming out—and someday Farnsworth's name may be as famous as those of fellow inventors Thomas Edison and Alexander Graham Bell.

The *Jefferson County TV and Pioneer Museum* has extensive displays about Farnsworth's life and work, including several handwritten journals, his Dictaphone, a Farnsworth television, much of his science book collection, and copies of just about anything ever written about the inventor. Other exhibits detail the early history of Jefferson County and its communities, including a Hall of Fame honoring local boys author Vardis Fisher and NFL great Larry Wilson. You also can see a jar of peaches canned in 1886! Museum hours are from 1:00 to 5:00 P.M. Tuesday through Saturday or by appointment. Suggested donation is $1.00 for adults and 25 cents for children. The museum is at 118 West First South in Rigby; just look for the high tower. The phone number is (208) 745–8423.

Feeling the need for relaxation? East of Idaho Falls near Ririe, *Heise Hot Springs* features a swimming pool with water slide and a soothing 105° F. mineral hot bath. But this popular resort doesn't stop there; visitors also can camp amid tall cottonwood trees, tee off on a nine-hole par twenty-nine golf course, grab a bite at the pizza parlor, or spread a picnic on the lawn. Heise Hot Springs is open year-round except November. For more information or current hours, call (208) 538–7312.

Mountain River Ranch, also near Ririe, is another spot offering a wide variety of entertainment and recreation. In summertime, a Wild West shoot-out takes place in the ranch's old frontier town, Rock Bottom Springs. After the "gun fight," horse-drawn wagons transport guests to the Meadow Muffin Dinner Theatre, where they enjoy a hearty chuck-wagon style meal of barbecue chicken ($19) or steak ($24), baked beans, corn on the cob, potato salad, garlic sourdough bread, lemonade, and Italian ice for dessert before settling in for more old-time Western entertainment. In wintertime, sleigh rides run nearly every night in December and weekends through February 14; meal options with these include Cornish game hen ($26) or prime rib ($34). Ask about reduced prices for children. The ranch also has a fee-fishing pond (no license needed), an RV park, and two rustic rooms for rent. For more information, call (208) 538–7337; write to Mountain River Ranch, 98 North 5050 East, Ririe 83443; or see www.mountainriverranch.com.

The *Cress Creek Nature Trail* is yet another worthy stop east of Ririe off the Heise Road. This well-marked path gives visitors a chance to learn about the flora, fauna, and geology of Eastern Idaho, all while enjoying some tremendous views. At one point the panorama stretches from the Caribou Mountain Range south of the Snake River all the way to the Beaverhead Range on the Montana border. The Blackfoot Mountains, Big Southern Butte and East Twin Butte, the Lost River Mountain Range, and the Menan Buttes can all be seen as well.

U.S. Highway 26 continues to follow the Upper Snake River toward its origin in Wyoming. The Swan Valley–Palisades area is one of Eastern Idaho's least populated and most scenic stretches. Several U.S. Forest Service campgrounds along Palisades Reservoir provide excellent bases for enjoying the region's good fishing and boating.

The Lodge at Palisades Creek is considered one of the top fly-fishing lodges in the West. This rustic-yet-elegant resort sits within casting distance of the South Fork of the Snake River and Palisades Creek, and the

I Scream, You Scream . . .

*T*he heavily Mormon country of Eastern Idaho and Utah reportedly has some of the highest ice-cream consumption rates in the United States. Some theorize this is because members of the Church of Jesus Christ of Latter-day Saints deny themselves other hedonistic pleasures like alcohol and caffeine. But it may also simply be because there's a lot of excellent ice cream made by places like **Reed's Dairy**, located on the western outskirts of Idaho Falls at 2660 West Broadway (just west of Broadway and Bellin, on the north side). Reed's makes about forty flavors, including such favorites as Cow Tracks (vanilla with peanut butter and chocolate chips) and Chunky Monkey (banana with nuts and chocolate chips). You'll usually have your pick of eighteen at any one time. Cones, shakes, sundaes, frozen yogurt, and sandwiches are available; there is informal seating inside and out, and self-guided tours are offered,

too. Reed's Dairy is open Monday through Saturday from 8:00 A.M. to 10:00 P.M. in the summer and until 9:00 P.M. the rest of the year. For more information call (208) 522–0123.

The **Rainey Creek Country Store** is another can't-miss spot on the region's ice-cream circuit. This convenience store at the junction of U.S. Highway 26 and Idaho State Highway 31 is famous for serving square ice-cream cones. Actually, it's the ice cream that is square—not the cones, but you get the idea. Owner Kent Wood and his staff scooped up 12,980 cones on the Fourth of July weekend in 2001, setting a new store record that may be broken by the time you read this. Rainey Creek offers twenty-four flavors including Idaho Huckleberry. Summertime store hours are 7:00 A.M. to 9:00 A.M. Monday through Saturday and 7:00 A.M. to 6:00 P.M. on Sunday. The rest of the year hours are 8:00 A.M. to 7:00 P.M. daily except Sunday. Phone (208) 483–2151.

Reed's Dairy

fly-fishing is so good that dinner is served until 10:00 P.M. to accommodate guests who wish to stay in the river well into the evening. Accommodations options include seven log cabins and a two-bedroom chalet, all overlooking the river. The lodge is spendy, as we say here in Idaho—about $3,000 per person for a weeklong stay in summertime—but the rate includes guide service, accommodations, and gourmet meals. (Rates are less for nonanglers. Overnight trips and guide service without accommodations are available, too.) For more information call (208) 483–2222 or write The Lodge at Palisades Creek, P.O. Box 70, Irwin 83428. The lodge's Web site is at www.tlapc.com, and its E-mail address is palisades@tlapc.com.

At Swan Valley, the traveler has a choice: Continue on Highway 26 to Alpine, Wyoming (the southern gateway to Jackson Hole), or take Idaho State Highway 31 over Pine Creek Pass, elevation 6,764. The latter provides access to Idaho's Teton Valley, the area we will explore next.

Teton Valley

Wyoming's Teton Range ranks among the world's most magnificent chains of mountains. The classic view of the Tetons is from the east, but Idaho's Teton Valley offers a less-crowded, equally scenic approach to the famed peaks. State Highways 31, 33, and 32 (in that order, from south to north) have been designated Idaho's *Teton Scenic Byway.* Along the way the drive winds through several small towns—Victor, Driggs, and Tetonia—oriented to outdoor recreation.

Driggs is the jumping-off spot for *Grand Targhee Ski & Summer*

Resort, just over the border in Alta, Wyoming, but accessible only via the Tetons' Idaho side. Targhee is well known for getting a pile of snow, typically more than 500 inches each winter, including plenty of powder. For the 2001–2002 season, the resort opened a new detachable quad lift serving Peaked Mountain and bringing its lift-accessed terrain to 2,000 acres. There are plenty of programs for skiers and snowboarders of all levels, including a special "Magic Carpet" serving the beginners' area. But Targhee is also a target of extreme skiers, with several instructional workshops typically planned each winter.

Grand Targhee is worth a visit in warmer weather, too. Take the chairlift to the top of Fred's Mountain for a great Teton vista. There's also good mountain biking, horseback riding, tennis, hiking, swimming, and a climbing wall, plus activities and childcare for kids of all ages. Resort staff even will arrange a fly-fishing, river-rafting, or soaring expedition nearby. Grand Targhee is also the site for several summer music festivals including the long-running Targhee Bluegrass Festival in mid-August. (Call for current dates.) For more information on Grand Targhee, call (800) TARGHEE; write to Grand Targhee Resort, Box Ski, Alta, WY 83422; or see www.grandtarghee.com.

With all the recreational riches at hand, it makes sense that businesses like *Reel Women Fly-Fishing Adventures* and *R.U. Outside* gravitate to the Teton Valley. Based in Victor, Reel Women offers fly-fishing lessons in Jackson Hole, trout-fishing trips in the Rockies, and international fishing adventures to such destinations as Baja California and Costa Rica. For more information call (208) 787–2657; see www.reel-women.com or write Reel Women, P.O. Box 289, Victor 83455. R.U. Outside specializes in offbeat, functional outdoor gear. It has a Teton Valley store at 455 South Main in Driggs, but if you can't get there, you can still shop via phone (800–279–7123) or on the Internet at www.ruoutside.com.

Food is taken seriously hereabouts, too: Whether you want to carbo load for a mountain bike trek or enjoy one of the most unusual dining experiences in the West, you will not go hungry in the Teton Valley. If you like a little entertainment with your meal, check out *Pierre's Playhouse* on Main Street in Victor. This family business, going strong in its fourth decade, presents 1890s-style melodramas Wednesday through Saturday mid-June through the Saturday before Labor Day. Each show is preceded by an all-you-can-eat Dutch oven dinner featuring chicken, potatoes, salad, scones, and coffee. While waiting for your food, you can always amuse yourself by reading the rules and regulations on the playbill; these include "Children left in the theatre over three days become the property of the villain," "Firearms may not be discharged in the

Author's Note

If you grew up in the '50s, '60s, or '70s, chances are you spent your share of summer nights parked in front of a massive outdoor movie screen, either fighting with your siblings or smooching with your sweetie. Drive-in movie theaters are dying out across much of North America, but there remain a fair number in the Gem State.

*Appropriately enough for Idaho, the one just south of Driggs is called the **Spud Drive-In**. The Spud's giant potato is a landmark throughout the region, and its hamburgers are pretty famous, too. For twenty-four-hour movie information, call (208) 354–2727.*

Elsewhere in Idaho, you'll still find drive-in theaters at Idaho Falls, Twin Falls, Boise, Mountain Home, Parma, and Lewiston.

direction of the stage," and "It is requested that liquor not be imported into the theatre in any other than a human container."

Proprietress Peggy Egbert plays the piano and presides over the merriment. She started the playhouse with her husband, Tom, in the early 1960s. Tom has passed away, but Peggy still runs the show, which attracts about a quarter of its audience from outside Idaho each summer. Cost is $15.00 for the show and dinner, or $8.00 for just the show. Dinner is served from 6:00 P.M. to 8:00 P.M., with the curtain at 8:00 P.M. Reservations are advised; call (208) 787–2249. The dinner theater is on the Web at www.pierresplayhouse.com.

The ultimate Teton Valley dining experience is at **Inn Lost Horizon** at Alta, Wyoming. Technically, like Grand Targhee, Inn Lost Horizon shouldn't even be included in an Idaho guidebook. But since the only road there runs through Idaho, the Gem State can make at least partial claim to these treasures. Chuck and Shigeko Irwin serve a ten-course Chinese-Japanese meal once each evening on Friday and Saturday. In between the courses of the three-hour meal, guests can wander through the Irwins' 6,000-foot home, taking in the Teton views. Cost is $40 per person, and diners are asked to reserve a spot by calling (307) 353–8226 about two weeks ahead of time. Complimentary RV parking is offered after dinner. The Irwins have a life—they like to travel extensively and spend a good bit of time out of town—so don't be too disappointed if Inn Lost Horizon is temporarily closed when you'd like to visit. Just consider it another reason to return to the Teton Valley.

The Teton Valley also has several unusual spots to bed down for one night or longer. The **Pines Motel–Guest Haus,** at 105 South Main in Driggs, is an unusual combination of mom-and-pop motel and bed-and-breakfast inn. Originally a two-story log cabin built about 1900, the building has been enlarged and is now home to John and Nancy Nielson and their family. Many travelers who stay at the Pines seem to wind up part of the Nielsons' extended clan, returning for holiday dinners and corresponding with the family. Outdoors, a stone fireplace, gas grill, lawn chairs, and play area offer summertime fun and relaxation. Local people and tourists alike turn out for Driggs's annual antiques show, held in the Nielsons' backyard almost every Fourth of July, and for ice-skating on the pond John builds most winters. Visitors needn't worry about bringing their own skates; the Nielsons have a collection with enough pairs to fit nearly anyone.

The Pines Motel–Guest Haus has seven rooms, including one suite with adjoining rooms, ranging in price from $35 to $70 double occupancy. Children twelve and under are welcome at no extra charge; pets are permitted for an additional $10. When requested, the Nielsons serve a big country-style breakfast on antique dishes in one of the original log-cabin rooms. The meal is $10 extra per person for guests (half-price for children twelve and under). For more information or reservations, call (800) 354–2778 or write the Pines Motel–Guest Haus, P.O. Box 117, Driggs 83422.

Moose Creek Ranch is famous for its wild mustangs, which are adopted, trained, and ultimately added to the remuda. This is a working dude ranch, where guests are encouraged to learn as much as they can about horse care during their stay. But it's not all chores: Moose Creek visitors also enjoy lots of riding, plus hiking, swimming, and white-water rafting. Visitors stay in comfortable cabins or a five-bedroom ranch home and enjoy great Western grub. Special kids' programs are available, too. The cost of a weeklong stay is about $1,200 for adults, with lower rates for children. Call (800) 676–0075 for more information or write Moose Creek Ranch, P.O. Box 350, Victor 83455. The ranch Web site is at www.moosecreekranch.com.

On the road to Grand Targhee, *Teton Tepee Lodge* caters to skiers and mountain bikers. It's a cross between a hostel and a guest lodge, with small but pleasant rooms radiating from a cavernous common area and a bunkhouse-style dorm downstairs. Winter rates (including a private room, lift passes and transportation to and from Grand Targhee, and all-you-can-eat breakfasts and dinners) run $435 per adult, double occupancy, for a three-day stay. The lodge also can be reserved in its entirety for reunions, weddings, and retreats. For more information call (800) 353–8176 or write Teton Tepee Lodge, Alta, WY 83422.

Yellowstone Country

*J*ust west of Tetonia the Teton Scenic Byway continues north on State Highway 32, terminating in Ashton, where the Mesa Falls Scenic Byway begins (see page 144). Highway 33 continues west to

Rexburg, largest city in the Teton Valley. En route plan a stop at the **Teton Dam Site,** just a mile and a half north of Highway 33 near Newdale. A big pyramid of earth is all that is left of the Teton Dam, which collapsed June 5, 1976, killing eleven people and causing nearly $1 billion in damage. (The nearby Idaho state highway historical marker erroneously puts the death toll at fourteen.) The dam—widely opposed by environmentalists—had just been completed and its reservoir was still being filled when the breach occurred, unleashing eighty billion gallons of water toward Wilford, Sugar City, Rexburg, and Idaho Falls. Fortunately most Teton Valley residents heard about the coming torrent and were able to evacuate before the waters swept through their towns.

The **Teton Flood Museum,** at 51 North Center Street in Rexburg, tells the tale in exhibits, photos, and a fascinating video called *One Saturday Morning.* (Ask at the front desk to view the tape.) Other displays at the museum showcase handmade quilts and a collection of more than 300 salt-and-pepper shakers. The Teton Flood Museum is open from 10:00 A.M. to 5:00 P.M. Monday through Saturday from May through early September, and 11:00 A.M. to 4:00 P.M. Monday through Friday the rest of the year. Admission is by donation. For more information phone (208) 356–9101.

While in Rexburg, don't miss the **Idaho Centennial Carousel,** located in Porter Park. The merry-go-round was built in 1926 by the Spillman Engineering Company of North Tonawanda, New York, and brought to

Global Hoedown

*L*ittle Rexburg, Idaho, is more globally minded than most towns of 17,250. Mormon-owned Brigham Young University–Idaho has several hundred international students and many American students who have served church missions all over the planet. But during the last week of July each year, Rexburg really starts to resemble a mini–United Nations. That's when about 300 folks from scores of foreign lands arrive to perform in the **Idaho International Folk Dance Festival,** a sort of Olympics for the arts. Past years' events have attracted dancers from Slovakia, India, Sweden, Malaysia, China, Russia, and dozens of other nations. In addition to daily dancing, visitors also can expect lots of Western—as in cowboy—entertainment, including a rodeo and barbecue. For more information or a schedule for the next festival, call (208) 356–5700 or write the Rexburg Chamber of Commerce, 420 West Fourth South, Rexburg 83440.

Idaho Centennial Carousel

Rexburg in 1952. By the late seventies, the old carousel had been severely damaged by vandalism and the Teton Dam floodwaters. Now, however, the carousel is completely restored and truly one of a kind. Sherrell Anderson, a master carver, replaced more than fifty broken legs and ten tails for the carousel's horses, then created twelve new horses that match the originals in style but are festooned with symbols of Idaho.

The lead horse, "Centennial," is decorated with the state tree (whitepine), the state bird (mountain bluebird), the state flower (syringa), the state gemstone (star garnet), and the state seal. On the opposite side, the "Chief Joseph" horse is a gray Appaloosa (Idaho's state horse) fitted with ornamentation including a bear-claw necklace and a shield bearing the portrait of the great Nez Perce leader. The carousel's center also is decorated with pictures and symbols from all over the Gem State, including scenes of Hells Canyon, Balanced Rock, and Harriman State Park, as well as a moose, grizzly bear, and white-tailed deer. The Idaho Centennial Carousel is open for rides from 12:30 to 7:00 P.M. Monday through Saturday during the summer months (except on days with bad weather). It can be reserved for group use; for more information call (208) 359–3020.

The *Menan Buttes,* rising south-west of Rexburg, are another National Natural Landmark and a fun spot for even the littlest hikers (although steep and challenging treks are available for those who want more adventure). The two 10,000-year-old buttes are composed of glassy basalt lava, found in only a few places in the world. The buttes are 800 and 500 feet high, with craters that measure a half-mile wide and about 300 feet deep. The buttes are north of the small town of Menan, or they may be reached by taking State Highway 33 west of Rexburg.

St. Anthony, northeast of Rexburg on U.S. Highway 20, is famous for the sand dunes north of town. Like the dunes at Bruneau in Southwestern Idaho, the *St. Anthony Sand Dunes* are among the highest in the United States, but the St. Anthony complex is much larger than that at

Bruneau—about 150 square miles total. The St. Anthony dunes are particularly popular with all-terrain vehicle enthusiasts. Small, rolling hills are suitable for beginners, and hills up to 500 feet in height offer challenges for more experienced riders. But because the dunes are under consideration for wilderness designation—and because sagebrush and other vegetation at the site provide critical habitat for deer, elk, and sage grouse—visitors must ride on the open sand only. For more information call the Bureau of Land Management (which oversees the dunes) at (208) 524–7500.

Ashton, another 14 miles east of St. Anthony on Highway 20, is the gateway to the **Mesa Falls Scenic Byway** (Highway 47), a beautiful 25-mile route that runs right by the viewpoints for Lower and Upper Mesa Falls and offers good views of the Teton Range, too. This is one scenic drive that takes barely longer than the more direct highway route, so by all means indulge.

At Lower Mesa Falls, an overlook appropriately dubbed Grandview provides a panorama featuring the Henry's Fork of the Snake River and the

Yellowstone's Back Door

A *side trip from the Mesa Falls Scenic Byway takes travelers into the little-known Bechler District of* ***Yellowstone National Park****—an isolated area marked by broad meadows and abundant waterfalls. Remarkably, this rich region was almost lost to a reservoir in the early twentieth century, when Idaho farmers prevailed on Congressman Addison Smith to seek the Bechler area's removal from Yellowstone National Park so a dam could be built for irrigation water. In hearings, Smith insisted to his peers that the region was nothing more than a swamp. But fortunately naturalist William Gregg got word of the scheme and launched a crusade to save the Bechler district. The dam idea was finally crushed by public outcry.*

To detour about 40 miles round-trip to "the Bechler," which sits astride the Idaho-Wyoming border, watch 4 miles outside Marysville (itself just east of Ashton) for the Cave Falls Road (1400 North) and follow it for 19 miles. A Forest Service campground sits just past the Wyoming border. Nearby, a picnic area affords a view of Cave Falls, which drop along the entire width of Falls River. An easy 1-mile trail leads through the pine forest to Bechler Falls. Longer trails in the region can take you to magnificent meadowlands and dramatic waterfalls, including Union Falls and Albright Falls; check at the Bechler ranger station (located at the end of a short spur road off the Cave Falls Road) for details and permits, which are required for overnight treks.

65-foot falls, which are seen at some distance. Camping and picnicking are available nearby. Upper Mesa Falls, on the other hand, are viewed up close and personal. By descending a series of walkways, it's possible to stand right at the brink of the 114-foot Upper Falls, bask in its thunderous roar, and probably see a rainbow. Benches offer the traveler an opportunity to sit and reflect on the falls and the tall pines all around. Big Falls Inn at Upper Mesa Falls, constructed around the turn of the century and used by travelers en route to Yellowstone National Park, recently reopened as a visitor information center. From Upper Mesa Falls the byway continues 12 miles to U.S. Highway 20, returning to the main route near Island Park.

Island Park is among Idaho's top recreation areas. Aside from being a town of some 200 people, Island Park is a geological feature—a caldera, or volcanic basin, the world's largest at about 20 miles in diameter. The caldera was created when a volcano originally situated in the area erupted continuously for thousands of years before finally collapsing. This is also the land of the Henry's Fork, considered one of America's premier trout streams. The river was named for Andrew Henry, who passed through the area in 1810 as part of a fur-trapping expedition and established a trading post. These days numerous outfitters offer guide services and equipment for anglers, snowmobilers, and other recreationists.

Big Springs, located northeast of Island Park, is the source of much of the Henry's Fork flow and the home of some truly impressive rainbow trout. A National Natural Landmark, the springs are one of a kind, issuing at the rate of 92,000 gallons per minute from the same rhyolitic lava flows that created the caldera. The Targhee National Forest has a campground at the site. No fishing is allowed at Big Springs, but the trout will happily accept handouts of bread tossed by visitors. The John Sack Cabin, listed on the National Register of Historic Places, sits nearby and is open to visitors during the summer.

The Island Park area has several guest ranches. One such spot, *Jacobs' Island Park Ranch,* is an authentic, working cattle spread. Visitors can watch cowboys on the job, or even help out on a cattle drive. Many guests, however, prefer to play, and the ranch offers horseback riding, boat tours of Island Park Reservoir, fishing, swimming, and nighttime entertainment by Western musicians. In wintertime, cross-country skiing and snowmobiling are available. Lodging rates range from $80 to $350 a night. For more information call (208) 662–5567; write Jacobs' Island Park Ranch, 2496 North 2375 East, Hamer 83425; or see www.jacobsranch.com.

Mack's Inn Resort, on the banks of the Henry's Fork between Island Park and West Yellowstone, Montana, is another spot Idaho families have enjoyed for generations. The resort sports a variety of accommodations ranging from cabins of several sizes to condos, along with an RV park. Recreational amenities include float trips, paddleboats, miniature golf, basketball, volleyball, horseshoe pits, and more. Call (208) 558–7272 for more information; write Mack's Inn Resort, P.O. Box 10, Mack's Inn 83433; or see www.macksinn.com.

Island Park can be a noisy place in winter, what with all the snowmobilers racing across the white fields of snow. But solace isn't hard to find for those seeking a more serene wintertime experience. *Harriman State Park* has some of the state's best cross-country skiing, and the park is closed to snow machines. That's largely because the park is also a wildlife refuge, home to bald eagles, trumpeter swans, sandhill cranes, elk, deer, moose, and coyotes. Skiers and snowshoers are likely to catch glimpses of these and other animals during any winter trip through the park.

Harriman is peaceful in summertime, too. Trails ranging in length from 1 mile to 5½ miles meander along the Henry's Fork, Silver Lake, and Golden Lake, or up to the top of a ridge where the Teton Range may be viewed. Again these paths are open only to nonmotorized use by hikers, mountain bicyclists, and horseback riders. Visitors may bring their own horse or rent one in the park.

Harriman State Park is also home to the *Railroad Ranch,* a collection of buildings erected in the early twentieth century by investors from the Oregon Short Line Railroad. Over time the ranch became a favorite retreat of prominent American industrialists and their families. It was E. H. Harriman, founder of the Union Pacific Railroad, who envisioned the ranch as a refuge for wildlife. Ironically, he never really got to enjoy the ranch, but his son and daughter-in-law, E. Roland and Gladys Harriman, spent six weeks of most summers at the ranch, and a cabin remains furnished much as they used it.

Over a half-century about forty buildings were constructed at the Railroad Ranch. Twenty-seven of these original structures still stand, and many are included in tours given during the summer months. No camping is available in the park, but you can rent the four-bedroom ranch manager's log house for $190 for four adults; extra adults are $10 a person per night. Fully furnished with a screened-in sun porch, knotty-pine walls, and a stone fireplace, it sleeps up to eight people and makes a great base for either a fly-fishing trip or winter outing. Like all accommodations at the park, it's accessible only by cross-country skis or snowshoes in winter. Harriman also has a bunkhouse that sleeps from fifteen to forty people at a per-person, per-night cost of $14, with a minimum fee of $210 per night. To rent either facility, you must write the park no earlier than October 1 for the following year and include a $25 reservation fee. Both rentals tend to fill up for the next summer by mid-October. Finally, Harriman has two yurts accommodating up to six people for $40 per night. For reservations or more information about Harriman State Park, call (208) 558–7368; write Harriman State Park, HC 66 Box 500, Island Park 83429; or see the Web site at www.idahoparks.org/parks/harriman.html.

From Island Park, it's possible to take back roads to the last area of Eastern Idaho on our itinerary, the opal mines of Clark County. A2, a county road, runs from just north of Island Park west to Kilgore and on to Spencer, which sits on I–15. Spencer is reportedly the only place in North America where opals are abundant enough to mine commercially. Several businesses in the Spencer-Dubois area sell finished gemstones and opal jewelry. The *Spencer Opal Mine* is open to the public for digging on summer holiday weekends (Memorial Day, the Fourth of July, and Labor Day); the first full weekend of August; and occasional other dates when group tours have been booked. The cost is $30 per digger per day for up to five pounds of opal-bearing rock; extra pounds cost $5.00 apiece. When the mine isn't open, the headquarters (open daily from 8:00 A.M. to 8:00 P.M. mid-May through September) has a "mini-mine" where visitors can pay $5.00 per person for one pound of rock.

The opals rest in layers at the mine, and visitors dig in windrows of opal-bearing rock ranging in size from gravel to small boulders. The mine recommends the following tools be taken to the site: rock hammer, three- or four-pound crack hammer, points and chisels, eight- or ten-pound sledge hammer, bucket, spray bottle, gloves, sturdy shoes or boots, and safety glasses (which are required). Bring drinking water and a lunch, too; water to wash the mined rock is available on-site.

For more information, call (208) 374–5476 or write Spencer Opal Mines, HCR 62, Box 2060, Dubois 83423. In the off season, the mine owners can be reached at (928) 859–3752.

Most people don't care for strangers traipsing through their home, but Joy and Ken Myers don't mind. The couple live in the *Spencer Rock*

House, built in 1919 and listed on the National Register of Historic Places. The home's most unusual feature is the spring water that runs through the basement year-round. Joy says Charles Hardy, who built the home, tried to keep the spring water out, to no avail. Today the spring and the home's 42-inch-thick walls make the basement excellent for food storage, about 45° F. in summer and 35° F. in winter.

The craftsman-style home also boasts many original details, including unusual light toggle switches, a sleeping porch, and a footbath in the powder room. To find the Spencer Rock House, drive under the interstate overpass, turn right, and drive down the hill past the Spencer Bar and Grill. Joy says it's OK to just stop by, but you can call ahead (208–374–5359) and let 'em know you're coming. Incidentally, Joy Myers, Spencer's city clerk, is a great source for local information. She says the 2000 census reported thirty-eight people in Spencer, "but we're having trouble finding them all." Spencer is in Clark County, which is Idaho's second least-populated. According to Joy, there are four people and twelve cows per square mile.

Dubois, south of Spencer on I–15, is the Clark County seat and a friendly outpost for wind-beaten travelers. WELCOME TO DUBOIS, the city-limits sign says. WE'VE NEVER MET A STRANGER YET. Many people passing through these parts make it a point to eat at *Charlie's R & R,* where they dish up a big ham-and-eggs breakfast, hamburgers, and chicken-fried steak. Charlie's is open from 6:00 A.M. to 9:00 P.M. Monday through Saturday, 8:00 A.M. to 6:00 P.M. Sunday. The phone number is (208) 374–5504.

PLACES TO STAY IN EASTERN IDAHO

IDAHO FALLS
Days Inn Stardust,
700 Lindsay Boulevard,
(800) 527–0274,
fax: (208) 529–8361

Hampton Inn,
2500 Channing Way,
(208) 529–9800,
fax: (208) 529–9455

Littletree Inn,
888 North Holmes,
(800) 521–5993,
fax: (208) 523–7104

Motel West,
1540 West Broadway,
(800) 582–1063,
fax: (208) 524–1144

Shilo Inn Suites Hotel,
780 Lindsay Boulevard,
(800) 222–2244,
fax: (208) 522–7420

Towne Lodge,
255 E Street,
phone/fax: (208) 523–2960

West Coast Idaho
Falls Hotel,
475 River Parkway,
(800) 325–4000,
fax: (208) 529–9610

RIGBY
South Fork Inn Motel,
425 Farnsworth Way,
(208) 745–8700

SWAN VALLEY
South Fork Lodge,
Highway 26,
(877) 347–4735,
fax: (208) 483–2121

IRWIN
The Lodge at Pallisades
Creek, (208) 483–2222
(see text)

VICTOR
Moose Creek Ranch,
215 East Moose Creek
Road, (800) 676–0075,
fax: (208) 787–2284
(see text)

DRIGGS
Best Western Teton West,
476 North Main Street,
(208) 354–2363,
fax: (208) 354–2962

Grand Targhee Resort
(Alta, Wyoming),
(800) TARGHEE
(see text)

Pines Motel–Guest Haus,
105 South Main,
(800) 354–2778 (see text)

Teton Tepee Lodge,
(Alta, Wyoming),
(800) 353–8176

REXBURG
Best Western Cottontree
Inn, 450 West Fourth
South, (800) 662–6886,
fax: (208) 356–7461

CJ's Motel,
357 West 400 South,
(208) 356–5477,
fax: (208) 656–9923

Days Inn,
271 South Second West,
(800) 329–7466,
fax: (208) 356–9242

ST. ANTHONY
Best Western Weston Inn,
115 South Bridge,
(800) 528–1234,
fax: (208) 624–3711

ASHTON
Jessen's RV Park/Bed &
Breakfast, 1146 South
Highway 20,
(800) 747–3356

Log Cabin Motel,
1001 Main, (208) 652–3956

ISLAND PARK
Jacobs' Island Park Ranch,
2496 North
2375 East (Hamer),
(208) 662–5567,
fax: (208) 662–5743

Mack's Inn Resort,
Highway 20,
(208) 558–7272,
fax: (208) 558–9305

Pond's Lodge,
(208) 558–7221

DUBOIS
Cross Roads Motel,
391 South Reynolds,
(208) 374–5258

PLACES TO EAT
IN EASTERN IDAHO

IDAHO FALLS
Brownstone Restaurant &
Brewhouse (brew pub),
455 River Parkway,
(208) 535–0310

D.D. Mudd (American),
401 Park Avenue,
(208) 535–9088

Garcia's (Mexican),
2180 East Seventeenth
Street, (208) 522–2000

Helpful Web sites

The Post Register (Idaho Falls newspaper)—
www.idahonews.com/

Idaho Falls Chamber of Commerce—
www.idahofallschamber.com

Island Park area information—
www.westyellowstonenet.com

Yellowstone National Park—
www.nps.gov/yell/

Worth Seeing

Idaho Falls Aquatic Center

The TRAC at Sandy Downs—*Idaho Falls*

Idaho's Vietnam Veterans Memorial—*Idaho Falls*

Kelly Canyon Ski Area—*east of Heise*

Hess Heritage Museum—*near Ashton*

O'Brady's (American),
1438 West Broadway,
(208) 523–2132

The Sandpiper
(steaks/seafood),
750 Lindsay Bouelvard,
(208) 524–3344

The Snake Bite (eclectic),
425 River Parkway,
(208) 525–2522

Most major fast-food
chains, mainly along East
Seventeenth Street, West
Broadway, and North
Yellowstone Highway.

SWAN VALLEY
South Fork Lodge
(American),
Highway 26,
(208) 483–2229

VICTOR
Knotty Pine (American),
58 South Main,
(208) 787–2866

DRIGGS
Inn Lost Horizon
(Japanese/Chinese), in
Alta, Wyoming,
(307) 353–8226 (see text)

The Royal Wolf (American),
65 Depot Street,
(208) 354–8365

REXBURG
Burger King (fast food),
1874 West 1500 South,
(208) 356–5128

Frontier Pies,
460 West 4 South,
(208) 356–3600

McDonald's (fast food),
175 East 350 North,
(208) 356–0060

Me n' Stan's (American),
West Main and South
Second Street West,
(208) 356–7330

ST. ANTHONY
The Relay Station
(American), 593 North
2600 East, (208) 624–4640

ASHTON
Frostop Drive-In
(fast food), 26 North
Highway 20,
(208) 652–7762

Trails Inn Restaurant
(American), 213 Main,
(208) 652–9918

ISLAND PARK
Chalet Restaurant
(American), Highway 26,
(208) 558–9953

Island Park Restaurant &
Saloon (American),
Highway 26,
(208) 558–7281

DUBOIS
Charlie's R&R
(American),
(208) 374–5504 (see text)

Central Idaho

W hen people think of Idaho, they think of mountains, wildlife, and white water. For many residents and visitors, Central Idaho—blessed with all these natural treasures and more—is the region that most epitomizes the Gem State.

Few highways traverse Central Idaho; those that do are separated and isolated by mountain ranges. We'll explore this region in a counter-clockwise fashion, starting on State Highway 28 north from the ghost town of Gilmore to Salmon and environs. From Salmon, we'll head south on U.S. Highway 93, offer a few suggestions for sights in the Lost River Valley, then pick up Highway 75 for its trip to the Sawtooth National Recreation Area and Sun Valley. We'll finish by crossing the high desert on U.S. Highway 20.

For more Central Idaho travel information, call (800) 634–3347 or write the Central Idaho Rockies Association, P.O. Box 2420, Sun Valley 83353.

Lemhi River Valley

S tate Highway 28 is also known as the *Sacagawea Memorial High-way*—so named because the Lemhi River Valley, which Highway 28 parallels from the town of Leadore north to Salmon, was the birth-place of one of America's greatest heroines, Sacagawea. (Scholars say this is the correct spelling, even though many people prefer "Sacajawea.") This Shoshone Indian woman was an invaluable asset to the Lewis and Clark Expedition nearly two centuries ago, as we shall see.

Central Idaho was the site of a major mining boom in the late nineteenth and early twentieth centuries, and the ghost town of *Gilmore* stands in mute testimony to those days. To get there watch for the historical marker telling of Gilmore near milepost 73, then take the road west immediately across the highway. Gilmore sat about a mile and a half west over a gravel, washboarded road, and its two dozen or so remaining buildings come into view almost immediately. ENJOY BUT DO NOT DESTROY, weathered signs warn the visitor. Look for the remnants of an old railroad bed. This was

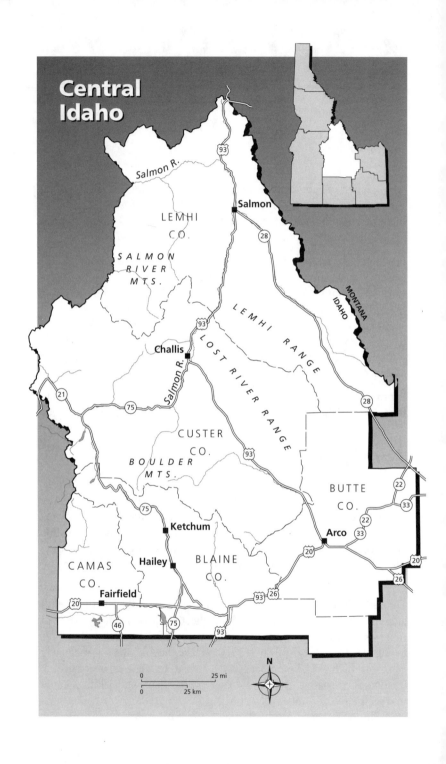

the Gilmore and Pittsburgh Railway—a branch railroad from Montana—which helped Gilmore's mines produce more than $11.5 million in silver and lead before a power plant explosion ended operations in 1929.

A most rewarding side trip is possible from Highway 28 to **Lemhi Pass,** where Meriwether Lewis became the first white American to cross the Continental Divide in August 1805. Traveling ahead of the rest of the Lewis and Clark expedition, Captain Lewis was searching for the Shoshone Indians in hopes they could provide horses to help the Corps of Discovery travel overland. On August 12, Lewis's party moved west into the mountains from what is now Montana's Clark Canyon Reservoir, following what Lewis called a "large and plain Indian road ... I therefore did not despair of shortly finding a passage over the mountains and of tasting the waters of the great Columbia this evening." Soon after, Lewis and his men reached a stream that he dubbed "the most distant fountain of the mighty Missouri in search of which we have spent so many toilsome days and restless nights." After pausing for a drink from the stream, Lewis and his men continued to the top of the ridge, where Lewis later wrote he saw "immense ranges of high mountains still to the west of us with their tops partially covered with snow." It was a point of reckoning for the expedition. Lewis had crossed the divide, but the sight of those mountains meant there would be no easy passage to the Columbia.

The day after reaching Lemhi Pass, Lewis and his party came upon several Shoshones, who led the whites to their chief, Cameahwait. Lewis convinced the chief to accompany him back over the pass, where Clark and the rest were waiting with their baggage. It was to be a most extraordinary meeting, for it turned out that Cameahwait was the long-lost brother of Sacagawea, the Shoshone woman who—together with her husband Charbonneau and their infant son—had accompanied the Corps of Discovery after their winter stay in the Mandan Villages of North Dakota. Because of this family coincidence, the expedition was able to get the horses it needed.

To visit Lemhi Pass turn east at the small settlement of Tendoy. The steep and winding 26-mile loop drive to the pass isn't recommended for large RVs or vehicles towing trailers, but most pickup trucks and passenger vehicles in good shape will make it with no problem. (The Montana approach to the pass is much less steep; apparently a busload of Lewis and Clark buffs made it to the top that way.) Face west at the pass to see the ridge upon ridge of mountains Lewis described. At 7,373 feet, Lemhi Pass is the highest point on the Lewis and Clark Trail and one of the most pristine, too. It's a great place to watch a sunset, and should you decide to stay the night, the small and primitive Sacagawea Memorial Campground is close at hand. Another campground sits 7.5 miles from the summit on the Agency Creek Road. Agency Creek, run by the Bureau of Land Management, has a vault toilet and picnic tables. Before returning to the highway, note the grave of Chief Tendoy, an Indian leader who commanded respect and influence. The burial site is sacred to Indians, and visitation by the general public is not considered appropriate. The small store at Tendoy sells gas and food; it's another 20 miles north to Salmon, where all services are available.

River of No Return

Even though it has just one stoplight, the Lemhi County seat of Salmon is one of Idaho's busiest recreation gateways. This is the outfitting spot for many trips on the Main Salmon, Idaho's "River of No Return." Many raft excursions run several days, but if time is limited, *Kookaburra Guided Whitewater Trips* offers a full-day trip for $85 per person, including a tasty lunch. Call (888) 654–4386 or see Kookaburra's Web site at www.raft4fun.com.

Salmon salutes the area's most famous native daughter at the new Sacajawea Center, which opened in 2002 on the outskirts of town. The center, being developed in several phases, has interpretive exhibits and trails on the Lewis and Clark Expedition and Lemhi Shoshone tribal culture. For up-to-date information on visiting the center, call Salmon City Hall at (208) 756–3214 or the Salmon Valley Chamber of Commerce at (208) 756–2100.

The *North Fork Cafe,* at the little town of the same name on U.S. Highway 93, is the restaurant of choice among hungry Idaho river runners, anglers, and hunters. Breakfast offerings include eggs topped with homemade chili, plate-size pancakes, and corned beef hash and eggs. At lunchtime, guests chow down on a variety of sandwiches. Steaks, fish, chicken, and hickory-smoked barbecued ribs are among the dinner offerings, and don't forget the huckleberry pie—it's among the best in the state, although it's not available all the time. The North Fork Cafe is open from 6:30 A.M. to 10:00 P.M. in the summer and 7:00 A.M. to 8:00 P.M. daily except Tuesday during the winter. It's also closed the entire months of January and February. The phone number is (208) 865–2412.

CENTRAL IDAHO

TOP ANNUAL EVENTS

Sun Valley Ice Show (mid-June through September)

Sawtooth Mountain Mamas Arts and Crafts Fair, Stanley (mid-July)

Sun Valley Symphony (late July-early August)

Sacajawea Heritage Days, Salmon, (mid-August)

Wagon Days, Ketchum (Labor Day weekend)

Swing 'n' Dixie Jazz Jamboree, Sun Valley (mid-October)

Even if you're not planning a river trip on the Main Salmon from North Fork, you may want to drive the river road a ways anyhow. The road is paved for about 16 miles, then it's a good packed gravel byway. There's a small settlement at Shoup, which until just a few years ago had the last hand-cranked telephone system in the United States. Another 2 miles west, the Class III+ to IV *Pine Creek Rapids* are the highlight of most short river trips on this stretch of river. William Clark, making a reconnaissance trip in the area in August 1805, saw these rapids from a nearby bluff. The wild river, coupled with the canyon's sheer rock cliffs, convinced Clark he and Lewis would need to find a safer route west.

West of Pine Creek Rapids, a wayside has been built at the **Shoup Rock Shelter,** a site dating from perhaps 8,000 years ago. Pictographs can be seen here. The North Fork Road ends at River Mile 46, where the Corn Creek boat ramp marks the start of the Salmon's federally designated Wild and Scenic stretch. Permits are required to float the 79-mile section from here to Long Tom Bar. Near the put-in, *Salmon River Lodge* offers everything from drop-in meals to guided hunting, floating, fishing, and pack trips. Guests enjoy private quarters and bathrooms in a dormitory-style facility, and three home-style meals are served each day. Room rates are $61 to $88, and meals are extra. If you're just stopping in for a meal, ring the lodge on the old crank phone across the river, and they'll send the jet boat over to pick you up. For lodging reservations or more information, call (800) 635–4717; write Salmon River Lodge, P.O. Box 927, Salmon 83467; or see www.wildidaho.net.

South of Salmon on U.S. Highway 93, two notable Western-style resorts have lately come under the same management. Near the road, *Twin Peaks Ranch* ranks among the oldest dude ranches in the United States. Guests who have never been on horseback can learn to ride in the rodeo arena before setting off on gentle trails, while more experienced riders have the option of traveling high into the Idaho Rockies. Several stocked ponds provide challenge to anglers, and guided trips are offered to seldom-fished private streams. Twin Peaks also offers scenic and white-water floats on the Salmon River, as well as guided hunts for elk and deer. Twin Peaks caters to one-week stays, priced at $1,529 to $1,829 in summer, with reduced rates for children and for off-season stays. For more information call (800) 659–4899; write Twin Peaks Ranch, P.O. Box

774, Salmon 83467; or see www.twinpeaksranch.com. Twin Peaks also runs nearby **Williams Lake Lodge,** where the "Northern Rockies Outpost Vacation" includes riding, fishing, rafting, and a cattle roundup. For information call (877) 756–2007 or write Williams Lake Lodge, P.O. Box 1230, Salmon 83467.

Back on Highway 93, the **Greyhouse Inn Bed and Breakfast** is 12 miles south of Salmon. This beautiful Victorian building was once a hospital in Salmon and was trucked to its current location in the early 1970s. Proprietors Sharon and David Osgood offer four guest rooms in the main house, two with private baths. Or ask about more private accommodations in the Carriage House or Lewis and Clark cabins. The Osgoods provide a full breakfast to get guests primed for a day of hiking, hunting, floating, or fishing. Have them give you directions to Goldbug Hot Springs (sometimes called Elk Bend Hot Springs), on Warm Springs Creek about 11 miles away. It's one of the finest hot springs in Idaho. Rates at the Greyhouse are $70 to $90 a night. For current information call (800) 348–8097; write the Greyhouse Inn, HC-61 Box 16, Salmon 83467; or see www.greyhouseinn.com.

For lodgings of a different sort, check out the **Dugout Ranch,** homestead of Richard "Dugout Dick" Zimmerman. Dugout Dick has been on this piece of land 19 miles south of Salmon since 1948, and he says he helped put in the road and the bridge over the Salmon River. But it

Williams Lake Lodge

wasn't until 1969 that he started digging caves and multiroom tunnels out of the hillside. He now has about a dozen, and yes, they are available for rent at a cost of $10.00 to $35.00 a month or $2.00 to $5.00 a night. Rooms are outfitted with a woodstove and a bed, although visitors should bring their own sleeping bags.

Dugout Dick's accommodations are certainly spartan and not to everyone's taste, but a handful of people—including a couple from Idaho Falls and a teacher from Missoula—find the caves so cozy they consistently spend their weekends at the Dugout Ranch. One of Idaho's true characters, Dugout Dick has been featured on National Public Radio, in *National Geographic* magazine, and in several books. He'll be glad to tell you a few tales, too. If you stop by the ranch and find it deserted, don't worry—Dick is probably just out on his grocery run to Salmon. Have a look around, and he'll be back before you know it.

At Ellis—little more than a post office on Highway 93—the Pashimeroi River meets the Salmon. About 12 miles farther along the highway, watch for a ranch bearing a large TNT brand. No, this isn't the home of Ted Turner, but of Aly and Nancy Bruner, their daughters Taryn and Tawnie, and anyone else who happens along to stay at the family's *Rainbow's End Bed & Breakfast.*

Travelers truly are apt to think they've found the proverbial pot of gold here. The four-bedroom guest house can be rented by the room (starting at $225 per night) or in its entirety (for $1,000). Ask about discounted rates late November through early June. In summer, visitors can pick fat raspberries, catch trophy-size rainbow trout from a stocked pond, or relax in a lovely gazebo overlooking the Salmon River. (Bruner says the cast-iron gazebo, built in 1850, once belonged to President Ulysses Grant.) In fall, guests use the home as a base camp for elk-hunting expeditions into the nearby Salmon River Mountains and Lost River Range. In spring, the Bruners' place fronts one of the hottest steelhead fishing holes in Idaho.

Don't leave Rainbow's End without seeing some of the bronze sculptures created by Aly Bruner (who signs the works with his *nom de clay,* "*A. Matthews*"). Inspired by his childhood in multiracial North Carolina and by the works of French artist Louis Hottot, Aly has sculpted a series called "The Evolution of Jazz." His art has won numerous awards and can be seen at the Mad Dog Gallery in Challis and the Trails West Gallery in Ketchum. For more information on Rainbow's End or A. Matthews's artwork, call (208) 879–5999; write P.O. Box 1146, Challis 83226; or see the Web site at www. rainbowsendbb.com.

Seven miles farther down the highway in Challis, locals like to eat at **Antonio's Pizza and Pasta** at Fifth and Main uptown. Every Friday, Antonio's offers an all-you-can-eat soup, salad, and pizza bar from 11:00 A.M. to 3:00 P.M. for $4.25. The wide-ranging menu also includes calzones, sandwiches and burgers, and about a dozen dinner entrees. You won't leave hungry. Antonio's is open from 11:00 A.M. to 10:00 P.M. Monday through Thursday, 11:00 A.M. to 11:00 P.M. Friday and Saturday, and noon to 10:00 P.M. Sunday with somewhat reduced hours in winter. The phone number is (208) 879–2210. Just across the street, a little spot called **Cafe.com** serves a standard menu at breakfast and Mexican cuisine later in the day. It, too, is packed at lunchtime, and as the name implies, diners can surf the Internet after grabbing a bite.

At Challis, travelers need to choose between taking Highway 93 south to Arco or hopping off on Highway 75, which continues along the Salmon River. Either way, the scenery is glorious.

Highway 93 streaks south through the Lost River Valley. Fourteen miles southeast of Challis at about mile post 150, the road bisects **Grand View Canyon,** a short but impressive gorge forged about 350 million

The Borah Earthquake

*O*n the morning of October 28, 1983, an **earthquake** measuring 7.3 on the Richter scale rocked Idaho's Lost River region. This temblor was the strongest in the continental United States in a quarter-century, and it proved more powerful than the two high-profile California earthquakes in 1989 and 1994, which combined killed 123 people. But because Central Idaho is so sparsely populated, the damage was correspondingly less, though not insignificant: Two children were killed in Challis, and area residents lost property valued in the millions.

Geologically, the quake made its mark, too. A side road from Highway 93 leads to a viewing area where it's easy to see the scarp left in the quake's wake, 21 miles long and 10 to 14 feet high. This rock ledge at the base of the Lost River Range stands in raw testimony to the temblor.

Mount Borah gained 2 feet in elevation during the 1983 quake, which means it now stands at 12,662 feet. The mountain, earlier christened Beauty Peak, was renamed in 1933 for William Borah, the "Lion of Idaho," who served in the U.S. Senate from 1907 to 1940. Experienced mountaineers say Borah Peak can be climbed up and back in a day, but trekkers need to be well prepared mentally and physically for the strenuous, if not technical, ascent. Check with the Forest Service office on Custer Street in Mackay for more information—and to let them know of your plans. For more information call (208) 588–2224.

years ago. Another 20 miles south, plan a stop at the **Mount Borah interpretive area** to marvel at Idaho's highest mountain and learn about the 1983 earthquake that struck this area (see sidebar).

South of Mount Borah, watch for the Trail Creek Road sign and turn right for a "shortcut" to Sun Valley. Trail Creek Road (Forest Road 208) is open in the summer months and accessible to passenger vehicles, although the westernmost section descending into Wood River Valley is steep and rocky. It's a good idea to inquire locally or check with the Forest Service in Ketchum (208–622–5371) to assess road conditions.

Halfway to Sun Valley along Trail Creek Road, Forest Road 135 heads south from the byway toward **Wild Horse Creek Ranch,** another classic Idaho guest ranch now under new management. Year-round, the ranch offers a luxurious base camp for mountain activities ranging from fishing and hiking to cross-country skiing and snowmobiling. Ten guest rooms rent for between $100 and $125 a night, double occupancy, including breakfast. Kids can camp out in tepees if they like. Wild Horse Creek also can set you up with everything from a two-hour trail ride to an extended big-game hunt. For more information call (208) 588–2575 or write Wild Horse Creek Ranch, P.O. Box 398, Mackay 83251. Past the Wild Horse Creek turnoff, Forest Road 135 follows the East Fork of the Big Lost River to Copper Basin, spectacularly situated between the Pioneer Mountains and the White Knob Mountains.

Back on Highway 93, it's 26 miles from Mackay to Arco. But we'll now return our attention to Highway 75. Just as Highway 93 did north of Challis, Highway 75 hugs the Salmon River tightly here, making for slow but stupendously scenic driving. It's easy to spend an entire day lingering here and there along the 55-mile drive from Challis to Stanley. Interesting stopping spots along the way include **Torrey's Resort and RV Park,** which offers good food and cozy cabins at a popular float trip takeout west of Clayton, and the **Sunbeam area** with its history and hot springs.

To many Idahoans unable to take lengthy and often expensive river trips down the Main or Middle forks of the Salmon River, a day float down this stretch of the Salmon is a minivacation and a whole lot of fun. Quite a few excursions leave from Sunbeam Village, including those offered by **White Otter Outdoor Adventures.** Whether you want lots of whitewater rapids or a calm scenic float, the Salmon delivers. Fun-seekers have their choice of oar boats, where the guide does all the work; paddle rafts, in which floaters help propel the boat downriver; and one-person inflatable kayaks that can be maneuvered by just about anyone fourteen or older. Cost for a half-day float with snack (including taxes) is $64 per teen or adult and $53 for kids; full-day trips including a deluxe meal run $83 for adults and teens, $73 for the small fry. Children must be at least four years old—eight in high-water season—to go floating. Call (208) 726–4331 for reservations or more information. (Note: In attempts to protect salmon-spawning areas, Sawtooth National Recreation Area officials occasionally close this part of the river to boating. So check with outfitters or the SNRA at 208–727–5013.)

Several accessible hot springs are located along Highway 75 west of Sunbeam. East to west there's the very visible *Sunbeam Hot Springs,* complete with bathhouse; *Basin Creek Hot Spring,* located near a campground of the same name; *Campground Hot Spring,* actually located in the Basin Creek Campground (walk into the bushes at Site 4); *Mormon Bend Hot Spring,* good for late-summer soaking (since a river crossing is necessary); and *Elkhorn Hot Spring.* Although these springs are all located near the highway, soakers are apt to feel a million miles away as they lean back and gaze at the blue sky above.

The Stanley Basin

I f the Tetons are the West's most magnificent mountain range, Idaho's Sawtooths run a close second. Stanley, situated at the Highway 75–Highway 21 intersection, is the hub of Sawtooth country—in fact, it's the only place in the United States where three National Forest Scenic Byways converge. In summer there's camping, fishing, and boating on the Salmon River and at Redfish Lake, and there are hikes high into the mountains and adjacent wilderness areas. But for many people winter is prime time in the Stanley Basin because that's when snowmobiling season starts. The area has more than 200 miles of groomed trails and outfitters poised to help visitors with everything from snow machine rental to lodging and meals.

For example, *Sawtooth Rentals* charges $100 to $160 per day for a snow-mobile; expert guides, snowsuits, boots, helmets, and gloves are available for rent, too. The company also has its own motel, with rooms starting at about $55. For more information call (208) 774–3409.

Stanley is the departure point for most trips on the *Middle Fork of the Salmon River,* which many people regard among the world's premier white-water trips. The classic Middle Fork trip covers 105 miles of river over six days, with prices starting at about $1,500 per person. Many outfitters run the Main Salmon; for help in choosing and booking a trip, consider *Idaho Whitewater Connection.* Run by Greg Edson, a longtime river guide and past president of the Idaho Outfitters and Guides Association, and his wife Lori, IWC matches would-be river-runners with top outfitters working the Middle Fork, Main Salmon, Snake, and Selway rivers. IWC also arranges chartered trips for large groups such as family reunions. For more information call (208) 733–1921 or see www. idahorafting.com.

The *Idaho Rocky Mountain Ranch* south of Stanley ranks among the Gem State's most renowned guest ranches. Built in the 1930s, the ranch offers plenty of activities, although it sometimes seems visitors are happiest just relaxing on the huge front porch of the central lodge, with its view of the Sawtooth Mountains. Other on-site diversions include a hot springs swimming pool, horseback riding, horseshoes, volleyball, fishing, and wildlife viewing. Hiking, mountain biking, rafting, and rock climbing are available nearby as well.

Idaho Rocky Mountain Ranch has seventeen cabin accommodations and four lodge rooms, all with private baths. Breakfast and dinner are served daily, with four or five entrees featured nightly—a typical selection might include fresh Idaho trout, steaks, lamb, and pasta, along with homemade breads and desserts. Rates range from $105 to $135 per person per night, double occupancy, including breakfast and dinner, with lower per-night rates for longer stays. (A three-night minimum typically applies.) For more information, including updated prices, or for reservations, call (208) 774–3544 or write Idaho Rocky Mountain Ranch, HC 64, Box 9934, Stanley 83278.

Stop at the *Galena Summit overlook* for another great view of the Sawtooth Mountains and the headwaters of the Salmon River. It's hard to believe this tiny trickle of a stream becomes the raging River of No Return, the longest river flowing within one state in the continental United States. Some of Idaho's best telemark skiing can be found on the Stanley Basin (or Humble Pie) side of Galena. Gentler terrain is available in the vicinity of *Galena Lodge,* situated at the base of the mountain on the Sun Valley side. The lodge features hearty food along with ski rentals, lessons, and overnight ski-hut accommodations. From Galena Summit it's about a half-hour drive to the Sun Valley–Ketchum area.

Wood River Valley

The Wood River Valley is more famously known as Sun Valley–Ketchum, site of America's first destination ski resort. In 1935 Union Pacific chief Averell Harriman dispatched Count Felix Schaffgotsch to find the perfect setting for a European-style ski haunt. After scouring the West, the count finally found what he was looking for near the scruffy Idaho mining town of Ketchum. Ironically, when the Sun Valley resort opened in 1936, there was barely enough snow to cover the slopes. But today, Sun Valley has state-of-the-art snowmaking capabilities, and it's widely considered one of the best ski areas in North America.

Skiing is the big draw here, of course, but there are other reasons to visit, too. Eating is another favorite pastime in the Wood River Valley; without a doubt, the area is home to some of the state's best and most creative restaurants. The dining scene seems in a state of constant evolution, but a few perennial favorites include the upscale *Evergreen Bistro,* the casual *Pioneer Saloon,* and *Whiskey Jacques',* which features raucous live entertainment in addition to its menu of pizza, sandwiches, and salads.

But not all fine dining is done indoors. *A Winter's Feast* offers five-course gourmet dinners served by candlelight in two yurts: one from Mongolia and another from the Northwest. The experience is available December through April, with one seating per evening. Guests arrive at the yurt either by sleigh ride (at a cost of about $12 per person) or under their own power on snowshoes or cross-country skis. Once there, diners are likely to see elk and even an occasional mountain lion.

Colleen Crain, chef and owner of A Winter's Feast, develops several menus each season. A typical repast might include grilled shrimp with fireworks sauce, pumpkin seed ravioli drizzled with basil oil, romaine and maytag bleu cheese salad with fresh vinaigrette, whole-roasted beef tenderloin wrapped in caramelized onions, Idaho potato gratin with white wine and herbs, fresh grilled vegetables, and Linzer torte with crème anglaise. The menu changes yearly, so call for the current selections. The cost is about $60 per person, plus gratuity. Homemade breads, coffee, tea, and hot apple cider are provided, but wine is extra. Advance reservations are required; call (208) 788–7665.

In the summertime Sun Valley offers a wide selection of special events. The *Sun Valley Summer Symphony,* the largest free admission symphony in the Rockies, features concerts in a tent on the Sun Valley lawn and various other venues from late July to mid-August. Call (208) 622–5607 for performance dates and programs. But probably no local summer attraction is as unique as the *Sun Valley Ice Show.* The biggest stars in figure skating—Katarina Witt, Nancy Kerrigan, Brian Boitano, and Ilia Kulik, to name a few—appear each summer. General admission tickets run about $25 for adults and $20 for children under age thirteen; dinner buffet tickets also are available. Contact the Sun Valley Sports Center at (208) 622–2231 for more information.

Of course, Sun Valley is an excellent base from which to explore the neighboring Pioneer, Boulder, Smoky, Sawtooth, and White Cloud mountains. *Venture Outdoors,* a Wood River Valley-based outfitter, offers a variety of guided adventures ranging from its half-day "Take a Llama to Lunch" trek (priced at $85 per person) to multiday llama packing and mountain biking trips. Venture Outdoors also leads sea kayaking expeditions to locales as close as Magic Reservoir and as far flung as Baja California. For more information, see www.ventureout doorsidaho.com; call (800) 528–LAMA; or write Venture Outdoors, P.O. Box 2251, Hailey 83333.

Ernest Hemingway spent part of his last years in Ketchum, and fans of his writing will find several local spots worth a stop. First there's the *Hemingway Memorial* located along Trail Creek east of town; take Sun Valley Road east from the stoplight in downtown Ketchum, and watch for the sign on your right. A short path leads to a memorial as spare as Papa's prose, topped by a rugged bust of the author and embellished by this passage Hemingway wrote in 1939 while in Idaho:

> Best of all he loved the fall
> the leaves yellow on the cottonwoods
> leaves floating on the trout streams
> and above the hills
> the high blue windless skies
> ... now he will be part of them forever.

Hemingway first came to Idaho in 1939 and visited many times over the next two decades. In 1959 he and his wife Mary finally bought a home in Ketchum, but by 1961, apparently depressed over his failing health, he was dead, the victim of a self-inflicted shotgun blast. He is buried in the Ketchum Cemetery, located just north of the downtown area. Look for two pine trees growing closely together near the rear of the graveyard; there you'll find the plots of Ernest Miller Hemingway and his last wife, Mary. Like Jim Morrison's grave in Paris, Hemingway's burial site sometimes attracts people who want to spend some time with the writer's spirit. On one visit this author had been preceded by a pilgrim who had left behind a pack of Dutch Masters little cigars— three left out of the box as if in homage—and an empty bottle of Maker's Mark Whisky.

For more local history, check out the recently expanded *Ketchum-Sun Valley Heritage and Ski Museum.* Located in the former Civilian

Conservation Corps-built Forest Service complex at 180 First Street East in Ketchum, the museum has a great collection of early ski gear and pioneer memorabilia. Hours are 11:00 A.M. to 4:00 P.M. Monday through Friday and 1:00 to 4:00 P.M. on Saturday, with admission by donation. Call (208) 726–8118 for more information.

Sun Valley and Ketchum are full of interesting places to stay. If you'd like to sleep where Hemingway did, you can either go deluxe at the venerable **Sun Valley Lodge** or sleep cheap (for Sun Valley, anyway) at the **Ketchum Korral Motor Lodge.** The area also has several notable B&Bs, including the European-style **Knob Hill Inn.** A Relais & Chateaux-affiliated inn, the Knob Hill has twenty-four guest suites and rooms, each with a balcony and mountain views. The location is good, just a short stroll from downtown Ketchum. Rates run $195 for a king room, $250 for a fireplace room, $310 for a suite, and $385 for a penthouse suite; all include a buffet-style breakfast. For more information, see www.knobhillinn.com; write P.O. Box 800, Ketchum 83340; or call (800) 526–8010.

Preserving the Past

*H*eroes, rogues, scoundrels, and saints . . . they're all well represented at the **Blaine County Historical Museum,** located at Main and Galena Streets in Hailey. This is the repository for the Joe Fuld Political Button Collection, among the largest of its type in the world. Fuld was an early Hailey businessman who started collecting political memorabilia in the late nineteenth century and wound up with more than 5,000 items of campaign souvenirs, not just buttons but handkerchiefs, pencils, posters, an ashtray used by Teddy Roosevelt, even the inaugural ball program from 1881.

The museum also has a corner devoted to **Ezra Pound,** the iconoclastic writer born in Hailey in 1885. Pound's parents left Idaho when Ezra was only fifteen months old, but the poet seemed ever after to consider himself an Idahoan. Perhaps he felt the state's outpost image was one well suited to his own renegade reputation. Pound went on to pen thousands of poems (including the epic Cantos series), but he outraged many when he embraced fascism and started making anti-American broadcasts from Europe during World War II. Pound later renounced totalitarianism, and he is now best remembered as a champion of other writers, including T. S. Eliot and Ernest Hemingway.

The Blaine County Historical Museum is open from 11:00 A.M. to 5:00 P.M. Monday through Saturday (except Tuesday, when it's closed) and 1:00 to 5:00 P.M. Sunday Memorial Day weekend through September. Admission is by donation. Tours also can be arranged for groups of five or more October through May by calling (208) 788–2700 one day in advance.

Hailey and Bellevue, the two "lower valley" towns, are much less known than Ketchum and Sun Valley. That's not saying they lack in glitz, however: Actors Bruce Willis and Demi Moore may no longer be a couple, but both still live in the area and have several business holdings in town. Both also are on the board of *Company of Fools*, an up-and-coming theatrical troupe that presents most of its performances in Hailey at the Liberty Theatre. Willis has even appeared onstage in the company's productions of Sam Shepard's *Fool for Love* and *True West*. Company of Fools is the only Idaho theater with "constituent" status from Theatre Communications Group, which puts it in the same league with such top playhouses as the Guthrie in Minneapolis, Lincoln Center Theater in New York, and the Seattle Rep. For tickets or information on upcoming shows, call (208) 788–6520 or see the Web site at www.companyoffools.org.

Two blocks west of the stoplight on Hailey's Main Street, the *Povey Pensione* offers three bed-and-breakfast rooms with private baths. The inn is run by Sam and Terrie Davis, who rebuilt from the ground up a home originally constructed by John Povey, a carpenter from Liverpool, England. A full, hot breakfast is served each morning, with fresh fruit and muffins typically accompanying an egg casserole, French toast, or apple-stuffed German pancakes. Rates at Povey Pensione are $75 to $90 for two people, which includes breakfast. The inn is considered unsuitable for children under twelve, and smoking is permitted outdoors only. For reservations call (208) 788–4682; write Povey Pensione, P.O. Box 1134, Hailey 83333; or see www.poveypensione.com.

Camas Lilies and Lava Beds

South of Bellevue more vehicles topped with ski racks travel the intersection of Idaho Highway 75 and U.S. Highway 20 than any other in Idaho. Most are heading north to Sun Valley, of course, but a growing number are destined for *Soldier Mountain* near Fairfield. Lift tickets at Soldier Mountain cost less than half what they do at Sun Valley, so it's a good family bargain. The skiing's not bad, either, with three dozen runs and 1,400 feet of vertical drop. Soldier also offers snowcat skiing. For more information on current hours and prices, call (208) 764–2526.

Named for a fire lookout on the westernmost peak of the Soldier Mountain Range, the *Iron Mountain Inn* at 325 West Highway 20 in Fairfield specializes in charbroiled steaks and prime rib. The latter is served Friday and Saturday nights for $11.95 for eight ounces and $14.95 for twelve ounces. The Iron Mountain Inn is open from 11:00 A.M. to 10:00

P.M. weekdays and 8:00 A.M. to 10:00 P.M. weekends. There's an RV park on the premises, too. The phone number is (208) 764–2577.

This part of Central Idaho is known as the Camas Prairie for the beautiful blue flowers that were such an important food source for the Indians. (Yes, part of North Central Idaho near the Nez Perce reservation is known as the Camas Prairie, too.) The week before Memorial Day is generally the best time to see the flowers in midbloom; they're at their best the spring after a wet winter.

North of Fairfield the **Soldier Mountain Ranch** resort offers golf, fishing, tennis, swimming, and horseback riding in the summer and cross-country skiing and snowmobiling come winter. Couples seeking a romantic weekend should ask about the honeymoon suite in the main lodge, featuring a fireplace, sunken tub with mirrors all around it, and a European-style tiled bathroom boasting an oversized shower with two showerheads, all for $75 a night. The resort also has ten two-bedroom cabins that sleep four to six people renting for $145 a night, another cabin that can sleep twelve people for $200 a night, and a lodge suited to parties for up to seventy-five guests. The cabins are equipped with kitchens and fireplaces. Call (208) 764–2506 for more information or reservations.

East of the Highway 75/20 junction, drivers soon spy **Silver Creek,** a fly-fishing dream stream. This was Hemingway's favorite fishing hole, and avid anglers say it's one of the best anywhere in the world, period. The Nature Conservancy protects part of Silver Creek with a wonderful preserve that also features a short nature trail. Silver Creek runs close to the little ranching town of Picabo, which some lexicologists say is Indian for "silver water." If the town's name—pronounced like the children's game—sounds familiar, it's probably because Picabo's namesake is Picabo Street, the champion Olympic and World Cup skier who grew up plying the slopes at Sun Valley. Picabo actually grew up in another tiny Wood River Valley town, Triumph, and somehow that town's name seems apt for her, too.

U.S. Highways 20 and 26 come together at Carey. From here, it's 25 miles east to **Craters of the Moon National Monument.** From Native Americans to early white explorers to the Apollo astronauts, people long have been fascinated with the strange landscapes of this region. Indians probably never lived on the harsh lava lands, but artifacts found in the area show they visited, probably to hunt and gather tachylite—a kind of basaltic volcanic glass—for arrow points. In the early twentieth century, Boisean Robert Limbert extensively explored the lava flows; it was his work and an article he penned in *National Geographic* that led to

Craters of the Moon being named a national monument in 1924. In 1969 a group of Apollo astronauts preparing to go to the moon first visited Craters to get a feel for what the lunar landscape might be like.

The same experiences are available today. Though Craters has a popular 7-mile loop drive offering opportunities for several short hikes, it also has a surprisingly accessible designated wilderness area that receives much less use than the rest of the monument. The best time to visit is in the spring, when delicate wildflowers cover the black rock, or in fall after the often-extreme heat of the desert summer abates. In winter the loop road is closed to vehicular traffic but may be enjoyed by cross-country skiers or on snowshoes.

There are two predominant types of lava at Craters: the jagged aa (pronounced "ah-ah," Hawaiian for "hard on the feet") and the smoother pahoehoe (also Hawaiian, meaning "ropey" and pronounced "pa-hoy-hoy"). Both may be seen on the North Crater Flow loop trail, a good introduction to the monument's geology. Also consider an overnight stay in Craters's campground; the sites set amid the lava make an absolutely perfect setting for telling ghost stories (although you'll have to do so without a campfire; no wood fires are permitted, since the only available trees are the ancient and slow-growing limber pines). Craters of the Moon National Monument is 18 miles west of Arco. Admission is $5.00 per vehicle (or with a Golden Age, Golden Access, or Golden Eagle passport). For more information call (208) 527–3257 or see www.nps.gov/crmo.

The Arco area has lately staked a claim as one of the West's best *hang-gliding* sites. Most of the action takes place off nearby King Mountain due east of the tiny settlement of Moore, 8 miles north of Arco on U.S. Highway 93. For more information on hang-gliding and paragliding opportunities, pick up the King Mountain brochure, available at the Arco visitor center, 132 West Grand Avenue.

The lava lands surrounding Arco and Craters of the Moon are but a small part of the huge Great Rift section of Idaho, which covers nearly 170,000 acres across the eastern Snake River Plain. For a view of the whole expanse, try a hike or drive up *Big Southern Butte,* the 300,000-year-old monolith towering 2,500 feet above the surrounding landscape. To get to the butte, follow the signs west from Atomic City. The dirt road up Big Southern Butte is steep, with a 2,000-foot elevation gain and some 15+ percent grades. It's a challenging hike but one that can be accomplished in a long day's excursion or relatively easy overnight trip. The winds can be fierce atop the butte, but hardy, early-waking campers may be rewarded with a view of the Teton Range against the rising sun.

**PLACES TO STAY
IN CENTRAL IDAHO**

NORTH FORK
North Fork Motel,
Highway 93,
(208) 865–2412

One Hundred Acre Wood
Bed & Breakfast, north of
town on Highway 93,
(208) 865–2165

River's Fork Inn,
Highway 93,
(208) 865–2301

SHOUP
Salmon River Lodge,
30 miles west at
Corn Creek,
(800) 635–4717 (see text)

Smith House Bed &
Breakfast, Salmon River
Road, (800) 238–5915

SALMON
Greyhouse Inn Bed &
Breakfast, 12 miles south
on Highway 93,
(800) 348–8097 (see text)

Twin Peaks Ranch,
south on Highway 93,
(800) 659–4899,
fax: (208) 894–2429
(see text)

Wagons West Motel,
503 Highway 93 North,
(800) 756–4281, fax:
(208) 756–6575

Williams Lake Lodge,
south of Salmon,
(208) 756–2007

CHALLIS
Northgate Inn,
Highway 93,
(208) 879–2490

Rainbow's End Bed
& Breakfast, 7 miles north
on Highway 93,
(208) 879–5999,
fax: (208) 879–5998
(see text)

MACKAY
Bear Bottom Inn,
411 West Spruce Street,
(208) 588–2483

Wild Horse Creek Ranch,
20 miles west off
of Trail Creek Road,
phone/fax: (208) 588–2575
(see text)

STANLEY
Idaho Rocky Mountain
Ranch, south on Highway
75, (208) 774–3544,
fax: (208) 774–3477
(see text)

Mountain Village Resort,
Highways 21 and 75,
(800) 843–5475,
fax: (208) 774–3761

SUN VALLEY/KETCHUM
Best Western Kentwood
Lodge, 180 South Main
Street (Ketchum),
(800) 805–1001,
fax: (208) 726–2417

Clarion Inn of Sun Valley,
600 North Main Street
(Ketchum),
(800) 262–4833,
fax: (208) 726–3761

Heidelberg Inn,
1908 Warm Springs Road
(Ketchum),
(800) 284–4863,
fax: (208) 726–2084

Ketchum Korral Motor
Lodge, 310 South Main
Street (Ketchum),
(208) 726–3510,
fax: (208) 726–5287

Knob Hill Inn,
Highway 75 (Ketchum),
(800) 526–8010,
fax: (208) 726–2712
(see text)

Sun Valley Resort,
(800) 786–8259,
fax: (208) 622–3700

HAILEY
Airport Inn,
820 Fourth Avenue South,
(208) 788–2477,
fax: (208) 788–3195

Hitchrack Motel,
619 South Main,
(208) 788–1696

Wood River Inn,
601 North Main,
(208) 578–0600

BELLEVUE
High Country Motel,
626 South Main,
(208) 788–2050

FAIRFIELD
Soldier Mountain Ranch,
9 miles northwest,
(208) 764–2506,
fax: (208) 764–2927
(see text)

ARCO
Arco Inn,
540 Grand Avenue West,
(208) 527–3100

D-K Motel,
316 South Front Street,
(800) 231–0134

Lost River Motel,
405 Highway Drive,
(208) 527–3600

**PLACES TO EAT
IN CENTRAL IDAHO**

GIBBONSVILLE
Broken Arrow (Mexican),
Highway 93,
(208) 865–2241

NORTH FORK
Lewis & Clark Supper Club
(American), Highway 93,
(208) 865–2244

North Fork Cafe
(American), Highway 93,
(208) 865–2412 (see text)

One Hundred Acre Wood
(fine dining),
Highway 93,
(208) 865–2165

SALMON
BG's Burnt Bun (fast food),
Highway 93,
(208) 756–2062

Buddy's Family Dining
(American), 609 Highway
93 North, (208) 756–3630

CHALLIS
Antonio's (pizza/pasta),
(208) 879–2210 (see text)

Cafe.com (American/
Mexican), (208) 879–2891
(see text)

MACKAY
Amy Lou's Steakhouse
(American), Highway 93,
(208) 588–9903

Bear Bottom Inn (eclectic),
411 West Spruce Street,
(208) 588–2483

STANLEY
Mountain Village
(American),
(208) 774–3317

SUN VALLEY/KETCHUM
Evergreen Bistro
(contemporary American),
115 River Street West,
(208) 726–3888

KB's Burritos (Mexican),
Sixth and Washington,
(208) 726–2232

Pioneer Saloon
(American), 320 North
Main Street (Ketchum),
(208) 726–3139

Roosevelt Tavern (eclectic),
280 North Main Street,
(208) 726–0051

Helpful Web sites

Idaho Mountain Express
(Sun Valley–area newspaper)—
www.mtexpress.com

Sun Valley/Ketchum Chamber of Commerce—
www.visitsunvalley.com

Stanley-Sawtooth Chamber of Commerce—
www.stanleycc.org

Craters of the Moon National Monument—
www.nps.gov/crmo

Worth Seeing

Challis Hot Springs

Land of the Yankee Fork State Park—
near Challis

Sawtooth National Fish Hatchery—
near Stanley

Ketchum–Sun Valley Heritage and Ski Museum—
Ketchum

EBR-1 nuclear reactor site—*near Arco*

Wild Radish
(international),
200 South Main Street,
(208) 726–8468

Sun Valley Lodge Dining
Room (continental),
(208) 622–2150

HAILEY
Cafe at the Brewery
(eclectic), 202 North Main,
(208) 788–0805

DaVinci's (Italian),
17 West Bullion Street,
(208) 788–7699

McDonald's (fast food),
720 North Main,
(208) 788–5986

Red Elephant Saloon
(American),
107 South Main Street,
(208) 788–6047

BELLEVUE
Dos Amores (Mexican),
321 South Main Street,
(208) 788–2262

FAIRFIELD
Iron Mountain Inn
(American), Highway 20,
(208) 764–2577 (see text)

ARCO
Grandpa's Southern
Bar-B-Q (barbecue),
434 West Grand Avenue,
(208) 527–3362

Pickle's Place (American),
440 South Front,
(208) 527–9944

Index

INDEX

INDEX

INDEX

INDEX

Help Us Keep This Guide Up to Date

Every effort has been made by the author and editors to make this guide as accurate and useful as possible. However, many things can change after a guide is published—establishments close, phone numbers change, facilities come under new management, etc.

We would love to hear from you concerning your experiences with this guide and how you feel it could be improved and be kept up to date. While we may not be able to respond to all comments and suggestions, we'll take them to heart and we'll also make certain to share them with the author. Please send your comments and suggestions to the following address:

The Globe Pequot Press
Reader Response/Editorial Department
P.O. Box 480
Guilford, CT 06437

Or you may e-mail us at:
editorial@globe-pequot.com

Thanks for your input, and happy travels!